'This is a hugely important addition to the liter
mobility. Through a series of thought-provokir
that a university experience is both equally ex
advantage on its recipients is meticulously unp...... ,
This must-read book makes a significant contribution to debates on widening
participation and social justice at a time of heightened marketisation and stratification of global HE.'
— *Jacqueline Stevenson, Head of Research,*
*Sheffield Institute of Education, Sheffield Hallam University, UK*

'This is an important book that brings together many key scholars on the sociology
of higher education. It explores, in a detailed manner, the ways in which social
factors (and particularly class) continue to shape access to higher education, and
students' experiences both during their degree and as they move into the labour
market.'
— *Rachel Brooks, Professor of Sociology,*
*University of Surrey, UK*

'This book provides a most important contribution to the field of equity by inter-
rogating assumptions about the relationship between university access and social
mobility. It casts a much-needed light on significant questions of transitional
processes through and beyond higher education and the ways that inequities play
out in relation to graduate outcomes.'
— *Penny Jane Burke, Professor and Global Innovation Chair of*
*Equity Director, University of Newcastle, Australia*

'Waller, Ingram, and Ward have produced a timely and critical text challenging
the assumption that widening participation is achieved at the point of admission.
Through a thoughtful presentation of the higher education journey, we are presented
with an empirically rich and theoretically-driven account of the complex and durable
relationship between social class and higher education. This book is essential
reading for those concerned with social justice and higher education; it has added
a prominent voice to the on-going widening participation debate.'
— *Ciaran Burke, Lecturer in Sociology,*
*Plymouth University, UK*

# Higher Education and Social Inequalities

A university education has long been seen as the gateway to upward social mobility for individuals from lower socio-economic backgrounds, and as a way of reproducing social advantage for the better off. With the number of young people from the very highest socio-economic groups entering university in the UK having effectively been at saturation point for several decades, the expansion witnessed in participation rates over the last few decades has largely been achieved by a modest broadening of the base of the undergraduate population in terms of both social class and ethnic diversity.

However, a growing body of evidence exists in the continuation of unequal graduate outcomes. This can be seen in terms of employment trajectories in the UK. The issue of just *who* enjoys access to *which* university, and the experiences and outcomes of graduates from different institutions remain central to questions of social justice, notably higher education's contribution to social mobility and to the reproduction of social inequality.

This collection of contemporary original writings explores these issues in a range of specific contexts, and through employing a range of theoretical and methodological approaches. The relationship between higher education and social mobility has probably never been under closer scrutiny. This volume will appeal to academics, policy makers, and commentators alike. *Higher Education and Social Inequalities* is an important contribution to the public and academic debate.

**Richard Waller** is an Associate Professor of the Sociology of Education at the University of the West of England, Bristol. His research focusses on the intersection of education, social justice, and identity, and he has published a number of books, book chapters, and journal articles on these topics.

**Nicola Ingram** is a Senior Lecturer in Education and Social Justice at Lancaster University. Her research focusses on social class and gender based inequalities in education and she has published widely in this area.

**Michael R.M. Ward** is Lecturer in Social Sciences at Swansea University and is the author of *From Labouring to Learning, Working-class Masculinities, Education and De-industrialization.*

## Sociological Futures
Series Editors: Eileen Green, John Horne, Caroline Oliver, Louise Ryan

Sociological Futures aims to be a flagship series for new and innovative theories, methods, and approaches to sociological issues and debates and 'the social' in the twenty-first century. This series of monographs and edited collections was inspired by the vibrant wealth of British Sociological Association (BSA) symposia on a wide variety of sociological themes. Edited by a team of experienced sociological researchers, and supported by the BSA, it covers a wide range of topics related to sociology and sociological research and will feature contemporary work that is theoretically and methodologically innovative, has local or global reach, as well as work that engages or reengages with classic debates in sociology bringing new perspectives to important and relevant topics.

The BSA is the professional association for sociologists and sociological research in the United Kingdom, with an extensive network of members, study groups, and forums, and A dynamic programme of events. The Association engages with topics ranging from auto/biography to youth, climate change to violence against women, alcohol to sport, and Bourdieu to Weber. This book series represents the finest fruits of sociological enquiry, for a global audience, and offers a publication outlet for sociologists at all career and publishing stages, from well-established to emerging sociologists, BSA or non-BSA members, from all parts of the world.

**An End to the Crisis in Empirical Sociology?**
Trends and Challenges in Social Research
*Edited by Linda McKie and Louise Ryan*

**Bourdieu: The Next Generation**
The Development of Bourdieu's Intellectual Heritage in Contemporary UK Sociology
*Edited by Jenny Thatcher, Nicola Ingram, Ciaran Burke, and Jessie Abrahams*

**Drinking Dilemmas**
Space, Culture and Identity
*Edited by Thomas Thurnell-Read*

**Within and Beyond Citizenship**
Borders, Membership and Belonging
*Edited by Roberto G. Gonzales and Nando Sigona*

**Higher Education and Social Inequalities**
University Admissions, Experiences and Outcomes
*Edited by Richard Waller, Nicola Ingram, and Michael R.M. Ward*

# Higher Education and Social Inequalities

## University Admissions, Experiences, and Outcomes

Edited by
Richard Waller, Nicola Ingram,
and Michael R.M. Ward

Routledge
Taylor & Francis Group

LONDON AND NEW YORK

First published 2018
by Routledge

2 Park Square, Milton Park, Abingdon, Oxfordshire OX14 4RN
711 Third Avenue, New York, NY 10017

*Routledge is an imprint of the Taylor & Francis Group, an informa business*

First issued in paperback 2018

*British Library Cataloguing in Publication Data*
A catalogue record for this book is available from the British Library

*Library of Congress Cataloging in Publication Data*
Names: Waller, Richard (Sociologist), editor. | Ingram, Nicola. | Ward, Michael R. M., editor.
Title: Higher education and social inequalities : university admissions, experiences and outcomes / edited by Richard Waller, Nicola Ingram and Michael R.M. Ward.
Description: Abingdon, Oxon ; New York, NY : Routledge, 2017. | Includes bibliographical references.
Identifiers: LCCN 2017009518 | ISBN 9781138212886 (hardback) | ISBN 9781315449722 (ebook)
Subjects: LCSH: Education, Secondary—Social aspects—Great Britain. | Universities and colleges—Great Britain—Admission. | College students—Great Britain—Economic conditions. | College graduates—Employment—Great Britain. | Social classes—Great Britain. | Educational sociology—Great Britain. | Social mobility—Great Britain.
Classification: LCC LC191.98.G7 H53 2017 | DDC 378.00941—dc23
LC record available at https://lccn.loc.gov/2017009518

ISBN: 978-1-138-21288-6 (hbk)
ISBN: 978-1-138-35199-8 (pbk)

Typeset in Times
by Florence Production Ltd, Stoodleigh, Devon, UK

# Contents

**Getting on: classed experiences of higher education**                    81

5   A tale of two universities: class work in the field of
    higher education                                                        83
    DIANE REAY

6   How to win at being a student                                          99
    MATTHEW CHEESEMAN

7   Social class, ethnicity, and the process of 'fitting in'              116
    BERENICE SCANDONE

8   The 'Jack Wills brigade': brands, embodiment, and class
    identities in higher education                                        136
    VICKY MOUNTFORD

**PART III**
**Getting out: social class and graduate destinations**                   151

9   Higher education and the myths of graduate employability             153
    GERBRAND THOLEN AND PHILLIP BROWN

10  A glass half full? Social class and access to postgraduate study     167
    PAUL WAKELING

11  Participation in paid and unpaid internships among creative
    and communications graduates: does class advantage play
    a part?                                                               190
    WIL HUNT AND PETER SCOTT

12  Gendered and classed graduate transitions to work: how
    the unequal playing field is constructed, maintained, and
    experienced                                                           210
    HARRIET BRADLEY AND RICHARD WALLER

    Conclusion: social class, participation, and the marketised
    university                                                            231
    DAVID JAMES

    *Index*                                                               243

# Illustrations

## Figures

## Tables

# Contributors

**Dr Vikki Boliver** is a Reader in Sociology and Social Policy in the School of Applied Social Sciences at Durham University. Her research interests centre on social class and ethnic inequalities of access to higher education, with a particular focus on admission to highly selective universities.

**Dr Hugh Busher** of the School of Education, University of Leicester, UK, holds a PhD in the micro-politics of schools. Research interests include critical perspectives on people, power, and culture in educational institutions, students' and teachers' voices and identities, and hybrid learning communities. Recent research with Dr Nalita James focused on adult students' shifting learning identities on Access to HE courses.

**Prof. Harriet Bradley** is Professor of Women's Employment at UWE Bristol, having previously worked at Bristol and Sunderland universities. Recent books include the second editions of 'Gender' and 'Fractured Identities' (both Polity) and 'Social Class, Higher Education and Social Mobility', co-authored with the Paired Peers team (Palgrave). Her research interests include gender and work, young people's trajectories, and intersections of social inequalities, and she is a Labour councillor and a trade union activist.

**Prof. Phillip Brown** is a Distinguished Research Professor at Cardiff School of Social Sciences, and Distinguished Visiting Professor, Zhengzhou University, China. He has written, co-authored and co-edited more than 100 articles and 17 books, including The Global Auction: The Broken Promises of Education, Jobs and Incomes (Oxford University Press, 2011), with H. Lauder and D. Ashton.

**Dr Matthew Cheeseman** is Senior Lecturer in Professional Ceative Writing at University of Derby. He runs Spirit Duplicator (spiritduplicator.org), a small press. @eine on Twitter.

**Dr Susan Coulson** recently retired from a post as teaching fellow in sociology in the School of Geography, Politics and Sociology at Newcastle University. Her research interests have been mainly in the fields of domestic violence, gender inequality and non-standard work, particularly in the cultural sector.

**Dr Lisa Garforth** is a lecturer in Sociology at Newcastle University. Her main focus is on environmental futures. She has also worked on epistemic cultures and the organisation of science work, and is currently co-editing a special issue on the idea and practice of student engagement in the context of neo-liberal HE reforms.

**Dr Neil Harrison** is a Senior Lecturer in the Department of Education and Childhood at the University of the West of England. His research interests include social justice, the student experience, epistemology of impact and intercultural/transnational education. His co-edited book, 'Access to Higher Education: Theoretical Perspective and Contemporary Challenges' was published by Routledge in November 2016.

**Wil Hunt** is a Research Fellow at Warwick Institute for Employment Research, University of Warwick. His research covers a wide range of employment related issues, including: higher education and the graduate labour market, labour market change, precarious forms of employment, social inequality and labour market disadvantage.

**Prof. David James** is Professor in the School of Social Sciences at Cardiff University, and Director of the ESRC Wales Doctoral Training Partnership. He edits a leading international journal, the British Journal of Sociology of Education. His research focuses on the relationship between social inequality and educational institutions/processes.

**Dr Nalita James** is Associate Professor in Lifelong Learning in the Vaughan Centre for Lifelong Learning, University of Leicester. Her research interests include: access to higher education, adult education, lifelong learning, educational transitions, and educational policy. Together with Hugh Busher she has conducted research on access to higher education (funded by the British Academy and Aim Awards 2011–2013) and is published widely in this area. She is co-author (with Hugh Busher) of 'Improving Opportunities to Engage in Learning: A study of the Access to Higher Education Diploma' (Routledge, 2018).

**Dr Vicky Mountford** is currently based in Newcastle-upon-Tyne having completed her PhD thesis at Newcastle University, entitled 'Everyday Class Distinctions in Higher Education', which explored the classed identities and experiences of students in different institutions. She now works in teaching in Newcastle University and in supporting student social enterprise.

**Prof. Geoff Payne**, FAcSS, is a Research Associate at Newcastle University, and Emeritus Professor of Sociology, University of Plymouth. A former president of the BSA, his most recent books include The New Social Mobility (2017: Policy Press) and Social Mobility for the twenty-first Century (2018: Routledge) co-edited with Steph Lawler.

**Prof. Diane Reay** is a Professor of Education at the University of Cambridge with particular interests in social justice issues in education, Pierre Bourdieu's social theory, and cultural analyses of social class, race, and gender. She has just completed a book on Education and the Working Classes in the twenty-first Century to be published by Policy Press in 2017.

**Berenice Scandone** is a PhD researcher at the University of Bath, Department of Social and Policy Sciences. She is interested in classed and ethnic identities, and inequalities in education and social mobility. Her current research looks at the experiences and identities of British-born women of Bangladeshi ethnicity in higher education.

**Dr Peter Scott** is Senior Lecturer in employment relations at Portsmouth Business School, University of Portsmouth. His research interests include vocational education and training, internships, precarious and low-paid work, technological change, and the political economy of employment relations. He recently co-edited a book on Employment Relations under Coalition Government.

**Dr Gerbrand Tholen** is a lecturer in sociology at the Department of Sociology at City, University of London. His research interests are centred around education, skills, jobs, occupations, and the labour market. He has previously examined issues of skill utilisation, graduate work, elite education, labour market mobility, income inequality, skill formation, and the global labour market as well as social theory.

**Dr Richard Waller** has taught in further and higher education for over 20 years. He is currently an Associate Professor of the Sociology of Education at the University of the West of England, Bristol. His research, which tends to be qualitative in nature, focuses on the intersection between social class, identity, and education, and inevitably has a social justice dimension.

**Dr Paul Wakeling** is Senior Lecturer in the Department of Education, University of York, UK. He is a sociologist of higher education, with interests in social stratification and mobility. His recent research has investigated connections between university prestige, student characteristics, and graduate outcomes. He is an expert on access to postgraduate study and has advised several public bodies on this topic.

**Emily Wastell** is the Volunteer and Communications Coordinator at Success4All in Newcastle, an educational charity that supports Learning Hubs in areas marked by low educational achievement. Emily graduated from Newcastle University in 2013 with a degree in Sociology. Her undergraduate dissertation was based on a qualitative study of friendship, social class, and learning practices among undergraduates.

# Introduction

## Setting the scene

*Richard Waller, Nicola Ingram, and*
*Michael R.M. Ward*

As Waller *et al*. (2014: 701) noted, in the UK and beyond 'a university education has long been seen as the gateway to upward social mobility for individuals from lower socio-economic backgrounds', and as a way of reproducing social advantage for the wealthy. The number of young people from the highest socio-economic groups entering university in the UK has effectively been at saturation point for several decades since the Robbins Report (CHE, 1963) and subsequent growth of higher education (HE) from the late 1960s onwards. As a consequence, the expansion in youth participation rates from around 15 per cent in the mid-1980s (Chowdry *et al*., 2010) to something like three times that currently (Department for Business, Information and Skills [BIS] 2015) has been achieved by broadening the social base of the undergraduate population in terms of both social class and ethnic diversity. That said, this 'broadening' still leaves significant inequalities (as this edited collection outlines), and also much of it can be accounted for by the changing class composition of the UK in the last 50 or more years.

Meanwhile, a growing body of evidence exists which illustrates the continuation of unequal graduate outcomes in terms of employment trajectories in the UK (e.g. Milburn Commission, 2014). Internationally, the OECD's (2014) *Education at a Glance* report recently demonstrated how wider access to higher education and social mobility are not the same thing. While the UK leads most OECD counterparts in terms of university participation rates, the country is still painfully lagging behind in terms of graduate career outcomes. Meanwhile, at a local or national level there is continued evidence of traditional inequalities of graduate outcomes in terms of who gets which jobs, with the various reports from the Milburn Commission being to the fore in the UK, (e.g. 2009; 2012; 2014; 2016). In one of these reports, then UK Prime Minister David Cameron suggested that 'You only have to look at the make-up of the high levels of parliament, the judiciary, the army, the media. It's not as diverse; there's not as much social mobility as there needs to be' (2014:7).

The issue of just *who* enjoys access to *which* university, and the experiences and outcomes of graduates from different institutions remain central to questions of social justice, notably higher education's contribution to social mobility and to the reproduction of social inequality. It is no longer enough to simply expand the number of university places – 'more bums on seats', nor to broaden the social base of the undergraduate population, as laudable as these aspirations may be; we must look at who goes *where* in terms of both university study and post-graduation careers – i.e. '*whose* bum on *which* seat?', and understand just how these processes happen so they can be challenged. We must also understand how peoples' experiences of both coming to and being at university contribute to ongoing social inequalities (see Bathmaker *et al.*, (2016) and Savage *et al.*, (2015) for recent detailed discussions of this topic).

In organising this book we employ a structure first used by Phillip Brown in his 1987 book *Schooling Ordinary Kids*.[1] Brown's study was, as the book title suggests, one of young people at school. However, the three phases in the lifecycle of an undergraduate – admission to university ('getting in'), progression through university ('getting on') and graduation from university ('getting out') offer a coherent way of organising otherwise disparate chapters into clear parts.

This introduction chapter now offers an overview of the content of the three parts – there are four chapters in each – and these are followed by a concluding chapter from Prof David James, Executive Editor of the *British Journal of Sociology of Education*, who offers a view of where the preceding contributions take us, and where both research and reforms might go next in a context of increasing marketization.

## Part I: Getting in: higher education access and participation

Part One considers the practices, processes and issues students encounter while applying to and entering higher education institutions (HEIs). The four chapters focus on 'getting in' to university, in slightly different ways, but all take social class as a starting point and as a key element in terms of participation.

The part begins with Coulson *et al.*'s chapter which explores issues around non-traditional students' experiences of HE. In this chapter these authors reflect on their own experiences as social agents who, willingly or not, have participated in the reproduction of class in HE institutions. As Access Summer School Co-ordinators, Admissions Tutors, Examinations Officers and former students, they combine diverse observations in a case study which looks at examples of the underlying processes and social mechanisms governing university access and shaping student experiences and academic success. Using a discourse analytic approach, Coulson *et al.* illustrate how social class is separated from personal identity and biography in admissions procedures, restricting the relevance of socio-economic background to questions of access, not experience. Two case studies are then used to explore how expectations of the 'Student Experience', particularly around friendships, impact on academic performance in ways that consolidate class identities. The first case study looks at the experiences of a widening participation summer school scheme and the second focuses on interview data from a small sample of third year undergraduates. The unsettling evidence presented in the chapter points to the importance of the small, taken-for-granted social mechanisms which sustain social class differences in, and through, HE.

In Chapter Two Busher and James take a closer look at non-traditional mature students' experience of higher education. Their focus is on how non-traditional mature students on Access to Higher Education (AHE) courses have to struggle to assert themselves by entering university and escaping from precarious economic circumstances despite the social and policy contexts they face and their prior experiences of learning, which were often unsuccessful. This chapter draws on a study that was carried out in seven further education colleges in a region of England. It used mixed-methods, collecting questionnaire data from over 500 AHE students and interview data from seven student focus groups that ran in each college three times during the academic year as well as from 20 AHE tutors across all colleges. Busher and James clearly show that students' struggles with their socio-economic contexts helped them to identify and express what they wanted to achieve and find ways of achieving it. Their experiences on the AHE courses and their relationships with tutors, fellow students, family and friends helped them to change their identities as learners and as people during their time as AHE students.

In Chapter Three Boliver explores the widening access debated further by focusing on the participation rates of those from more and less socioeconomically disadvantaged backgrounds, in relation to highly selective universities. Boliver finds that historically, policy makers and researchers have focused on the barriers to wider access which occur prior to the point of application to university, but increasingly the impact of HE admissions decision-making is coming under closer scrutiny. This chapter explores empirically the extent to which admission to highly selective, highly prestigious Russell Group universities can be said to be meritocratic, in the narrow sense of determined by applicants' prior attainment alone. It also advances the case for a greater shift towards meritocratic admissions policies in the broader sense, via the widespread use of contextualised admissions policies which take due account of the often challenging circumstances in which people from socioeconomically disadvantaged backgrounds achieve the qualifications required to go to university.

In the final chapter of this part, Harrison's focus turns to the more traditional university attendees, young people aged 18–21. Harrison suggests that while a huge change in the funding of higher education from the public to the private sphere has occurred over the past twenty years, this has not coincided with a drop in the demand for HE. This demand has especially increased among working-class communities and others with limited economic resources. Counterintuitively, as the cost of higher education has risen it is higher socio-economic groups that have tended to see falls in demand, while low income students have proved largely immune to financial incentives (e.g. bursaries and fee waivers) designed to influence their choices. This chapter begins by employing quantitative data from official datasets to chart and explore classed patterns in participation. Harrison then turns to draw on related statistical data around qualifications and unemployment to

build a more rounded picture of the choices facing young people and other prospective students and suggest some alternative hypotheses for why participation
patterns have not followed the predictions made.

## Part II: Getting on: classed experiences of higher education

Part Two considers how a students' classed background affects their experience
of fitting in and 'getting on' at university. It involves four studies of different groups
of students experiencing life at various types of higher education institutions, and
how their experiences are framed by their family backgrounds.

The part begins with Diane Reay's chapter looking at the experiences of 17
working-class students at two very different types of English universities, one
of which is a financially struggling new university ('Northern'), and the other a
wealthy university in the prestigious Russell Group ('Southern'). Reay employed
both questionnaire and interview data in exploring a more nuanced notion of
student identity than is often presented in the literature. She employs theoretical
tools from a range of authors including Bourdieu and Lave and Wenger, in drawing
upon and combining ideas of learner identity and an understanding of the space
and place that the mature learners occupy within the two contrasting settings.
In Southern, where academic excellence, competitiveness and individual autonomy
are seen as the norm, the mature working-class students felt that being in the
'student bubble' gave them significant academic confidence, and as high achievers
from disadvantaged social backgrounds, they often felt they 'fitted in' at university
better than they had in their generally low achieving working-class schools. By
contrast, at Northern, where a general assumption abounds of lower levels of
academic ability among the wider undergraduate cohort, the mature students often
lacked confidence in their abilities and learner identities, and struggled as a
consequence. Reay concludes that 'Southern students had both the dispositions
and advantageous field conditions to totally immerse themselves in the field',
however 'this was rarely the case for Northern students', studying at a university
unable to afford the additional support systems available to their Southern counterparts.

Matt Cheeseman's chapter is an ethnographic study for which he immersed
himself into the lifestyles of students to explore their role in Sheffield's night
time economy. Cheeseman undertook follow-up interviews with some of the
students whose lives he was studying, and had regular meetings with them as well.
Unusually for a study of this nature, he also interviewed people in a range of other
related roles associated with the night time economy, including police officers,
university porters and staff from the pubs and clubs that the students attended.
He looked at how universities themselves marketed a picture of student life as
hedonistic, and the role that the residential tradition and spaces of HE supports
the *habitus* of student life. Cheeseman found that the colonising of the night time

economy by the geographically mobile middle-class undergraduate body resulted in the students distancing themselves from the less socially valuable or 'authentic' stay-at-home university experience of some working-class undergraduates. As well as employing theories from Bourdieu to understand his findings, Cheeseman utilises theories of 'performance' from Goffman, and of contemporary relationships from Giddens, Beck, and Bauman to explore the nature of friendships at universities. He also explores the inter-university rivalry and associated class stereotyping through an analysis of public performance and social rituals.

The third chapter in the part is from Berenice Scandone, and focuses on the experience of a group of 21 British born young women of Bangladeshi heritage, and their attempts to 'fit in' at a number of different universities. The young women, all of whom lived with their families in London and attended universities in the city, came from both working- and middle-class backgrounds. Scandone illustrates how perceptions and experiences of fitting in are informed by class, ethnicity, gender and religion, and she also highlights how these social inequalities are produced and reproduced through higher education. The young working-class Bangladeshi women in the study who attended more prestigious universities were frequently 'othered' by, and from, the majority of students by their ethnicity and their religion as well as by their social class. However, such processes and experiences aided the development of a high degree of resilience and self-reliance for a number of the cohort. Meanwhile, those at less prestigious institutions felt more 'at ease' at university, and that they fitted in better. However, Scandone highlights how both symbolic violence and their self-perception of cultural capital in particular impacted on the students' experiences of fitting in and getting on in higher education. Religion played a role too – the fact that cultural mores meant they lived 'at home' and did not consume alcohol, means the focus of the chapter is in a sense the diametric opposite of most of those in Cheeseman's study. There was evidence of a social mix at the universities where Scandone's students studied, but very little social mixing.

In Chapter Eight, the final one of the part, Vicky Mountford looks at how class differences are 'performed' through the choice of clothing brands by working- and middle-class students in the north east of England. Mountford explores the lived experiences of 'fitting in' and 'standing out' at two contrasting universities in one UK city, and how clothing brands and the associated lifestyles are seen as signifiers of classed identities, and what particular types of student normativities may consist of. She employed in-depth one-to-one interviews and focus groups with a total of 27 young British undergraduates across the two institutions. Mountford highlights how 'different brands work as prestigious objects' in the two institutions, and that the significance of the branded clothing is relative to the wearer and the context. The chapter highlights the surveillance and policing of representation of individual identities, and the processes by which value is attributed to items of clothing through their association with brand identities and the students' own classed values. The economic capital of the better off upper-middle-class 'rah' students was converted to the cultural capital represented by particular fashion brands and 'looks'. This process was often further denied to the generally working-class students who needed to go straight to work after their day at university, a fact which itself had framed the type of clothing they could wear on campus.

## Part III: Getting out: social class and graduate destinations

Part Three considers the processes involved in 'getting out' of university, which we argue is fundamental to understanding the fuller picture of inequality in Higher Education . . .

The part begins with Tholen and Brown's chapter, providing an overview of the issue of 'employability', which has recently become a key focus for HEIs within the UK, not least of all because they are now measured according to their success in graduate destinations. The chapter questions whether the delivery of 'employability' skills by universities can overcome or compensate for the reality of the congested graduate labour market. The myth of graduate employability and the exaggeration of claims to a 'graduate premium' on earnings are explored through a review of the evidence. The authors argue that the employability agenda is bound to fail because it is ultimately flawed, and because the problems of the graduate labour market are structural, rather than as a result of a graduate skills' deficit.

In Chapter Ten, Hunt and Scott consider the issue of paid and unpaid internships for creative and communications graduates several years after the point of graduation. They explore the role social class plays in early labour market opportunities. Drawing on data from a survey of 616 creative and communications graduates from a range of UK Higher Education Institutions the study post-university labour market experiences, including participation in internships. The findings show that class background does not play a significant role in the acquisition of an *unpaid* internship in these industries. However, it crucially impacts on access to *paid* internships, which in turn are more likely than unpaid internships to lead to a graduate job. Graduates from working-class background are less likely to gain a paid internship even when educational performance is taken into account, putting them in a disadvantageous position compared to their middle-class peers.

Chapter Eleven deals with an often neglected area in graduate destinations, that of further study. With a steep increase in postgraduate participation there is a need to consider whether there are inequalities in access at this level. Wakeling's research draws on three large scale UK datasets to investigate the relationship between social class and postgraduate study in Britain. He reveals that there is social class disadvantage at this level and although this is not as stark as at undergraduate level it is compounded by the type of institution attended for initial degree. The chapter further shows that working-class educational disadvantage in postgraduate access increases when further study is delayed beyond first-degree graduation. The findings highlight both the continued educational advantage that is conferred by undergraduate access to elite institutions and to the advantage of the privileged classes in gaining access to postgraduate study regardless of their attainment.

The final empirical chapter provides an in depth qualitative analysis of the complex labour market transitions of graduates from the *Paired Peers* longitudinal project. In a congested labour market both working-class and middle-class graduates face great competition for jobs. This chapter shows that, by and large, the 2013 graduates from this study faced these challenges with both apprehension and hope but that the pathways to employment were influenced by class, gender and type of HE institution attended. The chapter provides insightful reflections on the processes involved in entering desired employment post-graduation, including continuing education, seeking a work-life balance, seeking high status employment, and having the capacity to wait for the right opportunities. By exploring the details of these processes the gender dimension of aspiration and job seeking practices are strongly revealed.

Together these chapters bring together a range of research and insights into the various stages of Higher Educational experience and practice – through a focus on access, participation, and outcomes. They shed light on the landscape of social class inequalities within the UK Higher Education system, a picture that remains deeply etched despite continued policy efforts within the sector to narrow the gaps between the privileged and the disadvantaged. In what follows we see evidence of a system that continues to support and reproduce class-based inequalities regardless of policy initiatives that are supposed to alleviate disadvantage (such as OFFA access agreements). For those of us working within the sector, whether as teachers, practitioners or researchers, with a commitment to social justice, it is difficult to see how significant changes can be made to this picture without a drastic reworking of the canvass. The layering of soft policy initiatives (at the level of government and at the institutional level) on top of a selective system that separates the classes on the basis of supposed meritocratic processes is akin to 'putting a Band Aid on a bullet hole' (to paraphrase Taylor Swift). Higher Education receives less criticism about academic selection than any other area of the UK education system. There is a tacit acceptance of the 'necessity' of academic selection at this level and a lack of critique of the hierarchical system that ensues from these and other elitist practices. This book presents a range of rich data that provides evidence for the need for changes across the higher education sector if equality is indeed a genuine goal.

## Note

1   Other monographs or edited collections have adopted a similar approach to structuring the content, for instance, see also Haselgrove (1994) and Bathmaker *et al.* (2016).

# References

Bathmaker, A-M., Ingram, N., Abrahams, J., Hoare, T., Waller, R., and Bradley, H. (2016). *Higher education, social class and social mobility: The degree generation*. London: Palgrave MacMillan.

Brown, P. (1987). *Schooling ordinary kids: Inequality, unemployment and the new vocationalism*. London: Tavistock.

Chowdry, H., Crawford, C., Dearden, L., Goodman, A., and Vignoles, A. (2010). *Widening participation in higher education: Analysis using linked administrative data*. London: Institute for Fiscal Studies.

Committee on Higher Education [CHE] (23rd September 1963), *Higher education: report of the Committee appointed by the Prime Minister under the Chairmanship of Lord Robbins 1961–63*, Cmnd. 2154, London: HMSO.

Department for Business, Information and Skills [BIS]. (2015). *Participation rates in higher education: academic years 2006 and 2007 to 2013 and 2014* (provisional). London: Department for Business, Innovation and Skills.

Haselgrove, S. (1994). (Ed.). *The Student Experience*, Society for Research into Higher Education and Open University Press: Buckingham.

Milburn, A. (2009). Panel on Fair Access to the Professions. 2009. *Unleashing aspiration: the final report of the Panel on Fair Access to the Professions* (also known as the Milburn Report). London: Cabinet Office.

Milburn, A. (2012). *Fair access to professional careers: A progress report by the independent reviewer on social mobility and child poverty*. London: Cabinet Office.

Milburn, A. (2014). *Elitist Britain? A report by the Independent Reviewer on Social Mobility and Child Poverty*. London: Cabinet Office.

Milburn, A. (2016). *State of the nation 2016: Social mobility in Great Britain*. London: Cabinet Office.

OECD. (2014). *Education at a Glance 2014: OECD Indicators*, OECD Publishing. Retrieved from http://dx.doi.org/10.1787/eag-2014-en

Savage, M., Cunningham, N., Devine, F., Friedman, S., Laurison, D., McKenzie, L., Miles, A., Snee, H., and Wakeling, P. (2015). *Social class in the 21st century*. London: Penguin.

Waller, R., Holford, J., Jarvis, P., Milana, M., and Webb, S. (2014). Widening participation, social mobility and the role of universities in a globalized world. *International Journal of Lifelong Education*, 33(6), 701–704.

Part I

# Getting in: higher education access and participation

# Chapter 1

# Admissions, adaptations, and anxieties

## Social class inside and outside the elite university

*Susan Coulson, Lisa Garforth, Geoff Payne, and Emily Wastell*

## Introduction

Social mobility, student diversity and fair access to universities are important issues in current UK public policy debate, and rarely out of the news (Payne, 2017). From the inside, however, it can feel that Higher Education Institutions ('HEIs') are failing to recognise how academic experiences and identities are shaped by *social class*. The sector is apparently convulsed with concern about educational inequality especially in the self-styled 'elite', research-oriented universities such as Oxford, Cambridge or the Russell Group (Russell Group, 2016), whose high status and marketing skills give them a predominant position in Higher Education ('HE') funding (Boliver, 2015). But is the sector in fact neglecting questions of social class, and perhaps even contributing to the continuation of classed inequalities? This chapter is rooted in a growing discomfort about how our own roles – as teachers, tutors, admissions and exams officers in several Russell Group universities – might contribute to the reproduction of, and silence about, classed HE experiences. It explores how attention to unequal educational opportunities and fair access are concentrated almost exclusively at the points of application and admission.

We begin by examining contemporary discursive constructions of fair access in the language of policy and in the formal symbols used on university application forms. This demonstrates that admissions procedures deal with issues of biography, schooling and personal identity largely without reference to 'class'. In the second part, interview data from a small sample of Third Year undergraduates shed light on the different experiences of those from public and state schools. We show how university networks, particularly friendships, impact on academic performance in ways that consolidate class identities and experience. Data from participants in a supported entry scheme for 'less advantaged' students is addressed in the third part. Here we explore non-traditional students' experiences of not fitting in. Juxtaposing these different aspects of one selective HE institution, our discussion highlights a difficult tension: while students' experiences and even their academic progress are deeply shaped by class, it is rarely acknowledged beyond admissions processes, which themselves work to separate students' achievements and identities from their classed backgrounds.

Our analysis of these textual and interview data is informed by a growing and increasingly nuanced body of Bourdieusian research and theorising about higher education (see Reay *et al.*, 2001; Archer *et al.*, 2003; Reay, 2006; Archer, 2007; Reay *et al.*, 2009, 2010; Bathmaker *et al.*, 2013; Loveday, 2015). This work offers powerful accounts of how social, economic and cultural capitals shape choices, experiences and outcomes in the HE field. Bourdieu's notion of the classed habitus (1984) facilitates the exploration of how working-class and non-white students choose universities and experience the HE system. It highlights how non-traditional students come to university with dispositions, habits, and preferences that leave them feeling they do not fit in, and explains why many feel uncomfortable in, or alienated from, elite institutions. Bourdieu's notion of field (1984) helps us to understand universities as classed institutions that reproduce wider classed structures, normalising and neutralising privilege.

By highlighting tensions between official policies to widen participation/fair access in elite universities, and sociological questions of classed experiences and identities, we demonstrate that current admissions processes and supported-entry schemes in Russell Group universities tend to treat socio-economic background as contingent and separable from the applicant. This amounts to a denial of the continuing relevance of students' classed identities and experiences at university. It enables universities to continue to operate as classed institutions which normalise high levels of cultural capital and educational privilege, and fail to attend to the complexities of working-class students' lived experiences once they are inside the university.

## Getting in: (not) doing class in UK university admissions

Since 2012, the replacement of the government block grant in England and Wales by increased student fees has contributed to growing concern about diversity of HE participation (Sutton Trust, 2013). This has led to greater scrutiny of universities' mechanisms for ensuring 'fair access'. All universities are expected to ensure their selection policies do not discriminate against qualified applicants on grounds of race, gender, poverty or origin. At the same time, however, increased competition for students has exacerbated distinctions between types of universities. In a period of rapid HE change, the Russell Group promotes its 24 members as high status, research-oriented institutions, whereas the 35 'post-1992' or 'new' universities formed from former Polytechnics and Scottish Central Institutions tend to emphasise their direct relevance to employment. This trait is even more pronounced among the similar number of former colleges more recently designated as universities. Higher levels of applications to the 'elite' universities mean that they can be more selective about their intakes, imposing (in most but not all subject areas) a 'higher tariff' entry requirement whereby students require the strongest A level grades or equivalent to enter (Graham, 2010; Scott, 2015).

In competitive contexts, university marketing departments and academic departments increasingly treat tariff levels as an indicator of the quality of the university and its programmes. University guides and league tables routinely use entry qualifications as a significant factor in how they rank UK universities (for just one example, see the Complete University Guide ranking methodology: www.thecompleteuniversityguide.co.uk/league-tables/methodology/). There is a wealth of evidence, however, that performance at A level is closely associated with differential educational opportunity and family background (e.g. Sutton Trust 2008, 2010, 2014; Higher Education Funding Council for England [HEFCE], 2014; Social Mobility and Child Poverty Commission [SMCPC], 2015) and that A level performance is only loosely related to degree-level performance (e.g. HEFCE, 2014). It is here that commitments to widening participation can come into tension with 'institutional culture(s) based on academic excellence' (Bravenboer, 2012: 122) and 'fair access' may come to refer narrowly to selection among those pupils with the best qualifications: 'As one prospectus states "the doors of this University are open to all students with the highest intellectual potential to succeed"' (Graham, 2010: 183).

Many high tariff universities have mechanisms in place that aim to acknowledge that social circumstances can contribute to lower A level achievement (as in the assisted-entry scheme at one UK Russell Group university discussed below, which enables academic selectors to offer lower entrance requirements to students with particular educational disadvantages). However, these mechanisms operate in a context deeply marked by investments in high tariffs as a marker of institutional quality and reputation. It is therefore no surprise that while HE entry has increased for 'disadvantaged' 18-year olds with lower qualifications (Universities and Colleges Admissions Service [UCAS], 2014: 78),[1] high tariff universities recruit lower proportions of those students from disadvantaged educational backgrounds than 'medium' and 'low' tariff universities (UCAS, 2014: 73). Nevertheless, the ratio of entrants from the most advantaged to the most disadvantaged groups has fallen only from about 9:1 to about 7:1 in high tariff universities in recent years (UCAS 2014: 80).

This ratio suggests some of the ways in which selective recruitment and widening participation can be in tension in selective universities. In the following section, we discuss how widening participation is currently constructed in these contradictory contexts, starting by examining the language of policies for fair access to universities in the UK and the ways in which 'contextual admissions' in HE operates as an access system.

## The language of fair access

The Office for Fair Access ('OFFA') has become increasingly important in managing policies of fair access to UK universities. OFFA aims to ensure that all learners have the chance to enter and succeed in HE and in particular seeks rapid widening of access to the 'most selective' HEIs (OFFA, 2016). Because it is now mandatory for HEIs charging the highest tuition fees to submit an Access Agreement to OFFA, it has a degree of power to hold universities' recruitment and admissions processes to account. Although OFFA can fine defaulting HEIs or limit the fees they charge, in practice these powers have never been invoked. However, as it presents the official Department for Business, Innovation and Skills' (BIS) policy for fair access (BIS, 2014), OFFA does have discursive power to frame the language and perception of fair access.

It is therefore interesting to note how rarely 'class' is mentioned in the 100 or so pages of OFFA's key strategy document (BIS, 2014): the term 'class' is used only five times, three of these in a single quotation from ESRC research. In contrast, there are over 100 references to less desirable social positions or identities, most commonly 'backgrounds', 'groups' or 'young people'. More than 50 of these references are qualified by labels like 'disadvantaged', 'low participation neighbourhoods', 'under-represented', or 'poorer' and 'low income background' (e.g. BIS, 2014: 6, 15, 17, 27, 39). 'Background' and 'the disadvantaged' are also used some 30 times on their own as shorthand synonyms for the complex social inequalities shaping access to HE. In the first five pages of OFFA's website, 'disadvantaged' is used five times, 'under-represented' four, 'low income' three and background twice. 'Class' is not mentioned.

The language of 'background' similarly features in the UCAS (2014) analysis of fair access and widening participation. Its detailed discussion of application and selection processes uses the POLAR (Participation of Area) scale to measure the proportion of young (under-21) participation in HE in UK wards and neighbourhoods. The proportion of pupils qualifying for free school meals is used as a proxy for socio-economic disadvantage at the school level. But as in OFFA's language, 'background(s)' is the single most frequently used term in discussions of educational participation and advantage – 23 times in UCAS's most recent document (UCAS, 2014). In the vast majority of usages, 'background' stands alone. Again, the word 'class' does not appear. Nor is this atypical of educational statistics: as the authoritative House of Commons Library has observed, 'the coverage of the socio-economic data had been falling for some years' (House of Commons, 2014: 1). UCAS for example gave up collecting information on class backgrounds in 2008 (House of Commons, 2010: 1), blaming incomplete data.

In policy discourse, then, the language of class is not used to frame unequal participation in HE. 'Background' and 'disadvantage' do the discursive heavy lifting, without invoking structural inequalities or systemic failures. Applicants *come* from different kinds of social and geographical places but these are not connected, nor are they as important as where applicants are *going*; their destinations and aspirations. On admission, class origin is left behind and can be ignored – if it was ever there. Background implies that applicants can be separated from their circumstances and will have equal chances to benefit from the class-neutral territory of HE. Background suggests that it is impolite, excessively analytical, or somehow judgemental to speak about the unequal material and cultural resources which shape individuals, and which in fact continue to operate in undegraduates' lives – what Goldthorpe (2013), in his discussion of the relatively weak effect of educational attainment on social position, describes as the 'stickiness' of class. In the sanitised language of OFFA and UCAS, it some times seems that the very desire to promote 'fair access' makes the factors causing unfair access all but unspeakable, as we show in the next two sections of this chapter.

## Contextual admissions as an access system

We turn now to look at analogous terms that are used in the operationalisation of university admissions processes: 'non-traditional students' and 'context'. The former is evident in special programs intended to provide support for local young people and attract them to apply to a university they might not otherwise have thought was for them. A typical example is the (pseudonymous) ENTRY (Entry for Non-Traditionally Represented Youth) scheme in which eligible students receive a conditional offer lower than the typical requirement for their chosen degree program. To qualify, students need to come from a 'non-traditional' background. 'Non-traditional' means coming from a non-university family, being entitled to free school meals or living in a HE low-participation neighbourhood.

The term 'context', as in the phrase 'contextualised admissions' (Supporting Professionalism in Admissions [SPA] 2012, 2013), is used more widely in admissions processes. SPA is funded by HEFCE, Universities UK and UCAS to set best practice in university admissions, so that the way context here refers to how university application and selection procedures can be adjusted to take into account the applicant's educational and socio-economic circumstances is endorsed across the HE sector. Contextual admissions enable subject selectors to evaluate applicants' achievements, abilities, and potential, by using quantitative data on neighbourhood levels of HE participation, school achievement relative to national averages, and percentage of school intake qualifying for free school meals. Qualitative or informal contextual information might also be provided by applicants themselves, or by their school. Contextual admissions can be seen as a way of translating the complexity of socio-economic difference and educational inequality (Reay, 2006) into a set of one-dimensional and often quantitative flags or markers.

This translation is materially visible on the paper-format university application forms used before UCAS and university systems recently went online. In one Russell Group university, the 'core' applicant information appears in four sections on the form. On the top left hand side are the applicant's *personal and educational details*. Below this is the applicant's *personal statement*, a short biographical sketch outlining educational and other successes, life experience and aspirations for university study. On the top right hand side *educational qualifications* and current courses of study are listed, including grades so far achieved. Below this is the academic *reference*, usually provided by the current school/college and often predicting grades for the public examinations that have yet to be taken.

The core of the application form, then, describes the applicant according to their own and their teachers' estimation. It tells us what they have got, and what their school thinks they are likely to get, in terms of public exam results. It may also tell us something about where they come from – admissions tutors may make inferences from the name or location of schools. Referees may provide information about the school catchment area and demographics, while students' personal statements sometimes say something about their family circumstances. But the majority of the information relating to students' origins (geographic, regional, educational, social, economic) comes from the so-called contextual data: icons, flags, and codes added to the form by UCAS and university admissions staff to indicate, for example, that an applicant is from a 'low participation neigh-bourhood', a participant in a supported entry scheme, or comes from a school in which the average post-16 qualifications achieved per student are below the national average.

The SPA's recommendations for contextual admissions present an abstracted vision of 'holistic assessment' in which applicant data and contextual information are used in the admissions process. But even in the SPA's idealised representation,[2] 'original' application data (qualification, personal statement, reference etc.) are graphically shown as completely separate from the contextu-alising information.

Despite the laudable aims of fair access, both the language and practice of contextual admissions tend to detach applicants from their social context. Context will be considered, but is contingent. The core remains the applicants' achievements, predicted achievements, and personal narratives. Class can be added or taken away. It is not a constituent part of the applicants' selves, their experience or their educational successes. This is an impoverished understanding of the relationship between socio-economic structures, culture and lifestyle, the social subject, and her educational opportunities and attainment (e.g. Archer *et al.*, 2003; Archer, 2007; Reay *et al.*, 2009, 2010; Boliver, 2011).

When class and context *are* (contingently) attached to applicants, only dis-advantaged applicants are 'contextualised'. There are no flags for socio-economic *advantage* or icons for educational *privilege*. Schools in deprived areas frequently preface their students' references by explaining the relative disadvantage of their intake. Public schools do not announce the context of exceptional advantage of their pupils. Contextual admissions mark disadvantaged applicants as different. Relative and absolute advantage remain unmarked, neutral, normative, and ordinary in the admissions system.

Without denigrating policies aimed at ensuring fair access and widening participation, or devaluing the work of university admissions teams seeking to make context count, the sociological question remains: how far do dominant discourses of fair access render structures of class privilege and individuals' classed experiences invisible via a vague language of background and context (Warmington, 2002; Tett, 2004)? The language and structure of the application form separate individuals' identities and achievements from their social, economic, and educational lives, and ignores what happens to applicants when they become undergraduates.

Although the first three authors shared a wide range of professional experience, our concerns were sharpened by the 'student's eye' perspective in Emily Wastell's semi-structured interviews with 12 female undergraduate students in their Third Year, collected as part of her Final Year dissertation. Her informants from a snowball sample were White British: six from private schools and wealthy families, and six from state secondary schools and 'ordinary' homes. Despite its inherent approximation – the educational dichotomy obviously cannot cover all types of student and classes – schooling here serves as a convenient and *explicit* surrogate for social class, i.e. unlike the vague language of fair access policies.

We were also able to compare the 12 students' accounts with special entrants from the ENTRY scheme, who by conventional sociological definition were working-class. A focus group of five students from the 2013/14 cohort was used to explore their experiences, revisiting after half a year the lists of hopes and fears they had made during the pre-entry Summer School. Longer, more wide-ranging individual interviews were also carried out with two ENTRY students in their Second Year. We of course recognise the considerable data limitations of our small purposive sample in one university, and therefore caution against over-generalisation: for example, the *Paired Peers Project* at the two Bristol universities shows how HEI environments vary (Bathmaker *et al.*, 2013, 2016). Nonetheless, the findings are sufficiently disturbing to warrant careful consideration. We deal first with the interview data collected from the Third Year students, and then in a following section, turn to a discussion of the ENTRY students.

## The consequences for students: class, expectations, and friends

Reflecting on their early expectations, the 12 Third Year informants talked about anticipating an excellent *social* life at university. They had envisioned an idealised student experience: 'epic', 'amazing', 'the time of my life'; going out every night, meeting and socialising with new people, while they acquired a degree in some unstated way. 'University' was perceived as an *experience* rather than an *academic institution*. This is perhaps unsurprising. Universities market themselves by showing the sun always shining on campus, where groups of happy (middle-class) students enjoy themselves. Academic work – where it briefly appears – is done in small friendly *groups* of similar fellow students. Group images of happy, young people enjoying the 'Student Experience' *together* speak of a 'vibrant nightlife', and an 'all round' experience, one long party for everybody. Commercial websites for young consumers like Carnage (www.carnageuk.com) or Younilife (www.younilife.com) reinforce the social aspects of student youth culture.

In our research, students' expectations of an exciting and pleasurable student experience influenced selection of universities. Academics may like to think choices reflect interest in scholarship, or that our intellectual reputations extend into the school-room. Sadly this was not so. Informants made almost no mention of academic quality, and then only in normative, passing references to 'Russell Group' or 'decent' universities, reflecting perceptions of institutional status. The few comments on the content of the degree program came late in the interviews, most often after interviewer prompts – 'I've got A*'s and A's at A Levels and I chose a course that I thought I'd really enjoy'.

Students from *private schools* seem to have been strongly influenced by their peer group, wanting to share their student experience with ready-made friends from school. They appear to be influenced by *fashions*.

> My friends and I would talk about it all the time, but we wouldn't just talk about where we were going, but where everyone else in college were going and which unis were most popular. See, the year before I went it seemed as if everyone in my area chose to go to Manchester University, and the year I was going everybody wanted to go to [this university] (Informant A).

They also picked the same, most expensive, hall of residence because 'it was going to be full of similar people . . . so I'll be able to make friends easy' (Informant B). Being comfortable with others sharing a recognisable background, and having a ready-made support group of friends, was further seen as desirable. This strategy seems successful in producing enjoyable, strong, long-lived and even intense inter-personal relationships.

> We'll do everything together we can't be separated. (Informant D)

> I had, like, four best friends by the end of the first week. (Informant C)

> Your university friends become more like family because you spend so much time with them and share everything with them. We'll all do it together. (Informant E)

Others thought getting on well with people was easier if they had things in common.

> You need to think about the type of people who are going to be there, and if you're going to get along with those people and fit in before you go. (Informant B)

> People who had the same background as me would be going there too which is important. (Informant E)

Being with people from similar backgrounds reduces social uncertainty, but also hints at dislike or fear of the unknown, of encounters with people who were different, e.g. 'others' from a social class who could not afford private schooling and higher priced accommodation. In their new environment, these privately-educated students quickly established a *closed* network, insulating themselves from interaction with other students whom they deemed as different from them.

*State school* students in our sample were more likely to choose universities as individuals, welcoming the prospect of meeting new people from different backgrounds, and showing little concern over choice of Halls.

> All of my friends were going to different places all over the country which we all really liked . . . university is about meeting loads of different people really isn't it. (Informant G)

> I remember being really excited and amused before going at the idea of all of my flat mates having different accents and none of us being able to understand each other. (Informant H)

> I didn't really mind which accommodation I got put in to. (Informant I)

> I just looked at which [residences] were closest to university and the town centre. (Informant J)

They did not expect exclusion from new relationships or that class backgrounds would be mobilised in social closure. They were surprised that making friends at university was so marked by class backgrounds like 'money or school or amazing things they've done' (Informant H).

> Just because you have money and maybe more life experience why does that mean we can't be friends? (Informant F)

> I knew that there was some sort of class divide. But I didn't think it really mattered. I didn't think that could stop people from making friends or feeling like you don't belong somewhere. (Informant I)

This was not how some thought the student experience was meant to be.

> I just remember hating myself in First Year. I used to watch people walk out of the flat door together going to the pub or something and I was never invited. (Informant J)

> It's just expected that you've met loads of great people and they're your best friends but it's not like that for me. When I see anyone I always tell them I'm having an amazing time and I love it. (Informant F)

Exclusion, inclusion and group cohesion worked in a casual and often taken-for-granted way through shared beliefs and cultural values.

Like one time it was great and then they started talking about how they are going to send their children to a private school because comprehensive [state] schools are rubbish. That really got to me and made me really annoyed. I didn't say anything because there was no point . . . I'm never going to belong here. (Informant I)

Her privately-schooled flat-mates assumed, and also reinforced each other's assumptions, that 'people like us' send our children to private schools.

## Responses to class isolation

Feeling isolated, un-liked, or simply not being fully admitted into the 'promised land' of the student experience, several state-educated informants opted out. This was not normal homesickness. As Informant F told us, her privately-educated house-mates:

. . . just don't get why I go home, but they never will because they're not like me and they've got loads of people around them that are like them with the same background and everything.

Informant J also preferred her home life to that of the institution:

I love going home because I get the chance to just feel like me again . . . . At home I get to see all my friends and I remember that I do belong somewhere.

By going home each weekend these students could re-assert their sense of worth and a happier, authentic identity through former friendships and family relationships.

However, this solution impaired on-campus and academic participation. These students became further isolated in lectures and seminars.

I hate waking up in the morning and thinking that I have to get up and sit in a lecture theatre on my own and watch everyone else walk in and sit in their groups . . . most of the people in the seminar are sat with their friends already and just talk amongst themselves and I don't really have the confidence around them to just join in so I usually end up just not going. (Informant F)

I do really struggle with my university work and I'm just not enjoying it at all. I don't feel like I can really get into any of my work because I'm constantly backwards and forwards . . . The only thing that keeps me going during the week is going home at the weekend. (Informant J)

Academic performance deteriorates if lectures and seminars become distasteful social experiences. For this sample of students at least, the *social* solution of going home interfered directly in *academic* performance. Low morale militated against engagement in learning; time spent going home was time lost for academic work; classes were missed. In our teaching experience, lecturers tend to notice these semi-absentee students only by their irritating non-attendance and, sometimes, poor performance. When engagement and interaction with staff are low, these students can become non-persons with invisible problems.

In contrast, privately educated students mobilised their peer groups to support their academic studies.

> When I'm in the library working with my course friends or in my house with all my housemates . . . we'll all sit in one room and we can listen to music and have regular breaks and make each other cups of tea. (Informant D)

Group identity sustained attendance and at least nominal participation:

> I always go to my lectures and seminars because you get to see all your friends . . . it's extra time to catch up with friends and talk about your nights out and what's happening and we'll usually go shopping or go out for lunch in between lectures. (Informant E)

Looking forward, some of them anticipate staying in the university city to maintain their successful friendships.

> I know so many people that are also staying who are continuing their study or applying for jobs. I'm so not ready to leave yet. (Informant A)

But state educated Informant J said she 'really can't wait to leave and just be in a place where I belong'. Others like her are demoralised and disaffected, wanting to leave the city, Higher Education and the graduate career rat-race.

> I did start applying for graduate jobs but . . . I'm not ready to move away from home to a different place again where I might not belong. (Informant I)

> I was going to do a Masters after but I don't see that happening. I don't even want to chance going through this again. (Informant F)

The characteristics of these groups can be highlighted by sketching two different adaptions (which we did not fully investigate). First some state educated students cope better by becoming 'colleagues'; partying, studying, and making friends *within their degree programme.*

> When my course started properly I made friends that way. Everyone was different, but we all had our course in common which bonded us I guess. There was a few of us that didn't really like our flatmates and stuck together and I went out on nights out and everything with them . . . it's been really fun, I couldn't ask for better friends. (Informant L)

They were *en route* to 'good degrees' whereas those who opted out under-achieved academically. Second, a minority of privately educated students engaged over-enthusiastically in their social life, at the expense of their degree performance. As one hard-working student from a state school observed of them,

> they live in a nice area but just not for me. It's for the more posh people at [this university] who are determined to be a social butterfly and your main aim in life is to know absolutely everyone. (Informant I)

While not claiming a complete typology of responses to the Student Experience, the interview data suggest post-admission adaptations can be summarised as in Figure 1.1. The figure shows how students from private schools either bond with others from privileged backgrounds and perform well, or 'integrate' too well socially to achieve a good degree. State-educated students either find support among students on their program and do well, or fail to integrate or maximise their potential.

Students arrive at university with a variety of motivations and expectations. Most hope that their degree will be the key to a highly paid job, social mobility and financial security. But their paths as undergraduates are very different. Many of the more privileged will have a great student experience with their friends in a city with its nightlife, knowing that family support and connections will help them achieve eventual success in the job market. Others will struggle to balance their studies and part-time paid work, taken on to support them during their studies and mitigate their debt burden when they graduate. A similar picture emerges from the experiences of ENTRY students at one Russell Group university, reported in the next section.

## The ENTRY students

ENTRY coordinators have begun to be aware that good jobs and social mobility are not guaranteed by university access alone. ENTRY students appear to have poorer career prospects. The figure for ENTRY students entering employment or further study 6 months after graduation (based on 2011 graduates) was around 89 per cent compared to the university-wide figure of 93.5 per cent. The proportion of the university's ENTRY students employed in 'graduate-type jobs' was 57 per cent, compared with 74 per cent of university-wide graduates. This suggests that the ways in which university is experienced, and careers subsequently embarked on, are strongly influenced by class background. A recent study supports this,

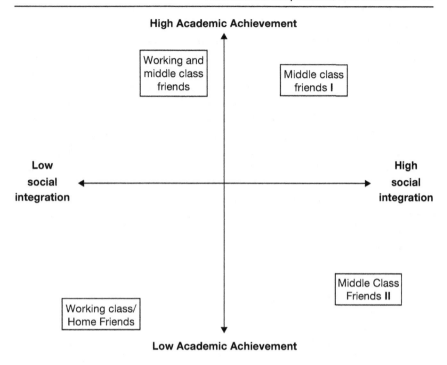

*Figure 1.1* Adaptations to a classed campus high academic achievement

suggesting that graduates' eventual earnings may also be affected by socio-economic background (Britton *et al.*, 2016). The mechanisms producing this class effect are as yet under-researched, but discussions with the Careers Service at the ENTRY university produced some possible contributory factors, including lack of confidence; poor awareness of the need for portfolio-building; little time for extra-curricular activities because of the need for part-time work; low levels of social, cultural and financial capital; and the desire to stay in the area despite its relatively limited job market. These factors echo findings from the *Paired Peers* project (Bathmaker *et al.*, 2013).

The academic performance of ENTRY students, however, was *not* one of the reasons for these career differentials. Students entering the university through the ENTRY scheme do well academically: an unpublished university internal document reports that in recent cohorts, a higher proportion of ENTRY than non-ENTRY students gained an Upper Second or a First. The withdrawal rate is also lower than for the university as a whole – a considerable achievement, given that national withdrawal rates for the widening participation cohort are typically higher than for other students (see e.g. Moore *et al.*, 2013: 51). We must look elsewhere for an explanation, which leads back to the students' classed experiences, and the interaction of upbringing and experience of Higher Education.

All the ENTRY students had looked forward to joining societies, taking part in social activities, meeting different people, making friends and doing something worthwhile. While one – the most confident of the group – served on the staff-student committee, the others had not joined groups or societies. The reasons they gave included expense, lack of time, feeling unwelcome, not fitting in, and uncertainty about the value of such activities. Most were unaware of the CV-enhancing qualities of volunteering, playing sport and other extra-curricular pursuits. Instead they felt that these might prove a distraction from their studies and prevent them spending time with families and pre-university friends.

Although universities portray Freshers' Week as the best of a student's life, a brilliant start to a great student experience – parties and fun, joining in, making friends for life – our ENTRY students found the reality disheartening and overwhelming. They lacked the money, experience and knowledge to engage successfully with the kind of social life familiar to more privileged students. Most did not immediately find friends and some found themselves in awkward social situations:

> This girl said she would go with me to a comedy night, but when we got there she disappeared. The guy on the stage pointed to me and said 'What's wrong with you, not got any mates?' I just went home and that was it, I never went to anything else.
>
> (Focus group participant)

Some resorted to going out with a group from their halls of residence with whom they had little in common and felt out of place. Others, who had opted to live at home, were put off by the prospect of going home alone late at night. Several said they were uncomfortable about going drinking with people they didn't know, preferring to spend time with family or local school friends. Some already had part-time jobs that ate into their free time, so their expensive Freshers' passes (costing around £75) were wasted. This also resulted in a feeling of separation from other students with no need to work and who could not identify with those who did.

We were startled at the extent to which making friends, or failing to, affected the ENTRY students' academic lives. Like the Third Year state school under-graduates, all had looked forward to meeting different kinds of people and forming new friendships with students from other parts of the country with different backgrounds and life experiences from their own. In reality, they found many students were not necessarily interested in making friends with them and rejected their approaches. This could take the form of polite, but vague, interest followed by excuses; or in some cases, more privileged students' outright refusal to associate with those unlike themselves.

This happened both in social situations and in the classroom. Some were met by silence when they tried to chat with a group of students; others talked about some students refusing to work with them when assigned to small group activities in class. All had experienced 'classist' comments in seminars, finding themselves regarded as outsiders. Suddenly seeing themselves through others' eyes and not measuring up, some ENTRY students began to lose confidence, developing a sense of isolation and fear of being seen on their own:

> You don't want to look like a loser, even if that's what you feel you are. I hated going to a lecture or seminar if I didn't have anyone to walk in with. If I didn't have someone to go with, I didn't go. It got harder and harder and in the end I just stopped going.
>
> (Focus group participant)

Poor attendance is a sore point with academic staff, who tend to regard it as the result of excessive partying. It came as a surprise to learn that for a substantial minority of students it is the opposite – the feeling of inadequacy brought about by their inability to fit in with other students and have fun – that caused them to disengage.

It is not unusual for local ENTRY students to continue living at home, at least in their first year. By minimising financial costs, they may reduce the need for part-time work, gaining more time for their studies. The safety net of family and 'home' friends also mitigates some of the social challenges. Conversely, home students find it difficult to become immersed in university life, missing out on participation in extra-curricular activities, especially at night. Not only does this have implications for portfolio-building, but a long commute may become a reason for poor attendance. Commuting, however, can also have a positive side:

> Once I'm in for the day, that's it. I don't have anything else to do or anywhere to go, so I just go to all my classes and get some work done in the library.
>
> (Focus group participant)

Other ENTRY students in halls of residence reported experiencing homesickness, even when home was only an hour or less away. They were not used to being away from family, friends, and familiar ways, and found they had to walk a tightrope between maintaining former relationships and trying to forge a new life at university. Particularly in the case of romantic relationships with a partner not at university, students could experience conflicts between loyalty to their partner and the desire to focus on their studies. They felt under pressure to go home at weekends, the expectation being that after obtaining their degree they would return home for good, and life would continue as before. Some students perceived this as a threat to academic and career success. The level of stress brought one student close to leaving university.

ENTRY students, coming from poorer families, worried about money and debt. Nearly all had part-time jobs, but term-time paid work gave the students anxiety about their studies while work over the summer meant few opportunities for travel or other CV-enhancing experiences. The two students who felt the most detached from university life did 20 and 25 hours of paid work a week. They felt academically disadvantaged, lacking confidence in their ability compared with more privileged students who had a 'better' education, even though these students often seemed disengaged from their studies, as one participant put it 'always texting in class and stuff'. The increased anxiety and fear of low grades made it even more difficult for ENTRY students to concentrate on their studies or find time for other experiences. Not surprisingly, they lacked the confidence to succeed in the job market.

## Concluding observations

It seems reasonable to speculate that many 'non-traditional' students will have the same experiences as the small ENTRY group. They encounter not only students from more advantaged homes, with more material and cultural resources, but a university system of procedures, places and personnel largely organised on the assumption that working-class origins are left behind on entering the campus. Elite universities are middle-class institutions (Reay *et al.* 2009, 2010). And yet, as our analysis of the discursive constructions of fair access in admissions policy language showed, there is no formal recognition of the importance of class, the way it operates as a system, or even how it is represented, in the selection process.

Questions have to be raised about the effectiveness for social mobility of widening participation schemes at elite universities if the effects of class are not recognised. University policies and staff increasingly seek to recognise students' financial difficulties; part-time paid employment; family problems and bereavements; the anxieties of young adult life. But rarely in everyday university life are these problems acknowledged as classed, nor is it routinely recognised that class has consequences for academic performance. Concentrating on meritocratic ideals to the point where we are blind to class barriers does not remove increasing social inequalities. We need to put more effort into extra support and confidence-boosting: helping students see that a poor secondary education is a structural fault, not an individual one; providing remedial support, for example in writing; enabling them to understand the demands of the job market, careers and portfolio building; and understanding that the moral hurts of social class continue inside HE.

We have tried to show in this chapter how elite university admissions processes draw on and contribute to a discursive framing in which disadvantage is contingent and background can be detached from individuals on entrance. Class then becomes difficult to recognise and reflect on in relation to students' everyday university experienc es, even for professional sociologists. But if some students are not fully engaging with their studies, that is perhaps because universities are not fully engaging with their classed selves, identities and experiences. Despite rigorous attention to widening participation in university admissions processes, some students are never fully admitted.

## Notes

1  Also see Boliver's chapter in this volume.
2  www.spa.ac.uk/resources/how-contextualised-admissions-used?section=126

## References

Archer, L. (2007). Diversity, equality and higher education: A critical reflection on the ab/uses of equity discourse within widening participation. *Teaching in Higher Education, 12*(5–6), 635–653.

Archer, L., Hutchings, M., and Ross, A. (2003). *Higher education and social class: Issues of inclusion and exclusion.* London: Routledge.

Bathmaker, A-M., Ingram, N., and Waller, R. (2013). Higher education, social class and the mobilisation of capitals: recognising and playing the game. *British Journal of Sociology of Education, 34*(5–6), 723–743.

Bathmaker, A-M., Ingram, N., Abrahams, J., Hoare, T., Waller, R., and Bradley, H. (2016). *Higher education, social class and social mobility: The degree generation.* London: Palgrave MacMillan.

BIS (Department for Business, Innovation and Skills). (2014). *National Strategy for Access and Student Success in Higher Education.* Retrieved August 20, 2015 from www.gov.uk/government/publications/national-strategy-for-access-and-student-success

Boliver, V. (2011). Expansion, differentiation and the persistence of social class inequalities in UK higher education. *Higher Education, 61*(3), 229–242.

Boliver, V. (2015). Are there distinctive clusters of higher and lower status universities in the UK? *Oxford Review of Education, 41*(5), 608–627.

Bourdieu, P. (1984). *Distinction: a social critique of the judgement of taste.* London: Routledge.

Bravenboer, D. (2012). The Official Discourse of Fair Access to Higher Education. *Widening Participation and Lifelong Learning, 14*(3), 120–140.

Britton, J., Dearden, L., Shephard, N., and Vignoles, A. (2016). *How English domiciled graduate earnings vary with gender, institution attended, subject and socio-economic background.* IFS working paper W16/06. London: Institute for Fiscal Studies. Retrieved April 12, 2016 from www.ifs.org.uk/uploads/publications/wps/wp1606.pdf

Goldthorpe, J. (2013). Understanding – and misunderstanding – social mobility in Britain: the entry of the economists, the confusion of politicians and the limits of educational Policy. *Journal of Social Policy, 42*(3), 431–450.

Graham, C. (2010). *Institutional commitment to widening participation.* Unpublished PhD Thesis, Birmingham: Birmingham University. Retrieved March 11, 2016 from www.etheses.bham.ac.uk/1117/1/Graham10PhD.pdf

Higher Education Funding Council for England (HEFCE). (2014). *Differences in degree outcomes: Key findings.* Bristol: HEFCE. Retrieved March 12, 2016 from www.hefce.ac.uk/pubs/year/2014/201403/#d.en.86821

House of Commons. (2010). *Higher education and social class.* SN/SG/620. London: House of Commons Library.

House of Commons. (2014). *Oxbridge elitism.* SN/SG/616. London: House of Commons Library.

Loveday, V. (2015). Embodying deficiency through 'affective practice': shame, relationality, and the lived experience of social class and gender in higher education.

*Sociology.* Published online before print June 30, 2015, doi: 10.1177/003803851558 9301.

Moore, J., Sanders, J., and Higham, L. (2013). *Literature review of research into widening participation to higher education: Report to HEFCE and OFFA by ARC Network.* London: HEFCE. Retrieved April 4, 2016 from www.offa.org.uk/wp-content/uploads/2013/08/Literature-review-of-research-into-WP-to-HE.pdf

Office for Fair Access (OFFA). (2016). *About OFFA* [Online], Retrieved March 20, 2016 from www.hefce.ac.uk/pubs/year/2014/201403/#d.en.86821

Payne, G. (2017). *The new social mobility.* Bristol: Policy Press.

Reay, D. (2006). The zombie stalking English schools: social class and educational inequality. *British Journal of Educational Studies, 54*(3), 288–307.

Reay, D., David, M., and Ball, S. (2001). Making a difference? Institutional habituses and higher education choice. *Sociological Research Online, 5*(4). Retrieved March 6, 2016 from www.socresonline.org.uk/5/4/reay.html

Reay, D., Crozier, G., and Clayton, J. (2009). 'Strangers in paradise': working class students in elite universities. *Sociology, 43*(6), 1103–1121.

Reay, D., Crozier, G., and Clayton, J. (2010). 'Fitting in' or 'standing out': Working class students in UK higher education *British Educational Research Journal, 32*(1), 1–19.

Russell Group. (2016). Russell Group Universities' Website, home page. Retrieved March 20, 2016 from http://russellgroup.ac.uk/

Scott, P. (2015). Meritocracy is in retreat in 21st-century higher education. *The Guardian,* Retrieved March 9, 2016 from www.theguardian.com/education/2015/sep/01/higher-education-class-degreeuniversity-inequality

Social Mobility and Child Poverty Commission (SMCPC). (2014). *State of the nation 2014: Social mobility and child poverty in Great Britain.* 2nd. Annual Report of the SMCPC. London: HMSO P002596716 10/14. Retrieved March 20, 2016 from www.gov.uk/government/publications/state-of- the-nation-2014-report

SPA (Supporting Professionalism in Admissions). (2012). *Fair admissions to higher education: research to describe the use of contextual data in admissions at a sample of universities and colleges in the UK.* Cheltenham: SPA. Retrieved August 20, 2015 from www.spa.ac.uk/information/contextualdata/

SPA (Supporting Professionalism in Admissions). (2013). Retrieved September 1, 2015 from www.spa.ac.uk/information/contextualdata/spasworkoncontextual/cdresearch2013/

Sutton Trust. (2008). *Wasted talent? Attrition rates of high-achieving pupils between school and university.* Retrieved March 19, 2016 from www.suttontrust.com/researcharchive/wasted-talent-attrition-rates-high-achieving-pupils-school-university/

Sutton Trust. (2010). *Responding to the new landscape for university access* Retrieved March 9, 2016 from www.suttontrust.com/researcharchive/responding-new-landscape-university-access/

Sutton Trust. (2013). *Independent commission on fees report.* London: Sutton Trust. Retrieved March 19, 2015 from www.suttontrust.com/researcharchive/independent-commission-on-fees-report/

Sutton Trust. (2014). *Richest parents four times more likely than poorest to pay for extra classes for their children Press Release 04.09.2014.* London: Sutton Trust. Retrieved March 19, 2016 from www.suttontrust.com/newsarchive/richest-parents-four-times-more-likely-than-poorest to-pay-for-extra-classes-for-their-children/

Tett, L. (2004). Mature working-class students in an 'elite' university: Discourses of risk, choice and exclusion. *Studies in the Education of Adults, 36*(2), 252–264.

Universities and Colleges Admissions Service (UCAS). (2014). *End of cycle report 2014: UCAS analysis and research*. Cheltenham: UCAS. Retrieved August 28, 2015 from www.ucas.com

Warmington, P. (2002). Studenthood as surrogate occupation: Access to HE students discursive production of commitment, maturity and peer support. *Journal of Vocational Education and Training*, *54*(4), 583–600.

# Chapter 2

# Struggling for selfhood

## Non-traditional mature students' critical perspectives on access to higher education courses in England

*Hugh Busher and Nalita James*

### Contexts and concepts

Although there is a growing literature on the experiences of mature students in Higher Education (HE) in England and Wales, little seems to be known empirically about the views and experiences of non-traditional mature students joining Access to Higher Education (AHE) diploma courses and how that affects their transitions in identity (Askham, 2008). Mature students are defined by the Department for Business, Innovation and Skills (BIS, 2012) as those over the age of 24 who are only eligible for loans to cover the costs of their course fees. However, the Universities and Colleges Admissions Service (UCAS) defines mature students as 'anyone over the age of 21 years who did not go to university after school or college' (UCAS, 2015: 3). As many reports to government on mature students use this latter benchmark, we also adopted this in our research. This chapter therefore seeks to add to the literature on mature students by focusing on those enrolled on AHE courses.

The vast majority of AHE courses are delivered in Further Education (FE) colleges. These colleges provide a range of academic and vocational education courses, and 'opportunities for lifelong learning' (Jephcote, *et al.*, 2008: 164), for students who choose to leave school at the age of 16 and other mature students. They are said to encourage an ethos that respects adult students (Jones, 2006). The colleges are neither part of the HE sector nor of the secondary school sector in England and Wales (Quality Assurance Agency for HE [QAA], 2015).

The AHE diploma courses, originally established in the 1970s in England and Wales to encourage more non-traditional mature students to become teachers, are specifically designed to 'provide a chance for adults with irregular education histories to raise their aspirations and enter higher education' (QAA, 2014: 5). This has been achieved by providing successful students with a Level Three qualification, that is an equivalent level to other Level Three qualifications including 'A' levels and Scottish Highers that permits entry to university courses across the UK. The AHE courses provide training in generic learning skills and study in a range of subject knowledge areas such as Nursing and Midwifery, Social Science, Arts and Humanities and Science and Technology (QAA, 2015). They are very intensive, being normally completed in under 1 year. The AHE diploma is awarded by regional award validating agencies for vocational education in England and Wales which are regulated by the QAA.

AHE students are a heterogeneous group of people (Waller, 2006; James, Busher, Piela, and Palmer, 2013; QAA, 2015). Their engagement with their courses is affected by their social and economic backgrounds (QAA, 2015) and the intersectionality of various social factors such as gender, class and ethnicity (Chandra, 2012; Youdell, 2012). Over 60 per cent of learners studying on AHE diploma courses, which have recently had in excess of 40,000 students a year (QAA, 2015), were mature, over the age of 25 years (QAA, 2014). Most of them (74 per cent) are women and 38 per cent come from areas described by the QAA as 'deprived' (QAA, 2015:1). These include many 'second chance' learners (McFadden, 1996; Waller, 2004; Fenge, 2011) who left school at 16 years to enter employment or who underachieved in their school leaving examinations.

The main strategy that many mature students choose to try to achieve their career aspirations is to look for ways to re-enter formal education and gain access to higher education so that they can develop their skills and knowledge (Burke, 2007; QAA, 2015) in order to secure jobs that they want. In part this is not only to gain greater personal satisfaction, but also to contribute more to other aspects of their adult lives such as sustaining a family (Field *et al.*, 2010). Re-engaging with formal education for many AHE students is accompanied with considerable risks (Gonsalves, Seiler, and Salter, 2011) because it impinges on other aspects of their adult lives such as employment, personal relationships with partners and the care of families (Johnston and Merrill, 2009). Furthermore, many mature students have to struggle with low self-confidence as learners because of previous unsuccessful experiences of formal education (Brine and Waller, 2004; Crossan, Field, Gallacher, and Merrill, 2003; Canning, 2010). Consequently, many have a sense of disadvantage especially when re-entering formal education (Reay, 2002; Dillon, 2010; QAA, 2015), although they also seem to develop a capacity to contest the social situations in which they find themselves (Reay, Crozier, and Clayton, 2009).

Courses for mature students can be important sites of transition and personal transformations (Waller, 2006; O'Donnell and Tobbell, 2007) although these are likely to retain elements of earlier identity constructions (Brine and Waller, 2004). Identity is not immutable but subject to constant development (Giddens, 1991; Bauman, 2000). These changes are brought about by people negotiating with social systems, processes and structures (Ecclestone, 2007; Hammersley and Treseder, 2007), such as educational courses and the labour and housing markets they inhabit, and reflecting on who they are (Cieslik, 2006), how they are affected by the social world around them and who they want to become, their career and life aspirations (Youdell, 2012). These reflections arise through people's internal conversations (Archer, 2003; Hammersley and Treseder, 2007) and conversations with others.

Asymmetrical power relationships impinge on how people live their everyday lives by constraining how they can act or forcing them to act in ways they might prefer not to (Foucault, 1977). For example, central government policy in England over at least the last decade has focused on developing the accountability of public sector institutions, such as schools and colleges, by constructing performative policies (Jeffrey and Troman, 2012) that measure the success of educational institutions by the results they achieve. In this view, efficient use of resources (Hodkinson, Ford, Hawthorn, and Hodkinson, 2007) is considered more important than the social value of education or of widening participation in it (Field *et al.*, 2010). Consequently, in the FE sector, AHE courses with poor completion and success rates, (QAA, 2014, 2015) or high costs, can be perceived by senior staff as of doubtful value to an institution's goals (Woodin and Burke, 2008). Such policies also emphasise the importance of hierarchy and supervision in FE colleges, diminishing the influence of ordinary teachers or students over college policy (Handley, Sturdy, Fincham, and Clark, 2006), but encouraging tutors to keep to the tight schedule of the AHE curriculum and scrutinise carefully the work of students as well as their attendance at seminars. This regimentation and surveillance impinges on students' lives in and out of college as the state tries to exert control over the bodies of its subjects through various agencies (Foucault, 1977).

Changes after 2010 in central government policy in England for education and to people's entitlement to in-work or out of work benefits also had a direct and inequitable influence on mature students themselves. Whereas people aged 19–24 years continue to have their course fees fully funded by central government, after 2013 older students could only gain government backed loans to cover their fees (BIS, 2010). Further, students had to fund their own living costs as central government gave no grants or loans for these. It meant AHE students had to either stay in or find employment, rely on their families (which many mature students found demeaning), or rely on state benefits, which many did not want to do (Busher, James, Piela, and Palmer, 2014). These constraints led AHE students into a variety of manoeuvres (Foucault, 1977) to negotiate with agents of the state, such as Job Centre officers, who regulated the allocation of in-work and out of work benefits, and FE college administrators by attending at their offices when students needed to be in employment or in their seminars. Meetings with the agents of the state frequently seemed to involve scrutiny or surveillance of students' activities and incomes, showing how state policies impinge on people's bodies (Foucault, 1977), and often seemed to threaten AHE students' struggles to gain further education and access to university by limiting the resources available to them (James, Busher, Piela, and Palmer, 2013). The demands of their courses led AHE students into manoeuvres of time to fit in their studies alongside family care and employment, often only being able to carry out independent study at evenings and weekends (Busher *et al.*, 2014).

In their struggles to transform their lives, AHE students encountered a range of significant others (O'Donnell and Tobbell, 2007) who helped them to cope with the pressures they faced and in order to sustain their commitment to their aspirations (Reay *et al.*, 2009). AHE course tutors helped students to enhance their self-esteem as learners by developing collaborative cultures on courses (Lave and

Wenger, 1991; Dillon, 2010), showing them how to construct successful learn-ing practices (Busher *et al.*, 2014) and interrupting models of incompetent learning which students may have held (Youdell, 2012). Many members of AHE courses worked together to solve problems in their studies and give each other emotional support, using face-to-face and online media (Busher, James, and Piela, 2015b). Yet other significant people for AHE students were their families to whom many felt strong allegiances (Johnston and Merrill, 2009).

The preceding discussion attempts to set out a conceptual framework to make sense of the struggles and affordances experienced by mature AHE students undertaking further formal education in FE colleges in order to gain entry to university. In the rest of this chapter, this framework is applied critically to a study that was carried out in 2012–2013 in a region of England. After outlining how the study was carried out, the subsequent section considers the aspirations that mature AHE students in the study held and how their initial choices of career were affected by social discourses of gender, age and social class and by the institutional cultures they encountered in schools. The chapter then considers how students struggled with their social and policy contexts, the economic conditions they experienced, the systems of the colleges and their courses in which they were embedded and the agents of the state with whom they had to negotiate. The final section of this chapter then investigates the importance of interpersonal relationships to AHE students trying to develop their self-confidence and skills as learners.

## The study that was carried out

The study on which the rest of this chapter is based took a social constructivist perspective (Lave and Wenger, 1991) to investigate the views of mature students 'with irregular education histories' (QAA, 2014: 5) on AHE courses who aspired to enter higher education. The study enquired about their learning experiences and shifts in identity and what affected these in particular socio-political contexts. It was carried out in seven rural and urban AHE providing institutions in a region of England in 2012–2013 and used a linked case study design (Miles and Huberman, 1994) and mixed methods to enhance trustworthiness by triangulating the perspectives of participants within and across colleges. The study gathered qualitative and quantitative data. The quantitative data came from 365 AHE stu-dents who completed a questionnaire in the autumn term and 166 AHE students who completed a different questionnaire in the summer term. The qualitative data was collected through seven institution-based focus groups, each of which had six to eight students, and who were predominantly white and female. These groups met three times during the academic year. Further qualitative data was collected through 20 semi-structured interviews with AHE tutors. The qualitative data was audio-recorded, transcribed, and analysed using open or inductive coding (Corbin and Strauss, 2008) powered by NVivo. The quantitative data was analysed with simple descriptive statistics. All the participants in this study gave voluntary informed consent to take part in the study, following the guidelines of the British Education Research Association (BERA, 2011).

The profile of the AHE students in the study was largely consistent with that portrayed nationally by the QAA (2014). Of the students who answered the autumn questionnaire, 254/365 (73.6 per cent) were female, although this proportion varied to some extent between the colleges in the study, and many came from lower socioeconomic backgrounds. The age spread of the participants was interesting. Of the students who answered the autumn questionnaire, 190/365 (52 per cent) were aged between 19 and 24 years while 168/365 (46 per cent) were aged 25 years or older. Most (89 per cent) of students had had experience of employment although only 223/365 (61 per cent) of students were currently employed when the study was carried out, albeit mainly in low paid jobs, and this proportion varied little between the colleges in the study. Only 10 per cent of these students had never had paid employment. Of the students who answered the autumn questionnaire, nearly 30 per cent (109/365) did not have Level Two qualifications, equivalent to the General Certificate of Secondary Education (GCSE) – the school leaving examination in England and Wales. On the other hand, 29 per cent (106/365) of the students had at least one qualification at Level Three. Of the students who answered the autumn questionnaire, the most popular AHE courses were Nursing and Midwifery 197/365 (54 per cent), Social Science 80/365 (22 per cent), Humanities 69/365 (19 per cent) and Science 62/365 (17 per cent).

The next section considers the aspirations that mature AHE students in the study held and how their initial choices of career were affected by social discourses around gender, age, and social class and by the institutional cultures they encountered in schools.

## Students' aspirations and inhibitions in being and becoming

AHE students in the autumn questionnaire gave three main reasons for joining AHE courses: *'to go to university'*, *'to better myself'*, *'to retrain or change career'*. However, gender affected their choices with more males than females choosing *'to go to university'* (females, 165/365 [45.3 per cent]; males, 220/365 [60.4 per cent]) or *'to complete my education'* (females, 138/365 [37.8 per cent]; males, 188/365 [51.6 per cent]). Further, more females 37/365 (10.2 per cent) compared to males 12/365 (3.3 per cent) gave *'for my family'* as the main reason for joining an AHE course. Age also appeared to influence people's reasons for joining AHE courses. Of the students who answered the Autumn questionnaire, the 19–24 year age group more often chose *'to better myself'* or *'to complete my education'* as reasons for joining AHE courses (88/365, 24.1 per cent), than any other age group. The same age group also more often chose *'to go to university'* (201/365, 55 per cent) as their main reason for joining than those aged 45 years and over (112/365, 30.8 per cent). On the other hand, more students aged over

35 years (116/365, 31.7 per cent) chose *'to retrain or change career'* as a main reason for joining an AHE course.

AHE students' decisions to return to formal education were linked to conversations with themselves (Archer, 2003) about their identities and their competing visions for their futures. For example, one participant explained, *'when I was at secondary school I always wanted to go into psychology, but left sixth form [did] hairdressing and I still [am] interested in psychology' (Student Coll. 4).* The students offered various explanations for why they did not pursue their aspirations when they were 16 years old. One set of explanations were age- and environment-related. Some students thought they were too young to decide at 16 years old or did not want to commit to a career *(Students Coll. 4 and 6).* *'At sixteen you just feel like you're so kind of up to here with education. I just kind of wanted to see what the world was about' (Student Coll. 5).* Yet other students related their choices to the views of their peers. *'[At sixteen] all the girls go (into) hair and beauty and all the boys want to go into the army' (Student Coll. 4).* A few were inspired by their friends. *'Seeing all my friends go off to university and aspire to be something more made me actually want to do it' (Student Coll. 7).*

Other explanations that students offered were related to their experiences of their schools as institutions. *'At my school it wasn't pushed to stay on and go to uni [versity]. Everybody just got jobs' (Student Coll. 4).* It was also reported by some that agents of the school, such as teachers, contributed to their negative experiences of their school's institutional cultures. *'I'm terrible at maths, but . . . no matter what teacher I got, they always just seemed so unapproachable and not particularly helpful' (Student Coll. 2).* Further, students' negative encounters with fellow students helped to create in some students a sense of being bullied *(Student Coll. 7).* This inhibited their confidence. *'I really love to learn by sort of asking questions and discussion, but at school [I was] just labelled as a nerd' (Student Coll. 5).*

Our AHE respondents' socio-economic backgrounds also had an important impact on their future choices as Reay, *et al.* (2009) also found in their study. Where students had lived when they were at school seemed to have greatly affected their experiences of education. *'School was horrendous. It was a really a bad neighbourhood and horrible, horrible school' (Student Coll. 1).* In other cases it was the families in which they grew up that affected their choices and views of schooling. *'I come from quite an underclass background. I had to go out to work to support my mum and my other sisters, literally had three jobs' (Student Coll. 2).* In other cases, it was related to problems in the family such as divorce. *'In education I did really, really well up until a few family problems and then kind of got lost' (Student Coll. 6).* Tutors on AHE courses also further commented that many of their female students had left school at the age of 16 to have children and then returned in their mid-twenties to formal education and this had a great impact on confidence levels (Busher, James, and Piela, 2015a).

In other cases, however, families were a source of support and inspiration. 'I've always wanted to go to university. [I] never really had the confidence until I met my husband. And now I've had my little boy. I want to set him a good example' (Student Coll. 7). Yet AHE students recognised that their families limited their choice of a college for their studies. As one student explained about her choice of college, 'For me it's convenient and I'm still holding down a job. So it's a matter of getting here, getting the children, and still keeping a job. I can't afford not to work' (Student Coll. 6). Families also influenced AHE students' choices of university in the same way, with AHE students mainly choosing to go those that were convenient to their homes and relatively easy to get to.

Having explored the aspirations and inhibitions of our respondents, this chapters next two sections move on to discuss how AHE students perceived their struggles with their social and policy contexts, the economic conditions they experienced, the systems of the colleges and their courses in which they were embedded. We also look at the agents of the state with whom they had to negotiate.

## Coping with economic conditions, colleges, and agents of the state

Experiences of the labour market challenged students' senses of agency and self-development, helping many to grow as individuals (Student Coll. 4), which may explain why 95/365 (26 per cent) of the respondents to the Autumn questionnaire claimed to be bored in their current jobs. In some cases, AHE students' jobs helped them to recognise the skills and knowledge they had gained that could lead to future careers (Gonsalves *et al.*, 2011). '*I want to be a primary school teacher. I was a riding instructor. So this is the first step because I don't even have GCSEs. So then hopefully go to university, do a PGCE*' (Student Coll. 6). The recession and economic downturn in the UK in 2008 encouraged some students to look again at formal education as a means of fulfilling their ambitions (*Student Coll. 6*) '*It's really difficult to get a job. If you've not got your qualifications what have you got?*' (Student Coll. 4).

In returning to education AHE students made considered choices in selecting the AHE diploma because it offered opportunities to 'second chance' learners (McFadden, 1996; Waller, 2004; Fenge, 2011) with low prior educational achievement. '*If you've been out of education and you want to get back into it, if there wasn't the Access Course I don't know another way of getting into university*' (Student Coll. 6). The AHE diploma course also offered other advantages, as AHE tutors pointed out (Busher *et al.*, 2015a). For example, when compared with 'A' level courses, which last 2 years in England and Wales, (and which some AHE students had previously undertaken albeit only partially successfully) the more compact nature of the course was an attraction. '*Access is only going to be like one year and then I can go straight to uni[versity]*' (Student Coll. 4). Other students thought the AHE course, '*sets you up well for university with the assignments and the deadlines and you have to get the work done. Whereas with 'A'-level [exams] I left it all sort of last minute*' (Student Coll. 5).

Nonetheless, in returning to formal education AHE students encountered various forms of regimentation (Foucault, 1977). This regimentation impacted on other demands on their time such as employment, family responsibility, and study (Field *et al.*, 2010), while senior institutional staff in their FE colleges mediated national education policies to try to maximise success rates on AHE courses. To mitigate these conflicts some colleges limited the contact hours on AHE courses so students could continue with their employment. '*This is the right place for me because they [only] do it over three days' (Student Coll. 2)*. This approach by colleges had a strange outcome for some students when they tried to negotiate unemployment benefit with local Job Centres, since the AHE courses appeared to be part-time because the private study elements of the courses were disguised, hidden in students' out of college hours. '*Our course is only fifteen hours, which means it counts as part-time [but] the College defines it as full-time' (Student Coll. 5)*.

However, in other aspects the college systems were less flexible in meeting AHE students' needs with colleges providing access to libraries and study support by staff at particular times which were not always convenient to AHE students who had to sustain jobs and family commitments. '*I work full-time and I come here to school full-time and it's tiring and it can be hectic. After college . . . I'll spend the whole night at work' (Student Coll. 6)*. Students' practices as students were carefully monitored by their tutors acting as agents of the colleges, giving evidence of what Foucault (1977) described as 'surveillance' as means for systems to keep people conforming to their norms. Unsurprisingly, students were expected to attend seminars in college at particular times which sometimes clashed with the demands of their employers, as might the submission dates/times of course assignments as various AHE tutors discussed (Busher *et al.*, 2015a). Some students had to dash away from college to pick up their children from school so were unable to undertake independent study in college.

Even with the difficulties we have outlined, some students acknowledged the support they received from their colleges. 'There's good resources, books and loads of computers, and there's always loads of staff around as well to help you out with anything' (Student Coll. 7). In five out of the seven colleges students were provided with web-based resources through a Virtual Learning Environments where tutors were supposed to create repositories of materials that students could access whenever they were undertaking their private study, such as at evenings and weekends. Many students welcomed the convenience of these virtual environments so long as the tutors kept them populated, (which apparently they did not always do), and as long as the students felt sufficiently IT literate to engage with them. 'When I'm not understanding, everything that we're doing will be on the Learn Zone' (Student Coll. 4). In addition, some colleges required tutors to make available to students their out of hours email and telephone addresses so that students could contact them if they needed help. This created particular pressures on tutors' use of professional and personal time (see Busher *et al.*, 2015a).

Despite the attempts of some colleges to minimise the impact of AHE courses on students' lives, attending the courses appeared to have deleterious effects, forcing students into various manoeuvres that they would have preferred not to make (Foucault, 1977). Some students had to reduce their hours of paid work once they had enrolled. *'I've had to drop down to twenty-five hours a week. I've got a house to pay for and a car to pay for and other bills' (Student Coll. 3)*. AHE tutors also noted the impact on their students of having to generate sufficient income to cover the costs of their courses and sustain the other aspect of their adult lives (Busher *et al.*, 2015a). In some cases, students simply stayed away from their courses when their employers asked them to work extra hours (Busher *et al.*, 2015a) while in other cases students simply worked long hours. For example, one student told us, *'Either quit my job and get benefits or keep working. I rather keep working otherwise I'm going to go insane with studying' (Student Coll. 2)*. A few employers were sympathetic about renegotiating students' hours of work (Student Coll. 3) but other employers were less helpful. *'I asked [for] my job to go part-time but they didn't allow it. So I had to leave, but this made me ineligible for Job Seekers Allowance' (Student Coll. 5)*.

Where students could not gain enough income through employment to cover the costs of their studies they had to engage with agents of the state, such as officials in Job Centres and administrators in FE colleges that controlled access to state payments or benefits for in-work and out of work people. Trying to gain state support involved students in various manoeuvres (Foucault, 1977) both in time and space (Paechter, 2004), in order to attend offices for scheduled meetings. These procedures subjected them to the regimentation of the benefits schemes with which they had to comply if they were to gain payments. The Job Centres were unsympathetic to students' needs in many cases. *'I got made redundant but the Job Centre were really, really difficult. [They] said that if a full-time job became available for me, that I'd have to quit the course and start the job' (Student Coll. 3)*. In other cases, as we outlined above, respondents reported that the Job Centres would not accept that AHE courses were full-time because their contact hours were limited and benefits were not available to students on part-time courses. Losing or not gaining benefits such as housing benefit and Job Seekers [unemployment benefit] was a major disaster for some students. *'It's going from that bit of financing where you can survive, to absolutely nothing and being at college all the time whilst still looking for work' (Student Coll. 5)*.

FE colleges also acted as agents of the state by regulating students' access to finance to cover their living costs, even students were told before their course started that they had gained college support for their fees, which was not always the case. The complexity of the national regulations caused confusion in some cases. *'At first they told me that I would be funded, but [at] enrolment they said, "No. You are not funded". [Now I struggle] to pay the rest of the tuition fee which at first they promised me' (Student Coll. 2)*. College support was strictly regulated and required various manoeuvres from students to access it. In one college there was a *'drop-in centre for student funds to help with . . . books, travelling' (Student Coll. 2)*, but students were not sure where it was. In another college it was reported to us that there was *'Like a hardship fund. So for me they're paying for the course fees. I get a bus pass and meal card. If it wasn't for that, I wouldn't be able to come here' (Student Coll. 6).* Bus passes could only be given to students who lived more than three miles from the college they attended. Some AHE students thought this was unfair. *'How you're meant to live and pay the rent and work [is] very difficult. My job is full-time' (Student Coll. 6).* They resented shifts in government policy that had reduced the level of funding for AHE courses. *'I think it was really rubbish to cut the Adult Learning Grant, because all of us have had to cut our hours at work' (Student Coll. 4).*

FE colleges were bound by the performative government policies that regulated their work (Hodkinson *et al.*, 2007) emphasising efficiency over the benefits of continuing education (Field *et al.*, 2010). Perhaps because of the relatively poor completion and progression rates of AHE courses (QAA, 2015), this led some colleges to treat AHE courses as marginal to their financial purposes, limiting the staff and spatial resources available to them. In one college the AHE course teaching base was given to business studies courses, to the chagrin of the AHE tutor and some students. One tutor stated, *'A couple of my students today, you know, said, "We're a prestigious course. Why are we being treated as though we're not?"' (Tutor Coll. 5).*

While coping with economic conditions, the administrative processes of the colleges and other agents of the state, our respondents also placed huge importance on their informal support networks. In the final section of this chapter, we investigate the importance of interpersonal relationships to AHE students trying to develop their self-confidence and skills as learners.

## The importance of 'others' for AHE students

Both the positive and negative influences of significant others were of major importance for AHE students. AHE students appreciated their tutors treating them with respect. *'[Tutors] understand that we're not school children who have no commitments outside college. We've all got families' (Student Coll. 1).* They also appreciated the approachability of many tutors. *'[If] you don't understand the assignment, you can go and talk to your tutor. He'll book you in for tutorial's (Student Coll. 7).* Tutors also modelled effective learning practices with and to the AHE students. *'You get a mark but you also get comments at the bottom of your work pointing you in the direction that maybe you should have gone down' (Student Coll. 4).*

The collaborative cultures that developed between AHE students and with many of their tutors helped them to cope with the intensity of the AHE curriculum and their personal situations (Busher *et al.*, 2014). Students welcomed the contrast with their experiences in school lessons. *'We weren't allowed to speak up in class. [But] we're encouraged now to kind of get involved and it really helps' (Student Coll. 2).* One student recounted how she was welcomed by other AHE students for researching the development of some assignments they had been given, stating *'you know what you're doing' [Laughter]. It's not like that when you're at secondary school because if you do good you get the mick took out of you' (Student Coll. 4).* These cultures reflected values shared between many AHE students. '*I think everybody who is here is here for a reason. So I need to get something out of it' (Student Coll. 6).* The collaborative cultures were elaborated through face to face interactions in class and through face to face study, '*so we go to the library, like a group of us, and get stuff done there, which is a good help' (Student Coll. 6)* as well as through online independent study and Facebook. However, not all students used these networks and some choose to work with alone and distanced themselves from others on their courses (see Busher *et al.*, 2015a; James, Busher, and Suttill, 2015).

Significant 'others' for AHE students also included their families and non-AHE students in their colleges. For example one respondent stated that '*there's absolutely no way I could do this without my partner. He has organised his whole working life around me being here' (Student Coll. 2).* Other AHE students talked about their partners and/or mothers undertaking childcare, cooking and house cleaning duties. However, some family members caused tensions for AHE students – the break-up of their marriages was referred to by a few female students – and many of those students who were single parents struggled with the additional workloads that the AHE courses brought. As a tutor informed us, '*you can see a pattern in terms of childcare and in finance. It's the ones that are on their own [who] have real problems [and] tend to struggle' (Tutor Coll. 6).*

Non-AHE students in the FE colleges were also significant. AHE students defined themselves as 'mature' and 'focused' unlike the other students whom they claimed had neither of these virtues (Warmington, 2002; James *et al.*, 2013). These 'others' were perceived neither as focused in their studies nor as 'mature' as AHE students and made it difficult for people to use college resources for serious study *(Student Coll. 5; Student Coll. 7).* It would appear that other students helped AHE students to define themselves by who they were not (Youdel, 2012).

## Conclusion

In this chapter we have shown that AHE students' struggled to transform their identities as learners and as people to have more fulfilling lives. These struggles led them back to familiar ground where they had been unsuccessful previously and which had undermined their confidence in being able to engage in formal education (Reay, 2002; Brine and Waller, 2004; Dillon, 2010). Despite the risks this entailed (Gonsalves *et al.*, 2011) the route they chose seemed to them the only way to become who they wanted to be and to enable them to achieve their aspirations, despite being encumbered in many cases with families and the other trappings of adult life (Johnston and Merrill, 2009). The structured and structuring series of choices and decisions students had to make to be able to participate in AHE courses, involved them negotiating arenas of unequal power relationships with educational institutions, the work place, the AHE curriculum and agents of the state, such as Job Centres. Through these processes students experienced the machinery of covert power that Foucault (1977) discussed, and regimentation by the curriculum and college system, surveillance by agents of the state (such as state benefit officers) and college tutors. This was accompanied by incidents where they were forced to carry out various manoeuvres that many would rather not have undertaken in order to get access to sufficient income and time for study to make it possible for them to undertake the AHE courses. These affected how they were able to live and impinged on their bodies (Foucault, 1977). They sustained their endeavours on the AHE courses by their determination to succeed because of their previous experiences of the labour market when holding only limited qualifications; the support of their families in many cases; the support of many of their tutors who helped to disrupt their previous experiences as unsuccessful learners (Youdell, 2012) as well as treating them with respect (Jones, 2006; Reay *et al.*, 2009). This was coupled with the collaborative cultures that they built with many of their fellow students. These cultures seemed to show many of the characteristics that are said to be constructed by communities of practice, whether formally set up or naturally occurring, in various types of organisations (Lave and Wenger, 1991; Busher *et al.*, 2014).

## Acknowledgements

### Funding

Aim Awards, a regional Award Validating Agency (AVA), Grant No.: **RS101 G0098**
The British Academy Grant No.: **RS141G0036**

### Research assistant and interns

Dr Anna Piela of Leeds Trinity University was the Research Assistant on the project and made a substantial contribution to its success.
Beth Suttill and Anne-Marie Palmer were research interns who sequentially made substantial contributions to the success of the project.

## References

Archer, M. (2003). *Structure, agency and the internal conversation*. Cambridge: Cambridge University Press.
Askham, P. (2008). Context and identity: exploring adult learners experiences of higher education. *Journal of Further and Higher Education, 32*(1), 85–97.
Bauman, Z. (2000). *Liquid modernity*. Cambridge: Polity Press.
Brine, J. and Waller, R. (2004). Working class women on an access course: Risk, opportunity and (Re)constructing identities. *Gender and Education, 16*(1), 97–113.
British Educational Research Association (BERA). (2011). *Revised ethical guidelines for educational research*. London: BERA.

Burke, P.J. (2007). Men accessing education: masculinities, identifications and widening participation. *British Journal of Sociology of Education, 28*(4), 411–424.

Busher, H., James, N., Piela, A., and Palmer, A.M. (2014). Transforming marginalised adult learners' views of themselves: Access courses in England. *British Journal of Sociology of Education, 35*(5), 800–817.

Busher, H., James, N., and Piela, A. (2015a). I always wanted to do second chance learning: identities and experiences of tutors on access to HE courses. *Research in Post-Compulsory Education, 20*(2), 127–139.

Busher, H., James, N., and Piela, A. (2015b). On reflection: Mature students' views of successful teaching and learning on access to higher education courses in England. *International Studies in the Sociology of Education, 25*(4), 296–313.

Canning, N. (2010). Playing with heutagogy: Exploring strategies to empower mature learners in higher education. *Journal of Further and Higher Education, 34*(1), 59–71.

Chandra, P. (2012). Marxism, Homi Bhabha and the omissions of postcolonial theory: Critique. *Journal of Socialist Theory, 40*(2), 199–214.

Cieslik, M. (2006). Reflexivity, learning identities and adult basic skills in the United Kingdom. *British Journal of Sociology of Education, 27*(2), 237–250.

Corbin, J. and Strauss, A. (2008). *Basics of qualitative research: techniques and procedures for developing grounded theory*, 3rd ed. Los Angeles, Calif. and London: Sage.

Crossan, B., Field, J., Gallacher, J., and Merrill, B. (2003). Understanding participation in learning for non-traditional adult learners: Learning careers and the construction of learning identities. *British Journal of Sociology of Education, 24*(1), 55–67.

Department for Business, Innovation and Skills (BIS). (2010). *Further Education – New Horizon: Investing in Sustainable Growth* (Crown Copyright). Retrieved November 26, 2016 from www.bis.gov.uk/assets/biscore/further-education-skills/docs/s/10–1272-strategy-investing-in-skills-for-sustainable-growth.pdf

Department for Business, Innovation and Skills (BIS). (2012). Government response to 'Students at the heart of the system' and 'A new regulatory framework for the HE sector'. Retrieved November 26, 2016 from www.bis.gov.uk/assets/biscore/higher-education/docs/g/12–890-government-response-students-and-regulatory-framework-higher-education

Dillon, J. (2010). Black minority ethnic students' journeys to higher education: Realisable or thwarted ambitions? *The International Journal of Learning, 17*, 219–231.

Ecclestone, K. (2007). An identity crisis? Using concepts of 'identity', 'agency' and 'structure' in the education of adults: Editorial. *Studies in the Education of Adults, 39*(2), 121–131.

Fenge, L. A. (2011). A second chance at learning but it's not quite higher education: Experience of a foundation degree. *Journal of Further and Higher Education, 35*(3), 375–390.

Field, J., Merrill, B., and Morgan-Klein, N. (2010). Researching higher education access, retention and drop-out through a european biographical approach: Exploring similarities and differences within a research team. *European Society for Research on the Education of Adults, Sixth European Research Conference*, University of Linköping, Linköping.

Foucault, M. (1977). *Discipline and punish: The birth of the prison*. Translated by A. Sheridan, London: Allen Lane.

Giddens, A. (1991). *Modernity and self-identity: Self and society in the late modern age.* Cambridge: Polity Press.

Gonsalves, A., Seiler, G., and Salter, D. E. (2011). Rethinking Resources and Hybridity. *Cultural Studies of Science Education, 6*(2), 389–399.

Hammersley, M., and Treseder, P. (2007). Identity as an analytic problem: Who's who in `pro-ana' websites? *Qualitative Research*, 7(3), 283–300.

Handley, K., Sturdy, A., Fincham, R., and Clark, T. (2006). Within and beyond communities of practice: Making sense of learning through participation. *Identity and Practice, Journal of Management Studies*, 43(3), 641–653.

Hodkinson, P., Ford, G., Hawthorn, R., and Hodkinson, H. (2007). Learning as Being. *Learning Lives Working Paper 6*. Leeds, University of Leeds.

James, N., Busher, H., Piela, A., and Palmer, A.M. (2013). Opening doors to higher education: Access students' learning transitions. *Final Project Report – Phase 2*, Leicester: University of Leicester.

James, N., Busher, H., and Suttill, B. (2015). "We all know why we're here": Learning as a community of practice on access to HE courses *Journal of Further and Higher Education*, 40(6), 765–779.

Jeffrey, B., and Troman, G. (2012). Introduction. In B. Jeffrey, and G. Troman (Eds.), *Performativity across UK Education: Ethnographic cases of its effects, agency and reconstructions*, Painswick: E&E Publishing.

Jephcote, M., Salisbury, J., and Rees, G. (2008). Being a teacher in further education in changing times. *Research in Post-compulsory Education*, 13(2), 163–172.

Johnston, R., and Merrill, B. (2009). Developing learning identities for working class adult students in higher education. In B. Merrill (Ed), *Learning to change? The role of identity and learning careers in adult education*. Frankfurt am Main: Peter Lang, 129–144.

Jones, K. (2006). Valuing diversity and widening participation: The experiences of access to social work students in further and higher education. *Social Work Education*, 25(5), 485–500.

Lave, J., and Wenger, E. (1991). *Situated learning: Legitimate peripheral participation*. Cambridge: Cambridge University Press.

McFadden, M.G. (1996). 'Second chance' education: Accessing opportunity or recycling disadvantage? *International Studies in Sociology of Education*, 6(1), 87–111.

Miles, M.B., and Huberman, M. (1994). *Qualitative data analysis: an expanded sourcebook*, Thousand Oaks, CA: Sage.

O'Donnell, V.L., and Tobbell, J. (2007). The transition of adult students to higher education: Legitimate peripheral participation in a community of practice? *Adult Education Quarterly*, 57(4), 312–328.

Paechter, C. (2004). Space, identity and education. *Pedagogy, Culture and Society*, 12(3), 3–7.

Reay, D. (2002). Class, authenticity and transition to higher education for mature students. *The Sociological Review*, 50(3), 398–418.

Reay, D., Crozier, G., and Clayton, J. (2009). Strangers in paradise: Working class students in elite universities. *Sociology*, 43(6), 1103–1121.

Quality Assurance Agency in Higher Education (QAA). (2014). The access to higher education diploma: Key statistics 2014. Gloucester: QAA. Retrieved November 26, 2016 from www.accesstohe.ac.uk/AboutUs/Publications/Documents/AHE-Key-Statistics-14.pdf

Quality Assurance Agency for Higher Education (QAA). (2015). *The Access to Higher Education Diploma. Key Statistics 2013–14*. Gloucester: QAA. Retrieved November 26, 2016 from www.accesstohe.ac.uk/AboutUs/Publications/Documents/AHE-Key-Statistics-14.pdf

University Council on Admissions (UCAS). (2015). *Applications by mature students*. Retrieved November 26, 2016 from www.ucas.com/ucas/undergraduate/getting-started/mature-students

Waller, R. (2004). I really hated school, and couldn't wait to get out! reflections on 'a wasted opportunity' amongst access to HE students. *Journal of Access Policy and Practice, 2*(1), 24–43.

Waller, R. (2006). "I don't feel like 'a student', i feel like 'me'"! The over-simplification of mature learners' experience(s). *Research in Post-Compulsory Education, 11*(1), 115–130.

Warmington, P. (2002). Studenthood as surrogate occupation: Access to HE Students' discursive production of commitment, maturity and peer support. *Journal of Vocational Education and Training, 54*(4), 583–600.

Woodin, T., and Burke, P.J. (2008). Men accessing education: Masculinities, class and choice. *Australian Educational Researcher, 34*(3), 119–134.

Youdell, D. (2012). Fabricating 'pacific islander': Pedagogies of expropriation, return and resistance and other lessons from a 'multicultural day'. *Race Ethnicity and Education, 15*(2), 141–155.

# Chapter 3

# How meritocratic is admission to highly selective UK universities?

*Vikki Boliver*

## Introduction

Widening access to UK universities has been high on the policy agenda for more than 70 years. The 1944 Education Act – best known for creating free, universal, and compulsory secondary schooling for all – introduced the first maintenance grants to enable students from poorer families to meet the day-to-day costs of going to university (Stevens, 2004). In the 1960s, the government-commissioned Committee on Higher Education led by Lord Robbins established the principle that '... all young persons qualified by ability and attainment to pursue a full-time course in higher education should have the opportunity to do so' (Committee on Higher Education, 1965: 49). The Robbins report led to the creation of thirteen new universities and thirty new polytechnic higher education institutions (Halsey, 2000), the mandatory provision of maintenance grants for students by local authorities, and a rapid increase in the HE participation rate from 5 per cent to 14 per cent within a decade (UGC, 1973).

Informed by the same meritocratic ideal as the Robbins report, the upgrading of the polytechnics to full university status following the 1988 Education Reform Act and the 1992 Further and Higher Education Act saw the HE participation rate increase again to 32 per cent by the mid-1990s (NCIHE, 1997). This ongoing political commitment to widening participation in higher education has been accompanied by a series of regressive policy measures implemented by successive UK governments since the late 1980s. These have included the introduction of student loans and the reduction of student maintenance grants from 1989 onwards, the introduction of tuition fees in 1998 and the subsequent increases in fees in 2006 and 2012 (DES, 1988; DfEE, 1998; DfES, 2003; DBIS, 2011). The latest statistics indicate that the HE participation rate for the UK now stands at over 40 per cent (DBIS, 2015) and that all young people from the most and least disadvantaged neighbourhoods are participating in HE at record rates (DBIS, 2014). At the same time, however, the evidence suggests that neither the more progressive era of HE policy in the UK, nor the more recent regressive era has produced much in the way of an equalisation of HE participation rates among those from more and less socio-economically advantaged backgrounds, least of all in relation to older, more prestigious institutions (NCIHE, 1997; Boliver, 2011).

Partly because inequalities in overall HE participation rates have remained so stubborn, debates about widening access to higher education have become more nuanced in recent years. First and foremost, analysts have become increasingly cognisant of the fact that in an era of mass participation in a highly diverse HE sector, it is important to focus not just on access to higher education in general, but on access to highly selective and prestigious universities as well. In particular, researchers and policy-makers are increasingly asking questions about why Oxbridge, the wider Russell Group of 'leading UK universities',[1] and Old (pre-1992) universities more generally remain so unrepresentative of wider society, much more so than most new (post-1992) universities (Boliver, 2013: 350). Second, there has been growing awareness of the need to look not only at the barriers to wider access which occur prior to the point of university application, but also to consider the potential role played by universities at the point of admissions decision-making. In particular, researchers and policy makers are increasingly asking to what extent university admissions can be considered meritocratic, both in the narrow sense of admissions decisions being determined by academic achievement alone without bias in favour of applicants from more socio-economically advantaged backgrounds (Sutton Trust, 2011; Zimdars, Sullivan, and Heath, 2009; Boliver, 2013; Noden, Shiner, and Modood, 2014; Boliver, 2015, 2016), and also in the broader sense of admissions decisions being taken in light of information about the socio-economic context of applicants' achievements in order to fully capture applicants' merit (Schwartz, 2004; Social Mobility and Child Poverty Commission, 2012; Boliver, Gorard, and Siddiqui, 2015).

Against this backdrop, this chapter explores empirically the extent to which admission to highly selective, Russell Group universities can be said to be meritocratic, in the narrow sense of determined by applicants' prior attainment alone. The chapter also discusses the case to be made for a greater shift towards meritocratic admissions policies in the broader sense, via the widespread use of contextualised admissions policies which take due account of the often challenging circumstances in which people from socio-economically disadvantaged backgrounds achieve the qualifications required to go to university.

## Recent trends in widening access to Russell Group universities

Before looking at admissions to prestigious, Russell Group universities, it is helpful, first, to take a look at the data on recent trends in the social composition of young full-time first degree entrants to these institutions. As Figure 3.1 shows, the percentage of entrants to Russell Group universities from state schools and colleges, remained flat at around 75 per cent in the 11-year period between 2002/3 and 2012/13, and although it has since increased by 3.3 percentage points to 79.1

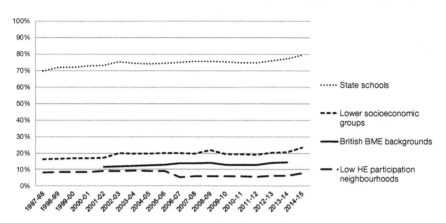

*Figure 3.1* Percentages of young full-time first degree entrants to Russell Group universities between 1997/98 and 2014/15 (calculated from HESA data)[2]

per cent in 2014/15 it continues to fall far short of the 93 per cent of 15-year-old school pupils attending state rather than private schools nationally (DfE, 2015). Similarly, the percentage of Russell Group entrants from lower social class backgrounds remained at around 20 per cent for more than a decade and although this figure rose to 23.3 per cent between 2013/14 and 2014/15 it is still significantly below the 37.1 per cent of 17–18 year olds in the UK population who come from lower social class backgrounds (LFS data for 2013). The percentage of students entering Russell Group universities from low HE participation neighbourhoods in fact fell from 8.8 per cent to 5.3 per cent in 2006/7 – the year that tuition fees were raised to £3000 a year, before being raised again to £9000 a year in 2012 – and has only recently begun to recover, reaching 7.8 per cent in 2014/15 compared to around 20 per cent of the wider national population. The representation of young people from black and minority ethnic (BME) backgrounds among entrants to Russell Group universities has increased slightly by some 2.6 percentage points between 2001/2 and 2014/5, but at 14.1 per cent remains below the figure of 19 per cent for the wider national population of young people (Nomis, 2013). Moreover, the aggregated statistic for BME students obscures the fact that while some ethnic minority groups, such as the Chinese and Indian groups, are statistically over-represented at Russell Group universities compared to their national population proportion, other groups, such as the Black Caribbean, Black African, Pakistani and Bangladeshi groups, are under-represented by as much as one half (Boliver, 2015).

## From entry rates to admissions chances

Of course the figures above relate to *entrants* to Russell Group universities, which conflate a number of different processes and outcomes. Ultimately entering a

Russell Group university is dependent sequentially on the following: (1) staying on in post-compulsory education and being on course to achieve the qualifications needed to be eligible for entry to a Russell Group university; (2) choosing to apply to a Russell Group university; (3) receiving an offer of a place having applied.[3] A wealth of research literature has been generated in relation to (1), and it is clear that a big part of the under-representation at Russell Group universities of students from socio-economically disadvantaged backgrounds and certain ethnic minority groups is poorer performance at school (DBIS, 2013). There is also ample evidence in relation to (2) which suggests that students from less advantaged backgrounds are less likely to apply to university generally and to more prestigious universities in particular (Boliver, 2013). Indeed, this factor drives much of the outreach work carried out by universities using funds committed to this endeavour in their Access Agreements. In relation to (3), which is the focus of this chapter, there is a growing body of empirical literature which has found that the Russell Group and other highly selective universities are less likely to offer places to applicants from state schools (Boliver, 2013; Noden, Shiner, and Modood, 2014; Boliver, 2016), lower social class backgrounds (Zimdars, Sullivan, and Heath, 2009; Boliver, 2013; Noden, Shiner, and Modood, 2014), low HE participation neighbourhoods (Boliver, 2016), and ethnic minority backgrounds (Zimdars, Sullivan, and Heath, 2009; Boliver, 2013; Noden, Shiner, and Modood, 2014; Boliver 2016) even after taking applicants' qualifications into account. The Russell Group has repeatedly dismissed these findings (Russell Group 2013; 2015a), even though they have been produced by academic researchers based at a number of their own institutions.[4]

## Analysing admissions data

It is possible to make some assessment of the degree to which admissions to Russell Group universities are 'meritocratic' in the narrow sense by analysing anonymised individual level applicant data supplied by the Universities and Colleges Admissions Service (UCAS). UCAS is the administrative body that assists universities in handling applications to almost all full-time higher education courses in the UK. The UCAS dataset analysed in the remainder of this chapter comprises a ten per cent random sample of all 'home' applicants to full-time undergraduate degree courses at UK universities commencing in 2010/11, 2011/12 and 2012/13. The working sample contains information on 68,632 UCAS candidates who collectively submitted 151,281 applications to Russell Group universities in the main admissions cycle. Individual applicants can submit up to 5 applications and so applications, rather than applicants, are taken as the unit of analysis. The Russell Group is defined for the purposes of this analysis as the 20 institutions that were members of the group during the admissions cycles under consideration.[5]

Several measures of the social background characteristics of applicants are available in the UCAS dataset. First, information about applicants' *school type* is used to distinguish between applicants from private schools, selective state grammar schools and non-selective state schools and colleges. Second, applicants' home postcodes have been classified according to the *young higher education participation rate* in their local area, divided into quintiles. Third, information is available about the *ethnicity* of applicants based on self-reports on UCAS forms. It is important to point out that ethnicity information is not communicated to admissions selectors at any point during the admissions decision-making process, although it is quite possible that admissions tutors would have an idea of the ethnic origin of some applicants from seeing applicants' names printed on their UCAS forms – a possibility driving David Cameron's pronouncement that UCAS forms should in the future be name-blind (Prime Minister's Office 2015) – and perhaps also from other pieces of information on their form such as home addresses, schools attended, and the substance of personal statements and references. Unfortunately, information on the social class background of applicants is not available in the UCAS dataset. However, information is available on gender and whether or not the applicant is a mature student – these are included as control variables in the statistical models presented later.

The main indicator of applicant 'merit' available in the dataset relates to attainment at A-level or in equivalent qualifications, as communicated to UCAS by the exam boards.[6] The Russell Group highlights that 'Independent school students enter higher education with better A-level grades than those from state schools'. (Russell Group, 2015b: 20) and that 'at A-level the gap between those achieving the highest grades from different ethnic backgrounds is substantial'. (Russell Group, 2015b: 21). The implications of these statements are that 'there is a smaller pool of highly qualified students' (Russell Group, 2015b: 21) from non-traditional backgrounds eligible to apply to highly selective universities in the first place, *and* that those from non-traditional backgrounds who do apply to Russell Group universities tend to be lower calibre applicants with respect to prior achievement. The first of these implications is largely correct and well documented by the available evidence, although it is important to note that (as the Russell Group publication acknowledges) students in selective grammar schools in the state sector do as well if not better at A-level than their privately educated counterparts on average, and that some ethnic minority groups such as the British Chinese and British Indian groups substantially outperform their white British counterparts at A-level (Russell Group, 2015b). However, the second implication lacks a substantial evidence base to support it, but can be tested empirically using UCAS data.

Of course, in addition to grades and subjects at A-level, admissions selectors may base their decisions on a range of additional criteria, including achieved grades at AS-level and at General Certificate of Secondary Education (GCSE); applicants' personal statements; teacher references; and in some cases subject-specific tests such as the UKCAT test for aspiring Medics and the LNAT test for prospective Law students and formal interviews with admissions selectors. Unfortunately, it has not been possible to include AS or GCSE attainment in the analysis due to restrictions placed by UCAS on the supply of data to external researchers.

Information about performance in further tests or interviews where applicable, and information about the nature of personal statements and references, is also unavailable for inclusion in the analysis.

Information is available, however, on whether or not the applicant had studied at A-level each of eight *'facilitating subjects'* identified by the Russell Group as often required for entry to courses at Russell Group universities. These facilitating subjects are Biology, Chemistry, English Literature, Geography, History, Languages, Mathematics and Physics (Russell Group, 2012).[7] The Russell Group has repeatedly claimed that:

> It is still the case that some students are not getting the right advice and guidance on the subjects to study, with the result that many good students haven't gained the qualifications they need for the course they want to apply for.
>
> (Russell Group, 2015b: 25).

This claim, made on anecdotal evidence in the Russell Group publication, is tested empirically below.

Further consideration is also given to the *popularity of the courses* applicants have chosen to apply to. The Russell Group has argued that 'There is evidence to suggest that students from state schools may apply disproportionately to the most competitive courses'. (Russell Group, 2015b: 31) and that 'The fact that BME students tend to apply in much greater proportions to the most competitive courses means that very many able students find that they are unsuccessful in securing a place'. (Russell Group, 2015b: 31). It is clear that, by mathematical necessity, applicants choosing more popular courses will be less likely to be offered a place, but the Russell Group provides little evidence as to how large and conclusive a role this plays in determining comparative admissions chances. The variables in the UCAS dataset make it possible to construct a measure of *course popularity* by calculating the initial rejection rate for each degree subject area at each Russell Group university present (in anonymised form) in the dataset.[8]

## How meritocratic is admission to Russell Group universities in the narrow sense?

Table 3.1 begins by comparing the raw rates at which applications to Russell Group universities from candidates from different school types, HE participation neighbourhoods and ethnic groups, are met with an offer of a university place. It is clear that raw offer rates are some fifteen percentage points higher for private and grammar school applicants compared to applicants from non-selective state schools and colleges, with a similar disparity for those from neighbourhoods with the highest and lowest young HE participation rates. The gap in raw offer rates is particularly large for British ethnic minority applicants from Black Caribbean, Black African, Pakistani and Bangladeshi backgrounds compared to the white

*Table 3.1* Applications to Russell Group universities (2010/11/12 entry)

| Applicant characteristic | Average offer rate | Average A-level points achieved by applicant | Average number of 'facilitating subjects' at A-level | Mean rejection rate for chosen course |
|---|---|---|---|---|
| **School type** | | | | |
| Private | 61.0 | 375 | 1.9 | 50.0 |
| Grammar | 65.0 | 372 | 2.1 | 44.8 |
| Non-selective state | 45.7 | 333 | 1.3 | 49.8 |
| **Local HE participation rate** | | | | |
| Top quintile | 55.4 | 363 | 1.6 | 49.7 |
| 4th quintile | 53.2 | 350 | 1.6 | 48.2 |
| 3rd quintile | 46.8 | 337 | 1.4 | 50.1 |
| 2nd quintile | 44.8 | 327 | 1.3 | 49.1 |
| Bottom quintile | 39.8 | 314 | 1.1 | 48.5 |
| **Ethnicity** | | | | |
| White British | 54.7 | 348 | 1.5 | 47.2 |
| Black Caribbean | 29.6 | 303 | 0.8 | 56.2 |
| Black African | 21.9 | 310 | 0.8 | 58.6 |
| Pakistani | 30.3 | 318 | 1.4 | 57.4 |
| Bangladeshi | 31.2 | 311 | 1.6 | 59.4 |
| Indian | 43.1 | 360 | 1.9 | 57.8 |
| Chinese | 49.6 | 413 | 2.0 | 54.2 |
| Mixed | 47.8 | 356 | 1.5 | 51.7 |

British group at between 25 and 33 percentage points. Applicants from Chinese, Indian and Mixed ethnic backgrounds also have lower offer rates than the white group, though the disparities are smaller at 5 to 10 percentage points.

Table 3.1 also makes clear that applicants to Russell Group universities from non-selective state schools and from lower HE participation neighbourhoods tend to have lower levels of achievement at A-level and fewer facilitating subjects at A-level than their more advantaged counterparts. However, these groups are not more likely to apply to the most competitive courses. A-level achievement levels are also lower for British ethnic minority applicants to Russell Group universities from the Black Caribbean, Black African, Pakistani and Bangladeshi groups in comparison to the white British group and black applicants have also typically studied fewer facilitating subjects at A-level. British ethnic minorities from the Indian, Chinese and Mixed groups, in contrast, have higher levels of A-level attainment and more facilitating subjects at A-level than their white peers on average. It is notable, however, that all British ethnic minority groups tend to choose courses that are more popular on average than their white peers.

Table 3.2 reports the results of a series of binary logistic regression models which predict the chances of an application to a Russell Group university being

*Table 3.2* Comparative odds of an offer of admission from a Russell Group university

| | Model 1 | Model 2 | Model 3 | Model 4 | Model 5 | Model 6 |
|---|---|---|---|---|---|---|
| **School type (Private)** | | | | | | |
| Grammar | 1.18* | | | 1.19* | 1.14* | 0.98 |
| Non-selective state | 0.54* | | | 0.67* | 0.86* | 0.80* |
| **Local HE participation rate (Top quintile)** | | | | | | |
| 4th quintile | | 0.91* | | 0.95* | 0.98 | 0.95* |
| 3rd quintile | | 0.71* | | 0.85* | 0.92* | 0.91* |
| 2nd quintile | | 0.65* | | 0.85* | 0.95* | 0.88* |
| Bottom quintile | | 0.53* | | 0.75* | 0.89* | 0.77* |
| **Ethnic group (White British)** | | | | | | |
| Black Caribbean | | | 0.35* | 0.51* | 0.61* | 0.76* |
| Black African | | | 0.23* | 0.38* | 0.45* | 0.54* |
| Pakistani | | | 0.36* | 0.41* | 0.51* | 0.64* |
| Bangladeshi | | | 0.38* | 0.44* | 0.51* | 0.74* |
| Indian | | | 0.63* | 0.61* | 0.62* | 0.84* |
| Chinese | | | 0.82* | 0.85* | 0.72* | 0.86* |
| Mixed | | | 0.76* | 0.80* | 0.80* | 0.88* |
| Other | | | 0.47* | 0.54* | 0.59* | 0.46* |
| Female | | | | 0.90* | 1.00 | 1.25* |
| Mature applicant | | | | 0.28* | 0.73* | 1.03 |
| **Application timing (15th January deadline)** | | | | | | |
| Early (By 15th October) | | | | 0.63* | 0.60* | 0.90* |
| Late (After 15th January) | | | | 0.41* | 0.39* | 0.44* |
| **A-level grades** | | | | | | |
| No. of A* grades | | | | | 1.46* | 1.61* |
| No. of A grades | | | | | 1.29* | 1.40* |
| No. of B grades | | | | | 1.20* | 1.18* |
| No. of C grades | | | | | 0.95* | 0.89* |
| No. of D grades | | | | | 0.74* | 0.71* |
| No. of E grades | | | | | 0.68* | 0.65* |
| **Tariff point equivalent to A-levels** | | | | | | |
| 420+ (A*A*A* or higher) | | | | | 1.37* | 2.58* |
| 360–419 (AAA to A*A*A) | | | | | 0.52* | 0.87** |
| 300–359 (BBB to AAB) | | | | | 0.41* | 0.71* |
| 240–299 (CCC to BBC) | | | | | 0.25* | 0.40* |
| <240 (CCD or lower) | | | | | 0.36* | 0.51* |
| **Facilitating subjects at A-level** | | | | | | |
| Biology | | | | | 0.89* | 1.20* |
| Chemistry | | | | | 0.96* | 1.09* |
| English Literature | | | | | 0.88* | 0.89* |
| Geography | | | | | 1.32* | 1.13* |
| History | | | | | 1.07* | 1.01. |
| Languages | | | | | 1.21* | 1.07* |
| Mathematics | | | | | 1.11* | 1.06* |
| Physics | | | | | 1.48* | 1.14* |
| Course popularity | | | | | | 0.95* |

Note: Data reports odds ratios. An asterisk indicates statistical significance at $p < 0.05$.

met with an offer of a place in light of the above social background and prior achievement characteristics of applicants. Models 1 to 3 simply reproduce what has been seen already in Table 3.1 – that before taking any other factors into account, the chances of being offered a place at a Russell Group university are substantially lower for applicants from non-selective state schools compared to private schools (expressed as an odds ratio of 0.54 to 1 in Model 1); for applicants from neighbourhoods with the lowest rates of young participation in HE compared to the top neighbourhoods (odds ratio of 0.53 to 1 in Model 2); and for applicants from all British ethnic minority backgrounds relative to the white group (with odds ratios ranging from 0.23 to 1 for Black African applicants to 0.82 to 1 for Chinese applicants in Model 3).

Model 4 includes school type, local HE participation rate and ethnicity in the same model together with gender, age group and timing of application. The odds ratios for school type, local HE participation rate and ethnicity increase towards unity in this Model but remain substantially below 1.

Model 5 adds applicants' grades at A-level and UCAS point scores for holders of other qualifications as well as whether or not applicants had studied each of eight 'facilitating subjects'. It is clear that higher grades substantially increase the likelihood of being offered a place at a Russell Group university: the odds of receiving an offer from a Russell Group university are improved by having a greater number of A*, A and B grades at A-level (1.46 to 1, 1.29 to 1, and 1.20 to 1 respectively) or by having a very high tariff point equivalency score for applicants who have entry qualifications other than A-level (1.37 to 1). It is also clear that five out of eight facilitating subjects are associated with improved chances of being offered a place, namely Geography, History, Languages, Mathematics or Physics. These controls for applicants' prior attainment increase the odds ratios for school type, local HE participation rate, and ethnicity towards 1, but substantial disparities in offer rates still remain.

Finally, Model 6 takes into account course popularity and finds that as the rejection rate increases by one percentage point the odds of receiving an offer of a place is reduced by 0.95 to 1. Importantly, controlling for course popularity appreciably reduces the extent of ethnic group differences in the odds or receiving an offer from a Russell Group university, indicating that ethnic minority applicants have lower offer rates than comparably qualified white applicants partly because they are more likely to apply to oversubscribed courses. However, even after controlling for numerical competitiveness, substantially lower comparative odds of receiving an offer persist for all ethnic minority applicants, as well as for applicants from non-selective state schools and low HE participation neighbour-hoods. For those from state schools and low HE participation neighbourhoods, controlling for course popularity in fact reduces the odds ratios to a degree, reflecting the fact that these groups of applicants to Russell Group universities are not more likely than their more advantaged counterparts to choose especially popular courses.

In summary, the above results suggest that admission to Russell Group universities is not meritocratic in the narrow sense of admissions decisions being determined by academic achievement alone. On the contrary, it would appear that applicants from more socio-economically advantaged backgrounds are more likely to be offered places than applicants from less advantaged backgrounds with the same grades and facilitating subjects at A-level.

It is important to note that research published recently by UCAS (2015: 59–76) suggests that offer rates from 'high tariff providers'[9] to applicants from ethnic minority backgrounds, low HE participation neighbourhoods, and the group eligible for free school meals are within the expected margin of error, once predicted A-level grades and specific degree subject and institution applied to, are taken into account.[10] UCAS's findings may seem to contradict those presented in this chapter, but in fact the two sets of findings taken together raise a number of important questions which require further empirical investigation. The UCAS research controls statistically for predicted A-level grades whereas this chapter takes into account actual grades achieved (due to the unavailability of predicted grades in the dataset available to me): if non-traditional students are more likely than others to have their A-level grades under-predicted, they may be less likely to be offered places at highly selective universities than their subsequent actual achievement at A-level would warrant. The UCAS research also focuses on applicants holding three or more A-levels whereas the analysis in this chapter includes holders of BTEC and Access to HE qualifications, who are more likely to be non-traditional students; if these latter qualifications are held in lower regard by highly selective universities this could systematically disadvantage non-traditional applicants. The UCAS research also focuses solely on 18 year olds applying for immediate entry to university rather than all applicants regardless of age; this is problematic given that a substantial number of non-traditional students apply as mature students and many students from advantaged backgrounds take gap years.

## Meritocratic admission to Russell Group universities in the broader sense

The foregoing analysis treats applicants' achievements at A-level and in equivalent qualifications as though they were objective measures of merit. For example, the achievement of AAA at A-level is assumed to imply the same thing about the aptitude and promise of an applicant regardless of their social background. But of course, the pre-university academic achievements of people from comparatively disadvantaged backgrounds will, by definition, have been achieved under more challenging social and economic circumstances than their more advantaged peers (Ward, 2014; 2015a; 2015b). As a consequence, the same grades achieved by applicants from disadvantaged and advantaged backgrounds cannot be treated as equivalent indicators of 'merit'. On the contrary, there is a strong case to be made for weighing formal qualifications against information on the socio-economic background of applicants and offering applicants from comparatively disadvantaged backgrounds university places conditional on lower entry requirements than are asked of their more advantaged peers – for example an offer conditional on AAB at A-level where the standard offer is AAA – or at least prioritising socio-economically disadvantaged applicants over more advantaged ones when making standard offers.

More than a decade ago the Schwartz Report (2004) advocated precisely this model of 'contextualised' admissions policies on the basis that 'it is fair and appropriate to consider contextual factors as well as formal educational achieve-ment, given the variation in learners' opportunities and circumstances' (Schwartz, 2004: 7; see also Universities UK, 2003). Since then there have been numerous high level calls for contextualised admissions policies to be rolled out more widely (Panel on Fair Access to the Professions, 2009; DBIS, 2011; Social Mobility and Child Poverty Commission, 2012; SPA, 2012; OFFA, 2013; CoWA, 2015). However, the evidence-base on which contextual admissions policies rest is still in its infancy. In particular, more work needs to be done to establish which are the most valid and reliable indicators of socioeconomic disadvantage, especially given that many indicators are area-based rather than individual-level measures, and some indicators are not currently available to universities at the point of admissions decision-making. More work also needs to be done to establish how well contextually-indicated students perform in higher education, in absolute terms and relative to their more advantaged peers, to enable universities to identify socioeconomically disadvantaged students who are likely to outperform compa-rably qualified peers from more advantaged environments and who may therefore warrant lower offers; or who can be expected to perform as well as comparably qualified peers from more advantaged environments and may therefore warrant prioritisation for standard offers; or who are likely to perform well in absolute, but not relative terms and may therefore require additional support to fully realise their potential. The evidence currently available suggests that school-level contextual indicators may be associated with better degree performances for students with equivalent levels of prior attainment (Smith and Naylor, 2001; McNabb, Pal, and Sloane, 2002; HEFCE, 2003; Naylor and Smith, 2004; Smith and Naylor, 2005; Ogg, Zimdars, and Heath, 2009; Kirkup, Wheater, Morrison, Durbin, and Pomati, 2010; Hoare and Johnston, 2011; Lasselle, McDougall-Bagnall, and Smith, 2014; Crawford, 2014a). However, individual-level and neighbourhood-level contextual indicators seem to be more often associated with poorer degree performances (Croxford, Doherty, Gaukroger, and Hood., 2013a,b,c; Crawford, 2014b; HEFCE, 2014; Bradley and Migali, 2015), suggesting that universities may need to do more to support socioeconomically disadvantaged students to achieve their full potential.

In its interim report, the Scottish Commission on Widening Access (CoWA) highlighted the fact that entry requirements have increased considerably in recent years and raised questions about whether very high grades are necessary for doing well at university or are largely a device used by popular universities to reduce the pile of eligible candidates to more manageable proportions (CoWA, 2015). Indeed, CoWA suggested that universities should consider revising down their base-line entry requirements – which would make many more socio-economically disadvantaged students eligible for entry – and redesign admissions criteria to take contextual factors into account more fully and to recognise the value of a diverse student population. More research is needed to establish how best to design such a system (or systems) to ensure that participation is widened without compromising student achievement. However, the fact that more than a third of UK universities currently take applicants' socio-economic context into account during the admissions process and over half of all universities state that they plan to use contextual data in the future (Moore, Mountford-Zimdars, and Wiggans, 2013; SPA, 2015) suggests that there is real scope for movement towards a university admissions system that is more meritocratic in this broader sense.

## Conclusions

Is admission to highly selective UK universities fair in the narrow sense of being determined by applicants' prior attainment alone? The empirical results presented in this chapter would suggest that the answer is no. However, this answer remains tentative in light of the evidence published by UCAS (2015) which suggests that the UK's third most selective universities make offers to applicants from ethnic minority backgrounds, low HE participation neighbourhoods, and those eligible for free school meals at rates that are within the expected margin of error once predicted A-level grades and specific course applied to are taken into account. Further research is clearly needed to explore whether non-traditional students are disadvantaged by an admissions system in which offers of university places are made on the basis of predicted rather than actual A-level attainment; by being more likely to hold qualifications other than A-level such as BTEC and Access to HE qualifications; or by being more likely to apply as mature students. Further research is also needed to explore whether state school applicants' offer rates are also within the expected margin of error once predicted grades and specific course applied to are taken into account (the UCAS research does not examine school type differences in offer rates in detail), and whether offer rates for all social groups appear equitable when focusing particularly on high-demand courses. This further research should be possible now that, following a hiatus of several years, UCAS intends to begin sharing detailed applications and admissions data with researchers again via the Administrative Data Research Network (ADRN) from 2017.

The analysis presented in this chapter, and the results of the UCAS research, both suggest that there is considerable scope for admission to highly selective universities to become more meritocratic in the broader sense of taking into account the often challenging circumstances in which people from disadvantaged backgrounds achieve the qualifications required to go to university. More research is needed on this score as well: to establish a solid evidence base regarding the trustworthiness of potential indicators of contextual disadvantage, and to identify where support systems may need to be put in place to support contextually disadvantaged students to realise their academic potential once at university. Given the persistence of inequalities in school attainment, contextualised university admissions policies represent one of the most promising means of widening participation in higher education, especially at highly selective universities.

## Notes

1  The Russell Group website bills its 24 member institutions as '24 leading UK universities which are committed to maintaining the very best research, an outstanding teaching and learning experience and unrivalled links with business and the public sector'. (http://russellgroup.ac.uk/. [Date accessed 20th March 2016].)
   The 24 members of the Russell Group are: University of Birmingham, University of Bristol, University of Cambridge, Cardiff University, Durham University, University of Edinburgh, University of Exeter, University of Glasgow, Imperial College London, King's College London, University of Leeds, University of Liverpool, London School of Economics and Political Science, University of Manchester, Newcastle University, University of Nottingham, University of Oxford, Queen Mary University of London, Queen's University Belfast, University of Sheffield, University of Southampton, University College London, University of Warwick, and University of York.
2  Data on entrants from state schools and colleges, lower socioeconomic groups, and low HE participation neighbourhoods is taken from HESA's *UK Performance Indicators on Widening Participation*, Table T1a for indicated years, available online at www.hesa.ac.uk/pis/urg. The 2014/15 data point for those from low HE participation neighbourhoods excludes Russell Group universities in Scotland (Edinburgh and Glasgow) and Northern Ireland (Queen's Belfast) because information for these institutions was absent from the relevant data table at the time of writing. Data on entrants from British ethnic minority backgrounds is taken from HESA's HEIDI database for the indicated years (data prior to 2001/2 is unavailable, as was data for 2014/15 at the time of writing). HESA data is used here with the required acknowledgement that 'HESA cannot accept responsibility for any inferences or conclusions derived from the data by third parties'.
3  Subsequently steps include (4) accepting that offer of a place, (5) achieving the grades needed for that offer of a place to be confirmed, (6) firmly accepting that confirmed place, turning up at induction week, and still being registered as a student on the HESA census date. These steps are likely to make a smaller contribution to the ultimate social composition of Russell Group universities, but are important areas for further research. They are, however, beyond the scope of this chapter.
4  The studies cited above were carried out by academic researchers at six Russell Group universities: Durham University (Boliver), Oxford University (Heath), University of Manchester (Zimdars), University College London Institute of Education (Sullivan), London School of Economics (Shiner, Noden), and Bristol University (Modood).
5  Durham University, University of Exeter, Queen Mary University of London and University of York joined the Russell Group in August 2012.
6  It is important to note that this is a measure of *actual* attainment at A-level, rather than predicted attainment which is what tends to be available to admissions selectors who make most offers on a conditional basis, requiring the applicant to subsequently achieve the academic entry requirements of their chosen course before their offer is confirmed. Unfortunately, UCAS was not willing to supply predicted grades data as part of the UCAS dataset analysed here. For the purposes of this analysis actual attainment in General Studies A-level is excluded.
7  It has only been possible to control individually for eight A-level generally 'facilitating' A-level subjects, rather than for specific combinations of A-level subjects which are prerequisites for admission to particular degree programmes. This is due to data supply

restrictions which mean that instead of information on the specific degree courses to which applicants are seeking entry the dataset only contains information about the broad degree subject areas to which applicants applied.

8   As noted above, the twenty-three degree subject areas identifiable in the data are relatively broad categories, and each comprises a large number of specific degree programmes with varying levels of numerical competitiveness. As a result, the numerical competitiveness variable used in the analysis that follows is subject to a certain degree of unmeasured heterogeneity, and so the extent to which numerical competitiveness accounts for ethnic group differences in the chances of receiving an offer of a place at a Russell Group university may be under- or over-estimated.

9   That is, the 40 or so institutions whose entrants have the highest UCAS point scores on average.

10  The UCAS publication does not report any similar analysis of offer rates by school type.

## References

Boliver, V. (2011). Expansion, differentiation and the persistence of social class inequalities in British higher education. *Higher Education, 61*(3), 229–242.

Boliver, V. (2013). How fair is access to more prestigious UK universities? *British Journal of Sociology, 64*(2), 344–364.

Boliver, V. (2015). Why are British ethnic minorities less likely to be offered places at highly selective universities? In C. Alexander, and J. Arday (Eds.), *Aiming Higher: Race, Inequality and Diversity in the Academy*, London: Runnymede Trust, 15–18.

Boliver, V. (2016). Exploring ethnic inequalities in admission to Russell Group universities. *Sociology, 50*(2), pp. 247–266.

Boliver, V., Gorard, S., and Siddiqui, N. (2015). Will the use of contextual indicators make UK higher education admissions fairer? *Education Sciences, 5*(4), 306–322.

Bradley, S., and Migali, G. (2015). *The Effect of a Tuition Fee Reform on the Risk of Drop Out from University in the UK*, Working Paper, Lancaster University: Department of Economics.

Committee on Higher Education. (1965). *Report* (The 'Robbins Report') London, HMSO.

Commission on Widening Access (CoWA). (2015). *Commission on Widening Access Interim Report*. Scottish Government: Edinburgh.

Crawford, C. (2014a). The link between secondary school characteristics and university participation and outcomes, Retrieved from www.ifs.org.uk/publications/7235

Crawford, C. (2014b). Socio-economic differences in university outcomes in the UK: drop-out, degree completion and degree class, Retrieved from www.ifs.org.uk/publications/7420

Croxford, L., Doherty, G., Gaukroger, R., and Hood, K. (2013a). Widening participation at the University of Edinburgh (1): entry, progression and degree outcomes of SQA-qualified entrants, Centre for Educational Sociology, University of Edinburgh *(CES Ref 1221)*

Croxford, L., Doherty, G., Gaukroger, R., and Hood, K. (2013b). Widening Participation at the University of Edinburgh (2): entry, progression and degree outcomes of A-level qualified students, Centre for Educational Sociology, University of Edinburgh *(CES Ref 1302)*

Croxford, L., Doherty, G., Gaukroger, R., and Hood, K. (2013c). Widening Participation at the University of Edinburgh (3): entry, progression and degree outcomes by subject area, Centre for Educational Sociology, University of Edinburgh *(CES Ref 1303)*

Department of Business, Innovation and Skills [DBIS]. (2011). *Students at the Heart of the System*, London: HMSO, Cm 8122.

DBIS. (2013). *Investigating the accuracy of predicted a level grades as part of the 2010 UCAS admissions process*. Research paper no. 20. London: Department for Business, Innovation and Skills.

DBIS. (2014). *National Strategy for access and student success in higher education.* (London, DBIS) April 2014.

DBIS. (2015). Participation rates in higher education: Academic years 2006/2007 – 2013/2014 (Provisional). (London, DBIS) 2nd September 2015.

Department for Education and Science [DES]. (1988). *Top-Up Loans for Students*, London, HMSO, Cm 520.

Department for Education [DFE]. (2015). Education and training statistics for the UK: 2015. Retrieved November 26, 2016 from www.gov.uk/government/statistics/education-and-training-statistics-for-the-united-kingdom-2015

Department for Education and Employment [DfEE]. (1998). *Higher Education for the 21st Century: response to the Dearing Report*, London, DfEE.

Department for Education and Skills [DfES]. (2003). *The future of higher education*, London, HMSO, Cm 5735.

Halsey, A.H. (2000). Further and higher education. In A.H. Halsey, and J. Webb (Eds.), *Twentieth century British social trends*. London: Macmillan. pp. 221–253.

Higher Education Statistics Agency [HEFCE]. (2003). Schooling effects on higher education achievement HEFCE 2003/32. Retrieved November 26, 2016 from www.hefce.ac.uk/pubs/hefce/2003/03_32.htm.

HEFCE. (2014). *Differences in degree outcomes: key finding*. Bristol: HEFCE.

Higher Education Statistics Agency [HESA]. (2014). Table SP5 – Percentage of UK domiciled young entrants to full-time first degree courses from NS-SEC Classes 4, 5, 6 and 7 by subject and entry qualification 2013/14. Retrieved November 26, 2016 from www.hesa.ac.uk/pis/urg

Kirkup, C., Wheater, R., Morrison, J., Durbin, B., and Pomati, M., (2010). Use of an Aptitude Test in University Entrance: a Validity Study, BIS Research Paper 26. Retrieved November 25, 2016 from www.bis.gov.uk/assets/biscore/higher-education/docs/u/10-1321-use-of-aptitude-test- university-entrance-validity-study.pdf

Lasselle, L., McDougall-Bagnall, J.M., and Smith, I. (2013). School grades, school context and university degree performance: evidence from an elite Scottish institution. *Oxford Review of Education, 40*(3), 293–412.

McNabb, R., Pal, S., and Sloane, P., (2002). Gender differences in educational attainment: The case of university students in England and wales. *Economica, 69*(275), 481–503.

Moore, J., Mountford-Zimdars, A., and Wiggans, J. (2013). *Contextualised admissions: Examining the evidence*. Retrieved November 25, 2016 from www.spa.ac.uk/sites/default/files/Research-CA-Report-2013-full_0.pdf

National Committee of Inquiry into Higher Education [NCIHE]. (1997). *Higher education in the learning society (The 'Dearing Report')*. London: HMSO.

Naylor, R., and Smith. J. (2004). Degree performance of economics students in UK universities: Absolute and relative performance in prior qualifications. *Scottish Journal of Political Economy, 51*(2), 250–265.

Noden P., Shiner M., and Modood T. (2014). University offer rates for candidates from different ethnic categories. *Oxford Review of Education, 40*(3), 349–369.

Nomis. (2013). Ethnic group by sex by age (Census 2011 data). Retrieved February 2016 from www.nomisweb.co.uk/census/2011/dc2101ew

Office for Fair Access [OFFA]. (2013). *How to produce an access agreement for 2014–15.* Bristol: Office for Fair Access.

Ogg, T., Zimdars, A., and Heath, A. (2009). Schooling effects on degree performance: A comparison of the predictive validity of aptitude testing and secondary school grades at Oxford University. *British Educational Research Journal, 35*(5), 781–807.

Panel on Fair Access to the Professions. (2009). *Unleashing aspiration: the final report of the Panel on Fair Access to the Professions.* London: Cabinet Office.

Prime Minister's Office. (2015). PM: Time to end discrimination and finish the fight for real equality. Press release 26th October 2015. Retrieved November 26, 2016 from www.gov.uk/government/news/pm-time-to-end-discrimination-and-finish-the-fight-for-real-equality

Russell Group. (2012). *Informed choices: A Russell Group guide to making decisions about post-16 education, 2012.* London: Russell Group.

Russell Group. (2013). *Research on university access.* Retrieved February 6, 2016 from www.russellgroup.ac.uk/news/research-on-university-access/

Russell Group. (2015a). *University access research.* Retrieved February 6, 2016 from http://russellgroup.ac.uk/news/university-access-research/

Russell Group. (2015b). Opening doors: understanding and overcoming barriers to university access. Russell Group. Retrieved February 6, 2016 from http://russellgroup.ac.uk/policy/publications/opening-doors-understanding-and-overcoming-the-barriers-to-university-access/

Schwartz, S. (2004). *Fair admissions to higher education: recommendations for good practice.* Report of the Admissions to Higher Education Steering Group. London: DfES.

Smith, J., and Naylor, R., (2001). Determinants of degree performance in UK universities: A statistical analysis of the 1993 student cohort. *Oxford Bulletin of Economics and Statistics, 63*(1), 29–60.

Smith, J., and Naylor, R., (2005). Schooling effects on subsequent university performance: Evidence for the UK university population. *Economics of Education Review, 24*(5), 549–562.

Social Mobility and Child Poverty Commission. (2012). *University challenge: How higher education can advance social mobility.* London: HMSO.

Supporting Professionals in Admission [SPA]. (2012). *Principles for the use of contextual data in admissions.* SPA: Cheltenham.

SPA. (2015). SPA's Use of Contextualised Admissions Survey Report 2015. SPA: Cheltenham.

Stevens, R. (2004). *University to Uni: The politics of higher education in England since 1944.* London: Meuthen.

Sutton Trust. (2011). *Degrees of Success: university chances by individual school,* London: Sutton Trust.

UCAS. (2015). *End of Cycle Report 2015.* Retrieved February 5, 2016 from www.ucas.com/sites/default/files/eoc-report-2015.pdf

University Grants Committee [UGC] (1973). *Statistics of education 1970, Volume 6,* London: HMSO.

Universities UK (2003) *Fair enough? Wider access to university by identifying potential to success.* London: Universities UK.

Ward, M.R.M. (2014). 'I'm a geek I am': Academic achievement and the performance of a studious working-class masculinity. *Gender and Education, 26*(7), 709–725.

Ward, M.R.M. (2015a). The chameleonisation of masculinity: Jimmy's multiple performances of a working-class self. *Masculinities and Social Change, 4*(3), 215–240.

Ward, M.R.M. (2015b). *From labouring to learning, working-class masculinities, education and de-industrialization*. Basingstoke; Palgrave Macmillan.

Zimdars, A., Sullivan, A., and Heath, A. (2009). Elite higher education admissions in the arts and sciences: Is cultural capital the key? *Sociology, 43*(4), 648–666.

Chapter 4

# Patterns of participation in a period of change
## Social trends in English higher education from 2000 to 2016

*Neil Harrison*

## Introduction

The UK higher education sector has rarely enjoyed policy stability, but the first 16 years of the twenty-first century have seen a series of important upheavals marking the latter stages of the 50-year evolution from a planned elite system to a mass market, as well as a shift from a public good to a private investment (Brown and Carasso, 2013). The overarching context of this chapter will be the sustained policy efforts during this period to create 'fairer' and 'wider' access to higher education institutions and, with a particular focus on elite universities where the social inequalities remain starkest.[1] It begins with a brief history of policy development, before moving on to examine national administrative data concerning applications and admissions by various proxies for socio-economic status, and exploring the role of ethnicity and entry qualifications. Due to the availability of data, the focus will mainly be on full-time young[2] undergraduates, although there is some discussion around mature and part-time students. Also, among the changes that have shaped higher education in the UK since 2000 has been the divergence of the national systems in terms of student financial support and other elements. Therefore, due to the constraints of space, this chapter will focus solely on England, which accounts for around 83 per cent of UK's undergraduate market.[3]

## Sixteen years of policy turbulence: a brief history

In many senses, the modern era of higher education in the UK begins with the publication of the *Dearing Review* in 1997 (National Committee of Inquiry into Higher Education [NCIHE], 1997). Intended to take stock after a period of rapid expansion of the sector and the abolition of the 'binary divide' between universities and polytechnics in 1992 (Ainley, 1994), Dearing concluded, *inter alia*, that there were very marked social divides in those who participated in higher education. For example, the children of those in the highest status occupations were around six times as likely to participate as those of the lowest, while application rates were notably lower from most minority ethnic communities (NCIHE, 1997).

While choosing not to pursue many of Dearing's other recommendations, the newly elected Labour Government seized upon this finding as the basis for a policy objective that would partly define their 13 years in office. They laid out their stall to continue the expansion of higher education started under the previous Conservative Government, while expecting the majority of the new demand to be drawn from lower socio-economic groups in order redress the inequalities identified by Dearing – an agenda that became known as 'widening participation'. However, ostensibly counter to this, one of their first decisions was to introduce tuition fees for the first time (means tested up to £1,000 p.a.) and to abolish student grants in favour of a single means-tested loan.

The widening participation agenda started to take shape in earnest from 2000. A policy aim was established that 50 per cent of young people should gain 'an experience' of higher education by the age of 30 (the figure then being around 35 per cent), with the publication of *The Excellence Challenge* (Department for Education and Employment [DFEE], 2000) laying the policy and resource foundations for what would become the Aimhigher programme in 2004. The main vehicle for delivery around widening participation, Aimhigher evolved from various predecessor programmes (e.g. 'Partnerships 4 Progression') charged with raising aspirations for higher education among groups that had been historically under-represented (Higher Education Funding Council for England [HEFCE], 2004). Working on a three-tier model with national, regional and sub-regional manifestations, Aimhigher developed and commissioned a wide range of activities with schools, colleges, universities and community organisations, including taster days, summer schools and tutoring/mentoring schemes (Passy and Morris, 2010; Moore and Dunworth, 2011; Doyle and Griffin, 2012).

*The Excellence Challenge* (DFEE, 2000) policy paper also heralded two other important developments. The first was the creation of 2-year 'foundation degrees' targeted primarily at learners in work who were seeking to upgrade their skills and knowledge through higher education, but who lacked the level of qualifications generally required for entry (Greenbank, 2007). The second was the tentative reintroduction of grants for low-income students, initially badged as 'opportunity bursaries' and limited to selected urban areas of deprivation (Hatt, Baxter, and Harrison, 2003), but rolled out nationally as 'higher education maintenance grants' from 2004 onwards.

Media stories about high-achieving candidates failing to secure places at elite universities prompted the government to commission a report into admissions practices (Schwartz, 2004), which concluded that there was no systemic issue and, by inference, the reason for the under-representation of students from lower socio-economic groups was that they lacked sufficient entry qualifications and had lower application rates. These findings have subsequently been challenged by writers such as Boliver (2013, 2016) and Jones (2012), who have identified continuing inequalities in elite universities' admissions through selection procedures and the use of 'personal statements' respectively. Shiner and Noden (2014) further conclude that disadvantaged young people are less likely to apply to elite universities, all else being equal (but see Mangan *et al.*, 2010). More widely, research around so-called 'contextualised admissions' suggests that universities have excessive confidence in an applicant's entry qualifications as a predictor of degree success, with students from state schools often outperforming those from private schools once in higher education at a given level of entry qualification (e.g. Hoare and Johnston, 2011; Moore, Mountford-Zimdars, and Wiggans, 2013), although attempting to overcome this creates new problems (Boliver, Gorard, and Siddiqui, 2015).

The publication of *The Future of Higher Education* White Paper (Department for Education and Skills [DfES], 2003a) and its companion report on widening participation (DfES, 2003b) marked a watershed for the Labour Government's policy development. On the one hand, they sought to reinforce the messages from the Dearing Review and *The Excellence Challenge* (DFEE, 2000) concerning the inherent inequalities in higher education participation, but, on the other, argued that an expanded sector was unaffordable for the public purse and that students should be expected to bear a higher proportion of the costs through tuition fees almost tripled to £3,000 p.a., although institutions could choose to charge less if they wished – very few did, thwarting expectations of a market in differential fees. This circle was to be squared through the provision of an expanded grant for low-income students to notionally offset the majority of their fees, a universal loan to ensure that no tuition fees were required upfront and a requirement for institutions to provide additional bursaries to disadvantaged students if they charged more than £1,125 p.a. in tuition fees. These bursaries quickly formed a hierarchical quasi-market, with elite universities generally offering significantly greater financial inducements than other institutions (Callender, 2010; Harrison and Hatt, 2012).

The fairness of this system would be enforced through the newly created Office for Fair Access (OFFA) and the process of requiring institutions to file so-called 'access agreements', laying out their commitment to widening participation through bursaries and outreach activities. However, OFFA's powers of intervention were limited to a largely monitoring and dissemination role which it continues to occupy as of 2016 (McCaig and Adnett, 2009; McCaig, 2015).

Despite these measures to bolster the financial circumstances of students from low-income backgrounds, the majority of commentators argued that the increase in tuition fees would have a profound impact on applications (e.g. Callender and Jackson, 2005; Jones and Thomas, 2005). It was argued that students from low-income families and from certain ethnic groups were more sensitive to costs and had a weaker connection to higher education, such that they would be disproportionately discouraged from applying. Indeed, the issue was an important one in the prelude to the 2005 General Election, with the Labour Government making a limited concession by enacting a minimum bursary of £300 as a statutory requirement. Ultimately, the provisions described with *The Future of Higher Education* (DfES, 2003a) were enshrined in the Higher Education Act 2004 and came into effect from 2006.

There was a short period of policy stability in the late 2000s. The predicted shockwaves from the rise in tuition fees did not occur, but there was also little sign of the radical improvements in the participation rates for disadvantaged groups that had been predicted as a result of Aimhigher (Harrison, 2011; Croxford and Raffe, 2014). This lack of progress was generally defined as a problem with targeting the widening participation agenda effectively and this became the focus of policy attention (HEFCE, 2005, 2007), although there were also questions about the metrics used to measure progress and a conflation of applications and admissions (Harrison, 2012). As part of the first wave of austerity following the global financial crisis, Aimhigher was scaled back from 2008 onwards, with the national and regional operations being largely abolished (HEFCE, 2008), before its full abolition in 2011. Interestingly, 2015 and 2016 have begun to see government policy coming full circle, with a limited restoration of elements of the Aimhigher programme – albeit at a fraction of the expenditure. The first example has been the creation of the National Networks for Collaborative Outreach (HEFCE, 2014) which encourage institutions to work together to increase applications from under-represented groups. The second has been the provision of funding to consortia for focused work in discrete geographical areas felt to be underperforming in terms of higher education admissions relative to school attainment, badged as the National Collaborative Outreach Programme (HEFCE, 2016).

With the rapid growth of higher education in the 2000s, albeit with little evidence for the social redistribution originally envisaged, the strain on a shrinking public purse increased further and the Labour Government commissioned Lord Browne to report on alternative funding mechanisms for higher education after the 2010 General Election. When the Browne Review (2010) did emerge, it argued for a radical shift in cost from state to student (Waller *et al.*, 2014), with most courses funded by tuition fees alone, with the state providing additional funding for subjects with additional overheads or national skills shortages. This was captured in the following year's White Paper prepared by the newly elected Conservative and Liberal Democrat Coalition Government: *Students at the Heart of the System* (Department of Business, Innovation and Skills [BIS], 2011).

The new system to be implemented from 2012 onwards, although somewhat strangely without an Act of Parliament, would see tuition fees almost triple to £9,000 p.a. for most students; a minority of institutions opted to charge less for some or all of their courses. Again, there was some attempt to soften the blow for disadvantaged students, with the extension of loans to cover fees, a more preferential loan repayment regime and the introduction of the ill-conceived and overly complex National Scholarship Programme (Carasso and Gunn, 2015; Bowes *et al*, 2016) which was cancelled 3 years later. This had the effect of focusing resources on a relatively small group of disadvantaged young people felt to have the 'potential' to attend 'elite' universities (McCaig, 2016). Indeed, this group has become an ever-present, if ill-defined and misunderstood, focus for higher education policymaking since they were identified as being 'missing' (Sutton Trust, 2004).

The other major policy shift at this time was the erosion and dismantling of the student number control system that had prevailed since the 1990s. Within a semi-managed market, institutions had been allocated annual numbers of students that they were permitted to recruit in order to prevent drastic shifts in demand that could destabilise the sector, compromise academic job security and undermine the wider roles of higher education in knowledge creation and exchange. From 2012, the government announced that institutions would be permitted to recruit as many students with high entry qualifications[4] as they wished, with all controls being abolished from 2014 onwards. This was widely understood to be a signal to elite universities to expand at the expense of lower status institutions, presumably in recognition of their supposed higher quality provision (Taylor and McCaig, 2013).

In addition, 2012 also saw a deregulation of entry to the higher education sector, with the Government offering a clear invitation to private providers to enter the market. A number of established reputable providers (e.g. the College of Law, now the University of Law) have done so, but there have also been concerns about unscrupulous and exploitative organisations taking advantage of the deregulation to harvest fees for substandard courses (McGettigan, 2014; Evans, 2015). This followed an earlier process of allowing many former 'colleges of higher education' to achieve university status, although the stratification with the market remains as strong as ever (Croxford and Raffe, 2015; Raffe and Croxford, 2015).

Finally, 2016 saw the publication of the *Success as a Knowledge Economy* White Paper which continued to position widening participation – by now comprehensively rebranded as 'social mobility' (Waller et al., 2015) – as a key government priority:

The Prime Minister has set two specific, clear goals on widening participation in higher education: to double the proportion of people from disadvantaged backgrounds entering university in 2020 compared to 2009, and to increase the number of black and minority ethnic (BME) students going to university by 20 per cent by 2020 (BIS, 2016: 14).

However, the White Paper is less than clear on how this will be achieved. It points to potential new powers for a reconceived OFFA (as part of the new Office for Students), 'name blind' applications and improvements in teaching quality and data sharing, although there is a tacit acknowledgement of a direct link between school attainment and higher education participation. More generally, the rhetorical emphasis on elite universities and high-achieving disadvantaged young people remains at the heart of government thinking and there is an underpinning confidence that the wisdom of the market will prevail.

The period from 2000 to 2016 has therefore been one of marked policy turbulence and mixed messages around the composition and function of higher education. On the one hand, there has been a sustained objective to diversify institutions' intakes, especially among the elite universities who are deemed to offer the greatest opportunities for social mobility and access to high-status

*Table 4.1* Summary of key English higher education policy developments – 2000 to 2016

| Year | Policy development |
| --- | --- |
| 2000 | Publication of *The Excellence Challenge*<br>Policy aim established that 50 per cent of young people should experience higher education by the age of 30 |
| 2001 | (Labour Government re-elected)<br>Creation of 'opportunity bursaries'<br>Creation of foundation degrees |
| 2002 | |
| 2003 | Publication of *The Future of Higher Education* White Paper |
| 2004 | Creation of national Aimhigher initiative<br>Reintroduction of means-tested student grants (replacing opportunity bursaries)<br>Publication of Schwartz Report on fair access to higher education<br>Passing of Higher Education Act 2004 |
| 2005 | (Labour Government re-elected)<br>Publication of 'participation of local areas' (POLAR) methodology |
| 2006 | Implementation of the Higher Education Act 2004<br>Tuition fee increase to £3,000 p.a.<br>Significant increase in student grants (to offset tuition fees)<br>Introduction of institutional bursaries<br>Creation of Office for Fair Access (OFFA) |
| 2007 | |
| 2008 | Scaling back of Aimhigher<br>Removal of funding for 'equivalent and lower qualifications' |
| 2009 | Publication of Milburn Report on fair access to professional careers |
| 2010 | (Coalition Government elected)<br>Publication of *Browne Report* |
| 2011 | Publication of *Students at the Heart of the System* White Paper<br>Cancellation of Aimhigher |
| 2012 | Tuition fee increase to £9,000 p.a.<br>Introduction of National Scholarship Programme<br>Relaxation of student number controls for high qualification students |
| 2013 | |
| 2014 | Abolition of National Scholarship Programme<br>Full deregulation of student numbers |
| 2015 | (Conservative Government elected)<br>Creation of National Networks for Collaborative Outreach<br>Publication of the *Fulfilling Our Potential* Green Paper<br>Announcement of abolition of means-tested student grants in favour of loans |
| 2016 | Creation of National Collaborative Outreach Programme<br>Publication of the *Success as a Knowledge Economy* White Paper |

professions (Milburn 2009). Very large sums (up to £500 million p.a., depending on what is counted) have been invested in this objective, initially borne by national government before being passed to individual universities. On the other hand, the personal cost of higher education to students has increased from around £1,000 p.a. to £9,000 p.a. – a move which is widely held to have restricted access from low-income families and deprived communities, although evidence for this is slight. There has also been a conspicuously elitist attempt to influence (or financially coerce) 'bright, but poor' applicants to choose high status universities, regardless of their own priorities, alongside a deregulation of the market that has proved challenging for the lower status institutions that attract the majority of students from the historically under-represented groups highlighted by Dearing (NCIHE, 1997).

Given this background, the remainder of this chapter will now examine statistical patterns in application to, and participation in, higher education over the period from 2000 to 2016, although most of the publicly available datasets span somewhat shorter periods than this. It will examine whether the impacts of the policy changes highlighted above can be seen within the data, either as abrupt fractures to long-term trends or in the form of those trends themselves. Needless to say, care will be taken not to over-extrapolate causality from large-scale quantitative datasets, but there is opportunity to test some of the claims made over the period by academic, political and journalistic commentators. Most of the data used is derived from that published by the Universities and Colleges Admissions Service (UCAS), which administers the higher education entry system in the UK. Additional data is also drawn from that published by the Department for Education (DFE), the Department for Business, Innovation and Skills (BIS) and the Higher Education Statistics Agency (HESA).

## Overall trends in participation

Since 2006, the number of new UK[5] full-time undergraduate students accepted has risen from 350,000 a year to 450,000 a year, while the number of applicants has risen from 420,000 a year to 600,000 a year. In other words, the sector has expanded rapidly over this period, both in terms of the supply of places and the demand for those places. This growth has been fuelled primarily by English institutions and by English domiciled students – we will return to trends by gender and ethnicity shortly. One readily apparent feature of this period, which can be seen in Figure 4.1, is the disruption to the general trend of applications between 2011 and 2013, associated with the increase in tuition fees in 2012.

Leaving aside this temporary aberration, the period has seen faster increase in applications (demand) than in acceptances (a proxy for supply). One feature of this has been that the acceptance rate – i.e. the proportion of applicants being offering and accepting a place – fell rapidly, from 81 per cent in 2008 to 73 per cent in 2010. This phenomenon has previously been documented by Coleman and Bekhradnia (2011), who argued that this marked the end of the 'Robbins' era of higher education where the supply of places had largely kept track with demand and where individuals would generally be able to secure a place, albeit not necessarily in their preferred subject or institution. However, a rise in the supply of places and the brief dip in demand have seen the acceptance rate rise once again to near the 2008 level.

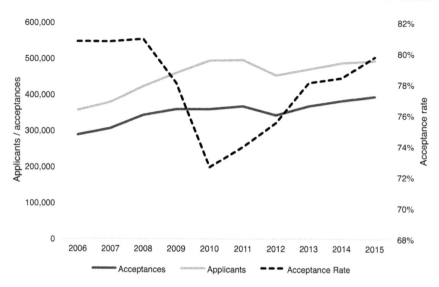

*Figure 4.1* Total applications and acceptances, with derived acceptance rate, for England from 2006 to 2015

Source: UCAS, 2016.

## Social class and participation

One of the challenges of analysing social class trends in participation in higher education is the absence of a reliable, valid and generally accepted measure. This chapter draws data from various sources using three different markers:

1.  *POLAR (Participation Of Local AReas) data* – this is an area-based measure developed by HEFCE (2005, 2010, 2012) from historical participation data for young people at the level of local government electoral wards. Each ward is allocated to one of five quintiles (with Quintile 5 having the highest historic participation rate) and applicants/students are assigned to a quintile through their home postcode. POLAR has gone through three revisions to keep pace with evolving data – the data used in this chapter is mainly from POLAR3, with POLAR2 used for data relating to before 2006[6]. POLAR data thus has issues in terms of validity as significant numbers of people from higher socio-economic groups live in low participation areas and *vice versa* (Harrison and McCaig, 2015).
2.  *Free School Meals (FSM) data* – this marker is derived from a young person's eligibility to receive free meals at school as the result of a means-test on their parents' income. The data is therefore at the individual level, but there are some questions about the reliability of the data in terms of take-up (Hobbs and Vignoles, 2007; Gorard, 2012). In addition, FSM data relates to income rather

than a more nuanced construction of social class or disadvantage. Nevertheless, this marker has gained importance as it has become administratively possible to link data from schools and higher education and it is now the main metric published by government (e.g. DFE, 2016a). However, this measure can only be reliably applied to students aged 18 or 19 on entry to higher education.

3. *Occupational data* – this relates to the student's occupation prior to higher education if they are 25 or over and to their parents' occupation (specifically the main earner) if they are younger. This has been the traditional means of examining social class in higher education, originally through the Registrar-General's scale (A/B/C1/C2/D/E), but more recently through the NS-SEC scale (from 1 to 7, with the former representing high-status occupations) used by the Office for National Statistics. This measure perhaps provides the most rounded indication of social class, but it has been dogged by issues of reliability as it is derived from statements made by applicants on their application forms which is often missing, inaccurate or impossible to code (Harrison and Hatt, 2009). NS-SEC data for institutional intakes is still published by the Higher Education Statistics Agency, but it has had declining importance attached to it over the period.

As can be seen from these summaries, each measure has shortcomings in terms of availability, the level of granularity and/or the extent to which it represents socio-economic status. It is important, therefore to problematise participation data and the meanings that can be attributed to it. For example, the area nature of POLAR is often ignored or misunderstood to be at a far finer granularity than is the case (Harrison and McCaig, 2015), such that any students living in low participation areas are assumed to be disadvantaged students from lower socio-economic groups.

## Acceptances

Figure 4.2 has been created from reports from UCAS (2012, 2015) and shows a number of trends in participation rates for 18 and 19 year olds between 2005 and 2014 for England, using the POLAR quintiles. First, the period saw improvements across all the groups, with the fastest being for Quintiles 1 (10.1 per cent) and 2 (9.6 per cent), compared to just 1.5 per cent for Quintile 5. The net result of this has been some narrowing of the 'gap' in participation between the areas with the lowest and highest historical rates – from 43 per cent in 2005 to 35 per cent in 2014. This is largely driven by a plateauing of participation from the areas with the highest participation, suggesting that demand has reached saturation here.

Second, there is a clear impact from the tuition fee rises in 2006 and 2012. In both instances, the participation rates of Quintiles 4 and 5 dropped; in 2006, Quintile 3 dropped as well. Conversely, the rates for Quintiles 1 and 2 (i.e. the lowest participation areas) rose in these years, which is a counterintuitive finding given the concerns expressed at the time about the impact of the changes on young

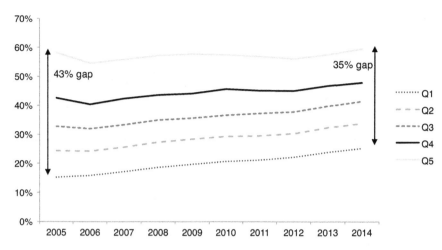

*Figure 4.2* Participation of English students aged 18 or 19 on entry by POLAR quintiles
(1 = lowest participation areas) from 2005 to 2014 entry cohorts

Source: UCAS, 2012, 2015.

people from lower socio-economic groups (e.g. Callender and Jackson, 2005; Jones and Thomas, 2005).

These short-term drops in participation for young people from relatively advantaged areas can potentially be explained by a proportion of 18 year olds who might ordinarily have chosen to take a 'gap year' between school/college and university not doing so, as can be seen in Figure 4.3.

In the years prior to the two increases, there is a sharp increase in participation from the Quintiles 3, 4 and 5, with a corresponding fall the following year. Quintiles 1 and 2 appear to have been largely immune to this effect, most likely as the phenomenon of gap years are most strongly associated with higher socio-economic groups and a period of travel or volunteering (Heath, 2007). Clearly, whatever the cause, the fluctuations in admissions in 2005 and 2011 were mainly a phenomenon of 18 year olds from more advantaged areas. Again, this would appear counterintuitive, as it positions more advantaged young people as more price sensitive with respect to higher education, which may reflect the limited or riskier alternatives available to their disadvantaged peers (Brynin, 2016; Harrison, 2016).

Figure 4.4 approaches a similar time period to Figure 4.2, but uses FSM eligibility as the marker for individual disadvantage (BIS, 2013, 2015; DFE, 2016a) as opposed to an area-based measure – note that this data is for young people from state schools only. A similar pattern can be identified, with a growth in participation for both groups. Those eligible for FSM saw their participation rate rise from 13 per cent in 2005 to 23 per cent in 2012, with the gap between

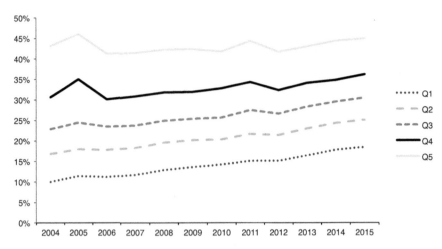

*Figure 4.3* Participation of English students aged 18 on entry by POLAR2 quintiles (1 = lowest participation areas) from 2004 to 2015 entry cycles

Source: UCAS, 2012, 2015.

groups falling from 20 per cent to 17 per cent over the same period. Once again, there is no evidence for a deterrent effect deriving from the 2006 or 2012 tuition fee rises. Interestingly, there was a small decline in participation for both groups in 2013 which is not seen in the POLAR data presented above.

It is notable that the speed of gap closing between the two reference groups (Quintile 1 vs. Quintile 5 and FSM vs. non-FSM) has been slower for the individualised data (Figure 4.4) than for the area-based data (Figure 4.2). This may suggest that some of the improvements within the POLAR data are due to relatively advantaged young people from low participation areas progressing to higher education (Harrison and McCaig, 2015; Harrison and Waller, in press). Also, the absence of data from independent schools may explain the absence of fluctuations around 2006 and 2012, as Figures 4.2 and 4.3 suggest that these are associated with the most advantaged groups.

Finally, Figure 4.5 shows data by parental occupation. Unlike the previous data, this is about proportions of the overall population of entrants rather than participation rates, although the story is largely congruent: there has been a steady, if unremarkable, rise in the proportion of students from lower socio-economic status homes (NS-SEC groups 4 to 7) over the period, with no reversals from the tuition fee rises in 2006 or 2012. The difference in proportions fell from 43 per cent to 33 per cent in this period, although it should be noted that data coverage also increased radically across this period, so some of the trend may be due to more complete data than an actual change.

In summary, data across three socio-economic measures of participation shows a consistent picture with a long-term trend of improvement in the participation of

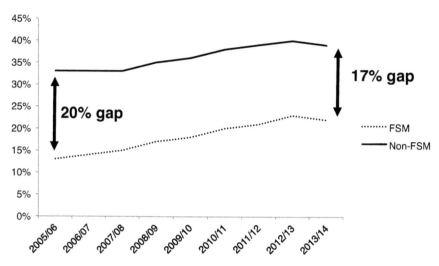

*Figure 4.4* Participation of English students from state schools[7] aged 18 or 19 on entry by eligibility for free school meals from 2005 to 2013 entry cycles

Source: BIS, 2013, 2015; DFE, 2016a.

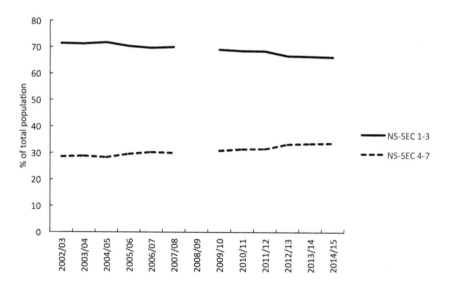

*Figure 4.5* Proportion of total entrant population of full-time undergraduates aged under 21 by NS-SEC groups for parental occupation for 2003 to 2014

Source: HESA, 2016.

(Note that data was collected in 2008/09 using a different approach and so are excluded here.)

disadvantaged young people and a growing share of the overall higher education market. Changes in tuition fees that were widely predicted to reduce demand from these groups seem only to have disrupted the trend for young people from more advantaged backgrounds; most likely, in the context of forgone 'gap years'. It is important to remember, though, that the tuition fee increases were offset to a degree by a variety of grants, bursaries and fee waivers for those from low-income households. One can therefore interpret the data above as either low price sensitivity for these groups or the success of the changes to the financial support offered – or some combination of the two.

## Applications

Admissions data is a function of demand (i.e. applications), supply (i.e. the number of places available) and the means of 'clearing the market' (i.e. the policies and processes by which universities decide which students to accept and whether students decide to take up those offers). Trends in admissions are not, therefore, a pure expression of demand from young people. For example, the improvements in participation from disadvantaged groups could represent the evolution of fairer admissions policies, rather than an increase in overall demand. Similarly, raw application figures are not entirely instructive as they themselves are a partial function of the underlying population of young people, which has been in a period of marked decline since the late 2000s. Detailed data on applications is less widely published than those on admissions, so it is useful to check the tentative analysis above against some of the data that are available. Arguably, this provides a purer measure of the success of widening participation policy than admissions.

Figure 4.6 shows the overall applicant numbers between 2006 and 2015, demonstrating the same basic trends as for admissions. The proportion of applicants from Quintile 5 dropped from 32.8 per cent to 29.7 per cent across the period, with that from Quintile 1 rising from 9.3 per cent to 11.5 per cent.

## Institutional status

Figure 4.7 shows the participation rates for English 18 year olds entering 'higher tariff'[8] institutions, divided again by POLAR quintiles. Immediately obvious is the strong stratification of this part of the sector, with rates for Quintile 5 being substantially higher (at around 20 per cent) than for all the other groups which are bunched between 3 and 13 per cent. In comparison with the overall figures shown in Figure 4.2, there is no apparent tuition fee rise effect for this subset of institutions. Instead, we see a rise in participation from 2012 onwards. This is most likely to reflect the change in student number control policies (Taylor and McCaig, 2013) that allowed these institutions to increase their intakes from the highest-achieving young people. The fastest relative increase has been among Quintile 1, although this reflects only an absolute increase from 2.3 per cent to 3.3 per cent. In other words, this group has moved from being around ten times as likely to

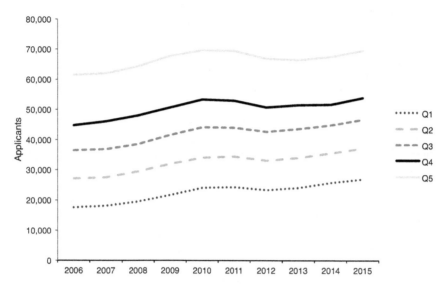

*Figure 4.6* Full-time applicants aged 18 or 19 by POLAR quintiles (1 = lowest
participation areas) from 2006 to 2015 entry cycles

Source: UCAS, 2016.

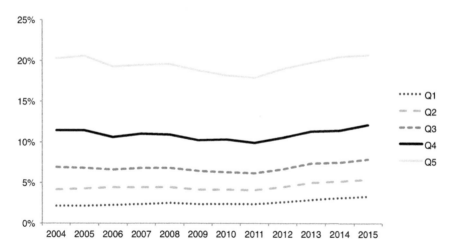

*Figure 4.7* Participation rate of English students aged 18 on entry in high tariff
institutions by POLAR quintiles (1 = lowest participation areas) between
2004 and 2015

Source: UCAS, 2012, 2015.

progress to higher tariff institutions than Quintile 5 to around seven times as likely. There is some trend in Quintiles 3, 4, and 5 for a decline in participation rate between 2008 and 2011 – no explanation is readily apparent for this, which is at odds with the rise seen in Figure 4.5.

In contrast, Figure 4.8 shows the same data for lower tariff institutions across a slightly shorter time period and presents a very different picture. There is very little difference between the groups throughout the period and nearly identical participation rates by 2014. Growth has been fastest for Quintiles 1 (from 5.5 per cent to 9.5 per cent) and 2 (7.8 per cent to 11.8 per cent). There is a clearly marked 'gap year effect' around 2012, especially for Quintiles 2, 3, 4, and 5, although it exists in Quintile 1 too.

Comparing these subset data with the full data in the previous section, we can draw two conclusions. First, the impact of the tuition fee changes was most marked among young people from higher socio-economic groups attending lower tariff institutions, who were less likely to delay their entry into higher education than usual. Second, the improvements in participation for young people from lower socio-economic groups has been concentrated in lower tariff institutions, although there have been some very modest increases in higher tariff institutions since 2011 when these were permitted to increase their recruitment.

This is reinforced in Figure 4.9, which shows the changes in participation rate over this period for different institutional types. The growth in participation in low tariff institutions shows a very clear relationship with the POLAR quintiles, with the highest growth in the areas with the lowest historic participation and practically no growth in young people from Quintile 5 areas. A similar, but less

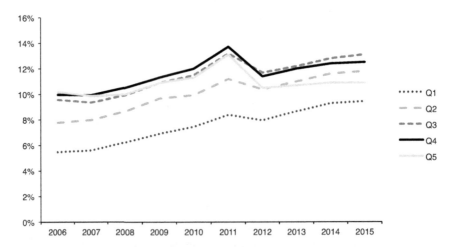

*Figure 4.8* Participation rate of English students aged 18 on entry in low tariff institutions by POLAR quintiles (1 = lowest participation areas) between 2006 and 2015

Source: UCAS, 2015.

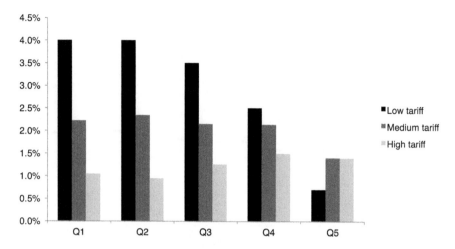

*Figure 4.9* Changes in participation rate between 2006 and 2015 of English students aged 18 on entry by POLAR quintiles (1 = lowest participation areas) and institutional status

Source: calculated from UCAS, 2015.

marked, pattern is present among the medium tariff institutions. However, among the higher tariff group, the growth is highest for Quintiles 4 and 5. Therefore, while the growth in participation in elite institutions for lower socio-economic groups is to be welcomed, it is very modest and contextualised within a parallel period of stronger growth for more advantaged groups.

This lack of progress in widening participation in elite universities is further reinforced by entry population data (HESA, 2016). The proportion of young entrants to the Russell Group[9] universities (prior to the recent expansion) from NS-SEC groups 4 to 7 rose from 19.9 per cent to 20.2 per cent between 2006 and 2014, while the proportion from POLAR Quintiles 1 and 2 rose from 5.9 per cent to 6.6 per cent. Of the sixteen institutions who were members in 2006, only nine have made significant positive progress diversifying their intake by parental occupation (with two falling backwards) and ten by area participation (with three getting worse). Croxford and Raffe (2015) describe this stratification as an 'iron law'.

## Role of ethnicity

The period covered by this chapter has seen a rapid change in participation patterns for students from BME communities. These were identified within the Dearing Review as generally having a lower propensity to enter higher education than the majority white community, although the Chinese and Indian populations had historically had very strong participation rates (NCIHE, 1997).

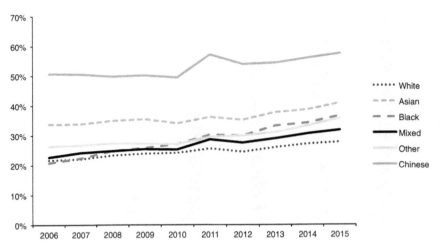

*Figure 4.10* Participation rate of English students aged 18 on entry by ethnic group between 2006 and 2015

Source: UCAS, 2015.

However, data now clearly suggests that this relationship has reversed. For example, Harrison (2013) reports that the size of the BME population in an area is now a positive predictor for higher participation rates, even once a range of academic, social and educational variables have been factored into the statistical model. Shah, Dwyer, and Modood (2010) suggest that this may be due to forms of 'ethnic capital' that actively promote education and qualifications as a method of intergenerational social mobility (Modood, 2012). However, there is also continuing evidence that many BME groups are less likely to receive an offer, once others are controlled for, than applicants from the white majority community (Noden, Shiner, and Modood, 2014; Boliver, 2013, 2016).

Figure 4.10 demonstrates this shift, with the White majority community having the lowest participation rate from 2007 onwards, as well as the one growing least quickly across the period (21.7 per cent to 27.8 per cent). The Black group has the fastest growth, moving from last to third place, and their participation rate increasing from 20.9 per cent to 36.7 per cent. Young people from Chinese backgrounds continue to have the strongest propensity to enter higher education by some way, with 57.6 per cent doing so in 2015.

## The role of qualifications

One of the lesser-known observations made under the auspices of the Dearing Review (Robertson and Hillman, 1997) is that young people with similar qualification profiles progress to higher education at approximately similar rates,

regardless of their socio-economic status. Coleman and Bekhradnia (2011) argue
that this relationship has remained stable over the intervening period, while
Crawford (2014) concludes that around 95 per cent of the differences in participation rates are encapsulated within the qualifications acquired at 16, leaving A
Levels and other Level 3 qualifications with a sorting role between institutional
types. HEFCE (2015) demonstrates that this hypothesis holds by gender, with
young men and women with varying A Level result profiles having almost identical
participation rates, despite women having higher rates overall. In other words,
young women are more likely to progress due to their prior attainment levels rather
than gendered differences in 'aspiration' or behaviour.

The period covered by this chapter has seen a sustained improvement in the
attainment of GCSEs[10] and equivalent qualifications at age 16. As can be seen in
Figure 4.11, this has been enjoyed across the socio-economic range, with similar
rates of growth for those eligible for FSM and those not; as with higher education
participation, there has been some modest narrowing of the gap.[11]

Also, mimicking trends in higher education participation, there have been
significant shifts in the GCSE attainment profiles for different ethnic groups. Figure
4.12 shows improvements across all the selected ethnic groups (see DFE 2010,
2014 for other groups), but with the slowest improvement being for the White
British group. Over this period, pass rates for Bangladeshi and Black African
young people overtook the White British group, while the Pakistani and Black
Caribbean groups narrowed the gap substantially (from 9.7 per cent to 5.0 per
cent and from 14.8 per cent to 7.2 per cent, respectively). Young people of Indian

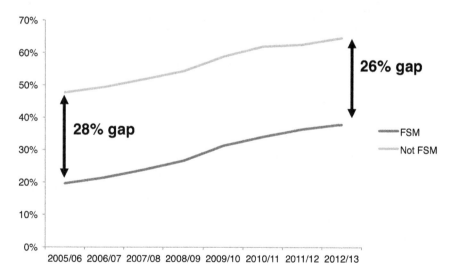

*Figure 4.11*  Proportion of young people achieving five GCSEs or equivalents including
English and mathematics at A* to C, by free school meals eligibility

Source: DFE, 2010, 2014.

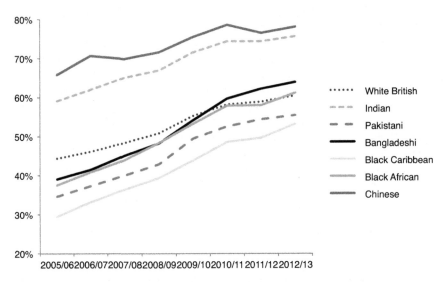

*Figure 4.12* Proportion of young people achieving five GCSEs or equivalents including English and mathematics at A* to C, by selected ethnic groups

Source: DFE, 2010, 2014.

and Chinese heritage maintained their position with the strongest pass rates, although somewhat less so in 2012/13 than in 2005/06.

Given that the white majority group now has the lowest higher education participation rate, this suggests that there is still a higher level of underlying demand from minority ethnic communities, given the relative GCSE attainment rates (see Strand, 2014 for a wider discussion of GCSE results for different ethnic groups).

## Mature and part-time students

Thus far, this chapter has focused on young, full-time entrants to higher education. This is in large part because the data relating to this group is more readily available and more easily analysed through participation rates – i.e. there is a known 'pool' of 18 year olds in each year who are broadly 'in the market' for higher education. Such a pool does not exist for mature students, while part-time students are heterogeneous and may be drawn from across all age groups. Furthermore, there are greater challenges in reliably allocating individuals to socio-economic groups (e.g. POLAR quintiles are calculated solely on the participation of young people).

Nevertheless, it is important to provide some commentary about these groups and some data are publicly available. Figure 4.13 shows overall application numbers and it can be seen that mature applicants showed a similar trend to younger

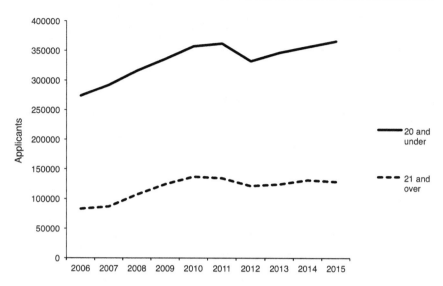

*Figure 4.13* Full-time applicants by age from 2006 to 2015 entry cycles in England
Source: UCAS, 2016.

ones, with growth from 2006 to 2010, followed by a reduction in demand in 2012 and growth after. However, the fall in 2012 was less dramatic (and preceded by a small drop in 2011) while the recovery since has been slower than for younger applicants.

There is no indication of a shift in social mix for mature entrants across this period, with the proportion being drawn from POLAR Quintile 1 areas remaining broadly constant at between 11.5 per cent and 12.5 per cent (HESA, 2016).

Part-time student numbers have dropped dramatically since 2012, however (Higher Education Policy Institute, 2015). As part-time applications are not generally made through the UCAS system, there is no central data collection on demand – only actual entrants. As can be seen in Figure 4.14, the number of mature part-time students has collapsed from a high point of 247,375 in 2008 to just 97,925 in 2014. Interestingly, this decline predates the 2012 tuition fee increase and is perhaps most likely to be related to the global financial crisis and the willingness and ability of employers in both the private and public sectors to pay for their staff to undertake part-time study. It is also clear that the abolition of funding for part-time students taking a second degree (so-called 'equivalent and lower quali-fications') from 2008 onwards has also contributed to this, although there has been some minor row-back to support students on part-time science and technology courses (Butcher, 2015). Conversely, young part-time student numbers were rising until 2011 and then fell rapidly with the tuition fee increase; they have not yet recovered.

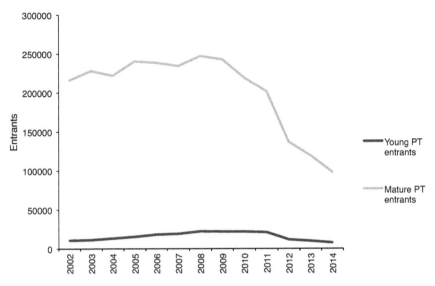

*Figure 4.14* Part-time entrants by age group from 2002 to 2014 in England
Source: HESA, 2016.

Perhaps counterintuitively, as mature part-time numbers have declined, the proportion of entrants coming from POLAR Quintile 1 areas has increased slightly from 6.7 per cent in 2006 to 7.9 per cent in 2014 (HESA, 2016). The proportion for young part-time students has remained stable at between 13 and 14 per cent.

## Conclusion

This chapter has presented data from a range of sources to shed light on trends in higher education participation between 2000 and 2016. On the whole, this story has been positive, with a sustained growth in the numbers of young people from lower socio-economic groups studying full-time and their overall participation rate. This seems, in part, to be driven by improvements in GCSE attainment, providing access to qualifications that then lead to entry into higher education. In particular, there has been a strong growth in the GCSE attainment of minority ethnic communities, which also appears to have translated into an increased demand for higher education. The situation for young people of a White British ethnicity has been less positive over this period, with a more muted rise in GCSE attainment and the correspondingly lowest propensity to enter higher education, particularly among men whose attainment is generally lower than for women.

This chapter has also demonstrated that predictions that the tuition fee increases in 2006 and 2012 would be a widespread deterrent to students from lower socio-economic groups were misleading. In fact, there is evidence that it is relatively advantaged young people have proved to be more price sensitive, especially if they were planning to attend lower status universities. This is, perhaps, due to them possessing career alternatives outside of higher education that were not readily available to disadvantaged students. Even among part-time students, the decline in numbers has coincided with stability or even a slight improvement in the social mix.

Most of the chapter has focused on younger students, but there have been marked trends in mature student participation too. While full-time mature student numbers have remained buoyant during the period, albeit with a slower recovery following the 2012 tuition fee rise, the number of part-time mature students has collapsed by over a half since 2008, possibly due to falling staff development expenditure among employers.

Finally, the growth in participation for young students has not been evenly distributed. Rather, it has been markedly concentrated within lower status universities. There has been remarkable little change in the social mix of elite universities within the period, with some even becoming less diverse. Given the policy attention and application of resources, this has to be viewed as a major failure, especially in light of research suggesting that discriminatory recruitment practices continue to operate in these institutions, as well as a failure to recognise the inequities of bare qualifications as entry markers except in a few institutions.

## Notes

1 The word 'institution' is used in this chapter to cover both universities and other colleges that offer higher education, while 'university' is reserved for those with recognised university status. The word 'elite' is used loosely as there is no established definition in place; common (and overlapping) markers include year of gaining university status, entry requirements, league table placement, number of applications for places available, research profile and self-assertion, including membership of the 'Russell Group' (see endnote 9 below).
2 The definition of 'young' varies according to the dataset used. In this chapter, data will variously be presented on 18-year-olds, 18 and 19-year-olds and under 21-year-olds, with this being clearly indicated in the text and on figures.
3 The Welsh and Northern Irish systems, accounting for 6 per cent and 2 per cent respectively, have not diverged significantly from the English system, but provide slightly preferential financial support; in addition, they use somewhat different markers for socio-economic status that are not directly comparable. The Scottish system (9 per cent) has always been somewhat different to the remainder through its separate qualifications system, but full responsibility for higher education policy has been devolved to the Scottish Parliament since 1999. It has not implemented the introduction of tuition fees, although this has interestingly not resulted in improved participation rates relative to the rest of the UK; indeed, Scotland has the lowest participation rates and slowest growth in participation (UCAS, 2014; HESA, 2016), although this is likely to be influenced by other social, educational, and geographical factors. A full discussion of the differing systems can be found in Croxford and Raffe (2014).
4 Initially grades of AAB or better at A Level, or the equivalent, then shifted to ABB from 2013 onwards.
5 'UK' here is used to mean those students treated as having 'home' status – i.e. it excludes international students studying in the UK.

6   The basic POLAR methodology has remained similar, but the allocation of local government wards to quintiles has shifted slightly over time with demographic changes and shifts in the participation rate. POLAR2 and POLAR3 data are not, therefore, directly comparable. However, the differences are minor and are unlikely to make a substantive difference to the analysis presented.

7   As this data excludes independent schools, it will underestimate the participation rate of young people not receiving free school meals to a degree.

8   A defined set of qualifications in the UK carry 'tariff points' towards entry to higher education, with institutions advertising the expected tariff for each course. 'Higher tariff' institutions are thus those with the most stringent entry requirements.

9   A self-identifying group of elite universities – in England in 2006: Birmingham, Bristol, Cambridge, Imperial College, Kings College London, Leeds, Liverpool, London School of Economics, Manchester, Newcastle-upon-Tyne, Oxford, Sheffield, Southampton, University College London, and Warwick. There has recently been an expansion, but the old membership was used for this analysis to maintain continuity.

10  General Certificate of Secondary Education: the main qualification taken at the of 16. The attainment of five 'good' passes is widely seen as giving access to qualifications that lead to higher education, including A Levels and BTEC diplomas.

11  From 2014 onwards, the definitions of which qualifications were deemed to be equivalent to GCSEs was radically overhauled and so more recent data is not directly comparable to those presented. The early indication is that this change has disproportionately affected young people who are eligible for FSM, reversing the closing of the attainment gap shown in Figure 4.11 (DFE, 2016b). Whether this will impact on higher education participation rates will become apparent in the near future when these young people reach the age of 18.

## References

Ainley, P. (1994). *Degrees of difference: Higher education in the 1990s.* London: Lawrence and Wishart.

Boliver, V. (2013). How fair is access to more prestigious UK universities? *British Journal of Sociology, 64*(2), 344–364.

Boliver, V. (2016). Exploring ethnic inequalities in admission to Russell Group universities. *Sociology, 50*(2), 247–266.

Boliver, V., Gorard, S., and Siddiqui, N. (2015). Will the use of contextual indicators make UK higher education fairer? *Education Sciences, 5*(4), 306–322.

Bowes, L., Moreton, R., Thomas,L., Sheen, J., Birkin, G., and Richards, S. (2016). *Evaluation of the National Scholarship Programme: Year 4 report.* Leicester: CFE Research.

Brown, R. and H. Carasso (2013). *Everything for sale? The marketisation of UK Higher education.* Abingdon: Routledge.

Browne, J. (2010). *Securing a sustainable future for higher education: An independent review of higher education funding and student finance.* London: Independent Review of Higher Education Funding and Student Finance.

Brynin, M. (2016). Higher education: Too risky a decision. In A. Mountford-Zimdars, and N. Harrison (Eds.), *Access to higher education: Theoretical perspectives and contemporary challenges.* Routledge/SRHE: Abingdon.

Butcher, J. (2015). Financial risk and inflexibility: part-time HE in decline. *Widening Participation and Lifelong Learning, 17*(4), 89–104.

Callender, C. (2010). Bursaries and institutional aid in higher education in England: Do they safeguard and promote fair access? *Oxford Review of Education, 36*(1), 45–62.

Callender, C., and Jackson. J. (2005). Does the fear of debt deter students from higher education? *Journal of Social Policy*, *34*(4), 509–540.

Carasso, H., and Gunn. G. (2015). Fees, fairness and the national scholarship programme: higher education policy in England and the coalition Government. *London Review of Education*, *13*(2), 70–83.

Coleman, R., and Bekhradnia. B. (2011). *Higher education supply and demand to 2020*. Oxford: Higher Education Policy Institute.

Crawford, C. (2014). *The link between secondary school characteristics and university participation and outcomes*. London: DFE.

Croxford, L., and Raffe, D. (2014). Social class, ethnicity and access to higher education in the four countries of the UK: 1996–2010. *International Journal of Lifelong Education* *33*(1): 77–95.

Croxford, L., and Raffe, D. (2015). The iron law of hierarchy? Institutional differentiation in UK higher education. *Studies in Higher Education*, *40*(9), 1625–1640.

Department for Business, Innovation and Skills [BIS]. (2011). *Students at the heart of the system*. London: BIS.

Department for Business, Innovation and Skills [BIS]. (2013). *Widening participation in higher education: August 2013*. London: BIS.

Department for Business, Innovation and Skills [BIS]. (2015). *The proportion of 15 year olds from low income backgrounds in English maintained schools progressing to HE by the age of 19: October 2015*. London: BIS.

Department for Business, Innovation and Skills [BIS]. (2016). *Success as a knowledge economy*. London: BIS.

Department for Education [DFE]. (2010). *GCSE and equivalent attainment by pupil characteristics in England: 2008/09*. London: DFE.

Department for Education [DFE]. (2014). *GCSE and equivalent attainment by pupil characteristics in England: 2012/13*. London: DFE.

Department for Education [DFE]. (2016a). *Widening participation in higher education: 2016*. London: DFE.

Department for Education [DFE]. (2016b). *Revised GCSE and equivalent results in England: 2014 and 2015*. London: DFE.

Department for Education and Employment [DFEE]. (2000). *The excellence challenge*. London: DFEE.

Department for Education and Skills [DfES]. (2003a). *The future of higher education*. Norwich: HMSO.

Department for Education and Skills [DfES]. (2003b). *Widening participation in higher education*, London: Department for Education and Skills.

Doyle, M., and M. Griffin. (2012). Raised aspirations and attainment? A review of the impact of Aimhigher (2004–2011) on widening participation in higher education in England. *London Review of Education*, *10*(1), 75–88.

Evans, G. (2015). Entrances and exits: Planning for failure in higher education provision in England. *Higher Education Review*, *48*(1), 68–90.

Gorard, S. (2012). Who is eligible for free school meals? Characterising free school meals as a measure of disadvantage in England. *British Educational Research Journal*, *38*(6), 1003–1017.

Greenbank, P. (2007). From foundation to honours degree: The student experience. *Education + Training*, *49*(2), 91–102.

Harrison, N. (2011). Have the changes introduced by the 2004 Higher Education Act made higher education admissions in England wider and fairer? *Journal of Education Policy*, *26*(3), 449–468.

Harrison, N. (2012). The mismeasure of participation: how choosing the 'wrong' statistic helped seal the fate of Aimhigher. *Higher Education Review*, *45*(1), 30–61.

Harrison, N. (2013). Modelling the demand for higher education by local authority area in England using academic, economic and social data. *British Educational Research Journal*, *39*(5), 793–816.

Harrison, N. (2016). Student choices under uncertainty: bounded rationality and behavioural economics. In A. Mountford-Zimdars and N. Harrison (Eds.), *Access to higher education: theoretical perspectives and contemporary challenges*. Routledge/SRHE: Abingdon.

Harrison, N., and Hatt, S. (2009). Knowing the 'unknowns': investigating the students whose social class is not known at entry to higher education. *Journal of Further and Higher Education*, *33*(4), 347–357.

Harrison, N., and Hatt, S. (2012). Expensive and failing? The role of student bursaries in widening participation and fair access in England. *Studies in Higher Education*, *37*(6), 695–712.

Harrison, N., and McCaig, C. (2015). An ecological fallacy in higher education policy: the use, overuse and misuse of 'low participation neighbourhoods'. *Journal of Further and Higher Education*, *39*(6), 793–817.

Harrison, N., and Waller, R. (In press). Success and impact in widening participation policy: what works and how do we know? *Higher Education Policy*.

Hatt, S., Baxter, A. and Harrison, N. (2003). The new widening participation students: Moral imperative or academic risk. *Journal of Access Policy and Practice*, *1*(1), 16–31.

Heath, S. (2007). Widening the gap: pre-university gap years and the 'economy of experience'. *British Journal of Sociology of Education*, *28*(1), 89–103.

Higher Education Funding Council for England [HEFCE]. (2004). *Aimhigher: Guidance notes for integration* (Report 2004/08). Bristol: HEFCE.

Higher Education Funding Council for England [HEFCE]. (2005). *Young participation in higher education* (Report 2005/03). Bristol: HEFCE.

Higher Education Funding Council for England [HEFCE]. (2007). *Higher education outreach: targeting disadvantaged learners* (Report 2007/12). Bristol: HEFCE.

Higher Education Funding Council for England [HEFCE]. (2008). *Guidance for aimhigher partnerships: updated for the 2008–2011 programme* (Report 2008/05). Bristol: HEFCE.

Higher Education Funding Council for England [HEFCE]. (2010). *Trends in young participation in higher education: Core results for England* (Report 2010/03). Bristol: HEFCE.

Higher Education Funding Council for England [HEFCE]. (2012). *POLAR3: Young participation in higher education* (Report 2012/26). Bristol: HEFCE.

Higher Education Funding Council for England [HEFCE]. (2014). *Guidance on national networks for collaborative networks* (Circular Letter 20/2014). Bristol: HEFCE.

Higher Education Funding Council for England [HEFCE]. (2015). *Young participation in higher education: A-levels and similar qualifications* (Report 2015/03). Bristol: HEFCE.

Higher Education Funding Council for England [HEFCE]. (2016). *National collaborative outreach programme: invitation to submit proposals for funding* (Report 2016/06). Bristol: HEFCE.

Higher Education Policy Institute [HEPI]. (2015). *It's the finance stupid: the decline of part-time higher education and what to do about it*. Oxford: HEPI.

Higher Education Statistics Agency [HESA]. (2016). *Performance indicators*. Retrieved February 12, 2016 from www.hesa.ac.uk/pis

Hoare, A., and Johnston, R. (2011). Widening participation through admissions policy – a British case study of school and university performance. *Studies in Higher Education* *36*(1), 21–41.

Hobbs, G., and Vignoles, A. (2007). *Is free school meals status a valid proxy for socio-economic status (in schools research)*? London: Centre for the Economics of Education, London School of Economics.

Jones, R., and Thomas, L. (2005). The 2003 UK Government higher education White Paper: a critical assessment of its implications for the access and widening participation agenda. *Journal of Education Policy, 20*(5), 615–630.

Jones, S. (2012). *The personal statement: a fair way to assess university applicants?* London: Sutton Trust.

Mangan, J., Hughes, A., Davies, P. and Slack, K. (2010). Fair access, achievement and geography: explaining the association between social class and choice of university.*Studies in Higher Education, 15*(3), 335–350.

McCaig, C. (2015). Marketisation and widening participation in English higher education: A critical discourse analysis of institutional access policy documents. *Higher Education Review, 48*(1), 6–24.

McCaig, C. (2016). The retreat from widening participation? The National Scholarship Programme and new Access Agreements in English higher education. *Studies in Higher Education, 41*(2), 215–230.

McCaig, C., and Adnett, N. (2009). English universities, additional fee income and Access Agreements: their impact on widening participation and fair access. *British Journal of Educational Studies, 57*(1), 18–36.

McGettigan, A. (2014). Uncontrolled expansion: how private colleges grew. *Times Higher Education*, 30th October, Retrieved October 23, 2016 from www.timeshighereducation. com/features/uncontrolled-expansion-how-private-colleges-grew/2016579

Milburn, A. (2009). *Unleashing aspiration: The final report of the Panel on Fair Access to the Professions*. London: PFAP.

Modood, T. (2012). Capitals, ethnicity and higher education. In S. Tomlinson, and T. Basit (Eds.), *Social inclusion and higher education*. Bristol: Policy Press.

Moore, J., and Dunworth. F. (2011). *Review of evidence from Aimhigher Area Partnerships of the impact of Aimhigher*. Bristol: Aimhigher/HEFCE.

Moore, J., Mountford-Zimdars, A., and Wiggans. J. (2013). *Contextualised admissions: examining the evidence*. Cheltenham: Supporting Professionalism in Admissions Programme.

National Committee of Inquiry into Higher Education [NCIHE]. (1997). *Higher education in the learning society* (known as the Dearing Report). Norwich: HMSO.

Noden, P., Shiner.M., and Modood. T. (2014). University offer rates for candidates from different ethnic categories. *Oxford Review of Education, 40*(3), 349–369.

Passy, R., and Morris. M. (2010). *Evaluation of Aimhigher: learner attainment and progression*. Slough: NfER.

Raffe, D., and Croxford. L. (2015). How stable is the stratification of higher education in England and Scotland? *British Journal of Sociology of Education, 36*(2), 313–335.

Robertson, D., and Hillman. J. (1997). *Widening participation in higher education for students from lower socio-economic groups and students with disabilities (NCIHE Report 6)*. Norwich: HMSO.

Schwartz, S. 2004. *Fair admissions to higher education: Recommendations for good practice.* Nottingham: Department for Education and Skills.

Shah, B., Dwyer, C., and Modood, T. (2010). Explaining educational achievement and career aspirations among young British Pakistanis: Mobilizing 'ethnic capital'? *Sociology, 44*(6), 1109–1127.

Shiner, M., and Noden. P. (2014). 'Why are you applying there?': 'race', class and the construction of higher education 'choice' in the United Kingdom. *British Journal of Sociology of Education, 36*(8), 1170–1191.

Strand, S. (2014). Ethnicity, gender, social class and achievement gaps at age 16: Intersectionality and 'getting it' for the white working class. *Research Papers in Education, 29*(2), 131–171.

Sutton Trust. (2004). *The missing 3,000: State school students under-represented at leading universities.* London: Sutton Trust.

Taylor, C., and McCaig. C. (2013). *Evaluating the impact of number controls, choice and competition: An analysis of the student profile and the student learning environment in the new higher education landscape.* York: Higher Education Academy.

Universities and Colleges Admissions Service [UCAS]. (2012). *End of cycle report 2012.* Cheltenham: UCAS.

Universities and Colleges Admissions Service [UCAS]. (2014) *End of cycle report 2014.* Cheltenham: UCAS.

Universities and Colleges Admissions Service [UCAS]. (2015) *End of cycle report 2015.* Cheltenham: UCAS.

Universities and Colleges Admissions Service [UCAS]. (2016). UCAS undergraduate end of cycle data resources. Retrieved February 12, 2016 from www.ucas.com/corporate/data-and-analysis/ucas-undergraduate-releases/ucas-undergraduate-end-cycle-data-resources

Waller, R., Holford, J., Jarvis, P., Milana, M., and Webb. S. (2014). Widening participation, social mobility and the role of universities in a globalized world. *International Journal of Lifelong Education, 33*(6), 701–704.

Waller, R., Holford, J., Jarvis, P., Milana, M., and Webb. S. (2015). Neo-liberalism and the shifting discourse of 'educational fairness'. *International Journal of Lifelong Education, 34*(6), 619–622.

# Part II

# Getting on: classed experiences of higher education

# A tale of two universities

## Class work in the field of higher education

*Diane Reay*

## Introduction

Widening Participation in Higher Education (HE) both in the UK and globally, has been driven by a concern to break down the exclusivity of university education (Blanden and Machin, 2004; McDonough and Fann, 2007). In spite of the relative success in increasing participation in HE generally, concerns remain about the social class gap in entry to higher education (Higher Education Funding Council for England [HEFCE], 2005; Wilkins and Burke, 2015). There exists an apparent polarisation of types of university attracting working-class and minority ethnic students (Sutton Trust, 2000, 2004, 2007) and considerable concern with student retention. The universities with the most success at Widening Participation have the highest drop-out rates (HEFCE, 2006) which has suggested a causal relationship and a tendency therefore to construct working-class students as problematic (Leathwood and O'Connell, 2003) and a risky investment for Higher Education Institutions (HEIs).

While there has been substantial research on retention issues (e.g. Tinto, 1993, 1996; Yorke and Longden, 2004) and increasingly the processes of university choice (Modood and Shiner 1994; Reay *et al.*, 2005; Gorard *et al.*, 2006; Harvey *et al.*, 2006; Clarke *et al.*, 2015) there is a minor but growing body of UK research that examines student experiences across the university sector (Archer and Hutchings, 2000; Harvey *et al.*, 2006; Mountford this volume), and within that a small percentage that compares and contrasts working-class students' experiences in different types of HEIs (Reay *et al.*, 2010; Bradley and Ingram, 2012). The importance of this work is increasingly evident when set within the context of research that examines the influence of attending different sorts of HEIs on graduate employability (Brown *et al.*, 2003; Tholen and Brown this volume; Bradley and Waller, this volume) and against the backdrop of a labour market in which half of recent UK graduates are employed in non-graduate jobs (Office for National Statistics [ONS] 2013).

Archer *et al.* (2003) study in one post-1992 university discussed constructions and concerns of risk, costs, and benefits of university participation. Bradley and Ingram's (2012) more recent research of an elite and a post-1992 university found that working-class students at both universities faced more constraints than their middle-class counterparts. The focus of this chapter is on how working-class students manage the academic in relation to their social selves across two institutions that are even more polarised in terms of social class and levels of resources than the two HEIs in Bradley and Ingram's study. The emphasis is on how they navigate and relate to the university both academically and socially in order to develop 'academic ability' and accrue educational knowledge (cultural capital) which they can turn into 'success'. Lave and Wenger (1991) present a socio-cultural theory of students' engagement with their learning, demonstrating the importance of the social as well as the learning contexts. However, their understanding of power relationships and structural concerns is limited (Fuller*et al.*, 2005). In order to develop an understanding of student experiences and interrelated processes that keeps power dynamics and structure, as well as agency, at the centre, the chapter deploys Bourdieu's (1983a) concepts of habitus, capital and field in the analysis of data.

## The research project

The Socio-cultural and Learning Experiences of Working Class Students in Higher Education, funded by the Economic and Social Research Council (ESRC), was a mainly qualitative study but it also utilised a quantitative questionnaire with a social class cross-section of 1,209 students. The focus was on undergraduate students, and began when they were in years 1 and 2; and took place in four very different Higher Education institutions in England. These were Northern, a post-1992 university; Midland, a pre-1992, civic, university; Southern, an elite university and a college of Further Education, Eastern College, where students were undertaking Foundation Degrees in conjunction with Northern University.

Students' social class was determined by: employing the Office for National Statistics (UK) Social and Economic Classifications of parental or mature student occupations, together with information on parents' and immediate family members' education profiles; identifying whether the students were first in their family to attend university; and also whether they received a grant or bursary which would indicate a low household income. We (the team also included Gill Crozier and John Clayton) collected some of this information via the questionnaire, but further refined the data on social class backgrounds during the interview process.

The research was in two stages. First we handed out questionnaire to all Y1 and Y2 students across the four institutions at the start of lectures and through on-line facilities. The purpose of the questionnaire was to find basic information about the student qualifications, social class, ethnicity, gender, motivation for choice of university, subject, career aspirations; views on their university experience both academic and social; and major challenges facing them on coming to university and through their time there. The information gathered allowed us to generalise on certain facets of student views and experiences. We also used this questionnaire to identify students for follow-up group interviews with students from a range of class backgrounds, but more importantly to locate our target group of working-class students.

From the questionnaires we identified 89 students: 48 middle-class and 41 working-class, for follow-up interviews conducted in both focus groups and one to one. We tried to obtain an equal spread across the four institutions, and to include as many working-class and male students as possible. Eight students were from minority ethnic backgrounds; 51 were women and 38 men. Accessing black and minority ethnic students was difficult in part because of limited numbers of these students in Southern and Northern institutions.

In stage 2 we identified 27 working-class students and followed them across two academic years. We interviewed the students at key decision making moments such as the beginning and end of term or at the start of a new module; before and after assessment periods, and kept in contact with them through e-mail and informal meetings. We aimed to gain insights into the students' perceptions of themselves and whether this changed over time and whether and how this impacted upon their attitude to their studies. We sought to access the social and psychodynamics of student relationships with their institutions and to gain insights into their views and feelings about their university experiences, friendships, learning experiences, and their motivations. We spent some time with the students in their environments to contribute to what Skeggs (1994: 72) describes as the 'geography of positioning and possibilities' in this way we aimed to map their cultural and learning experiences, both direct and indirect, and within the time scale of 12–18 months, chart their academic trajectories. We collected data from the students on their progress and asked them to draw a 'mind map' of their social and academic networks. All the student data is anonymised, and the names used are pseudonyms.

Over the course of the entire study we undertook 159 interviews: 143 with students and 16 with tutors, admissions officers, and widening participation officers. In addition, we observed 12 lectures and seminars in order to contextualise the interview data. This chapter draws on insights from our analysis of the whole data, but focuses specifically on the seventeen working-class students (out of a total of 41 working-class students interviewed) who attended two of the four institutions, Southern, the elite university and Northern, the post-1992 institution.

In the next section I focus on the wider field of HE, and how these 17 students, located in very different HEIs, are positioned within the field.

*Table 5.1* Statistical details of the 17 case study students in the two universities

| University | Total no. students | Female | Male | 18–21 | 22–25 | 26+ | BME | White | 1st in family |
|---|---|---|---|---|---|---|---|---|---|
| Northern | 8 | 6 | 2 | 4 | 0 | 4 | 0 | 8 | 8 |
| Southern | 9 | 5 | 4 | 8 | 0 | 1 | 0 | 9 | 9 |

## Incentives and disincentives of the field

Naidoo (2004) argues that fields are structured in hierarchy in the sense that agents and institutions occupy dominant and subordinate positions. These positions depend on the amount of specific resources (capitals) that are possessed in relation to other occupants. The UK HE field is a highly differentiated and hierarchical one (Brown, 2013) in which the prestigious Russell Group, of which Southern is a prominent member, and the Million+ Group, representing many of the 'new' universities, including Northern, denote dominant and subordinated poles (Bourdieu, 1993) within the wider field. The accumulation of power and distinction varies across the field, positioning students very differently within higher education. Southern students, in the elite institution located at the core of the wider field, are situated centrally in relation to axes of influence, status and achievement. Bourdieu (1983b: 345) asserts that 'there is nothing mechanical about the relationship between the field and habitus. The space of available positions does indeed help to determine the properties expected and even demanded of possible candidates'. The Southern students occupy a section of the field characterised by an elite academic habitus, where the academic dispositions 'expected, and even demanded' are those of excellence, autonomy, and competitiveness. Southern's positioning at the top of the UK university hierarchy provides its students with access to a rich distribution of different forms of capital, economic, social, cultural, and symbolic, even though, as working-class, the students in the sample were positioned marginally in relation to such dominant capitals. How ever, the Northern students were even more marginal, located in part of the field that was peripheral in relation to the main sources of academic power and distinction.

But there were other characteristics of the field that crucially impacted on students' ability to profit from their university experience. The degree to which students' learner identities became their main and strongest source of identity was powerfully influenced by the range and degree of structural constraints inscribed in the two institutions. In particular, the extent to which students either lived at home or in university accommodation was highly significant. In the questionnaire survey 70 per cent of the Northern students indicated that they lived at home, while in Southern all the students were in university accommodation.

These contrasting norms of living in university accommodation at Southern and living at home at Northern were reinforced by the very differing levels of labour market involvement in the two HEIs. Sixty-five per cent of the Northern students were undertaking paid work, and only 8 per cent at Southern. The working-class students at Northern were often precariously positioned in the new, unfamiliar field of HE, jostling work and family commitments with doing a degree. Often the first two overwhelmed and took precedence over studying, as individuals' biographies and stocks of capital remained in tension rather than alignment with the new field' (Davey, 2009). For the majority of our participants' social identities and relationships with peers, family, and work colleagues were inevitably prioritised over relationships to knowledge and the development of student learner identities.

In contrast, the Southern students centrally located in an elite segment of the field were much more insulated from adjacent fields of the labour market and working-class community. This separation and insulation was the reason all of our Southern, working-class students complained that being at Southern was 'like being in a bubble' (Reay *et al.*, 2009). However, they all benefitted academically and socially from being able to immerse themselves in the HE field with few of the distractions students attending Northern faced.

## Learner identities

However, it was not only labour market and family commitments, but also a sense of not having the requisite cultural capital to successfully navigate the field that made the HE experience often feel alien and difficult to manage for the Northern students. They spoke of being 'out of their depth' in the new learning regimes, of 'not being clever enough to be at university', and not having sufficient time to master the academic literature they were expected to become familiar with. Despite the fact that our sample was made up of those working-class students who had succeeded educationally, there was a clear disparity between the two institutions in the degree of confidence students brought to their studies. The working-class relationship to schooling has typically been one of failure (Willis, 1977; Weis, 1985; Reay, 2006) and this was still true for a majority of the Northern students. As Arthur, a white working-class History student at Northern, said:

My thoughts have always been, at my lowest point, it's always that I'm not capable of doing it.

And as Barbara, a white working class History student at Northern, suggested:

Academically-wise, I keep thinking I shouldn't be here, that you know I'm not up to the level that I should be.

Both Arthur and Barbara are mature students with, as Arthur points out, a considerable gap between school and university, but even the young students lacked confidence in their own academic ability:

> Unfortunately, my experiences of school always taught me that, I mean I was always a late learner, I never caught on particularly quickly but when I did it was always slightly later. So I was always brought up with the attitude that 'oh Fiona will never amount to anything'.
>
> (Fiona, a white working class Chemistry student, Northern)

In Northern we can see a disjuncture between established dispositions of academic insecurity and lack of confidence that are most often a consequence of working-class schooling, and those best suited to generate profit in the new HE field. In contrast, there was a stronger congruence between the originary habitus of the Southern working-class students, and the logic of practice of the HE field they had entered. The originary habitus of the Southern students had already begun to adapt and transform as a result of their educational success at school. They now had sufficient academic capital to succeed.

Growing confidence and strong sense of competence in relation to academic work was evident in all the Southern interviews. Linsey, one of our white working-class Southern Law students, admitted:

I do complain about the obsession with work but I'm also guilty of it. We are all workaholics even the ones pretending they're not working.

Jamie quipped 'we don't do laidback at Southern, here there is only geeky, geekier and even geekier', while Helen, the only mature working-class student in the Southern sample, joked 'We actually celebrate our geekiness here, it's geek paradise'.

In the references to being 'a geek' we see evidence of a specific academic habitus at Southern, one characterised by dispositions of earnest scholarly endeavour and single-minded commitment to academic study (Ward, 2014). All the Southern students gave a very strong sense of constant work and the intensity of the learning experience:

It was a massive culture shock, that it would be so much work, like I did 6 A levels and never did my work and then I come here and I actually have to learn how to work, they work you so hard, and everyone gets ill, tired, and you've got other stuff to do as well as that, and it's just knackering. The first year, I was ill every time I went home afterwards, like I had to spend a week in bed with tonsillitis or whatever . . . .

(Amy, white working-class Engineering student, Southern)

Amy is typical of the Southern students. At Southern there are lots of mentions of 'getting up to speed' and then of 'keeping up the pace' in a context where 'we get 9 or 10 essays a term' (Jamie). And this intensity of the learning experience is often contrasted to the relatively relaxed experience of students at different universities.

While the students at Northern did talk about an intensification of work over the degree period none of them compared learning to 'a race to the top' or 'the survival of the fittest' as did two of the Southern students. The Southern academic habitus was also one permeated by intense competitiveness. Jamie lamented that:

If you were the best at your secondary school . . . you're certainly not going to be the best here. There will be a lot, probably a lot of people, who are putting in the same amount of effort and doing just as well if not better, so you just have to get on with it and do the best that you can . . . you are constantly trying to beat off the competition.

(Jamie, white working-class Law student, Southern)

And:

> There's a lot of competition involved. I have joined the University Law Society and it's all based on competitions, we have lots of knock out competitions with mock trials.
>
> (Jim, white working-class Law student, Southern)

In contrast, competitiveness was discussed in very different terms in Northern, as a quality that for four of the female students, felt alien and inauthentic:

> I hate competitiveness and I would um, I would definitely um, I'd end up failing I think because I just don't feel like I've got that competitiveness in us. I feel like it's quite cruel to be. I mean it's nice to have a challenge, but at the same time I don't think that um, it's not nice to be first, like it doesn't make you better to be the first, to get there first.
>
> (Deborah, white working-class Engineering student, Northern)

Here we can see signs of 'the egalitarian habitus' of Garth Stahl's (2015) working-class boys who shunned competitiveness in order to retain a collegial, egalitarian ethos among their peer group.

While the Northern students expressed anxieties around skills, competencies and techniques of learning, this was far less the case for Southern students. In Southern, past anxieties around schooling had rarely been to do with learning and learner identities. Most of the Southern students struggled to some degree in their earlier schooling not with learning, since all were already excelling academically, but rather, with fitting in and feeling valued by the peer group. They were already 'fish out of water' (Bourdieu and Wacquant 1992: 127) by the end of secondary school (Ward 2015). Consequently, Southern, despite its elitism and middle, even upper class, ethos, represented a more valuing learning environment than school for them:

> I was so used to having to like make your own way and work really really hard if you wanted to be noticed, but you get here and here it's just like everyone's listening to you – "we want to hear what you think" rather than you having to be like hand in the air for half an hour.
>
> (Nicole, white working-class Law student, Southern).

> To come here and meet people and no one makes fun of you because you're clever . . . whereas before you'd have to pretend not to be clever.
>
> (Linsey, white working class Law student, Southern)

What characterised all nine Southern students was that they were educational self-starters. For them learning was an individualised process in which they had to develop dispositions of independence and self-reliance. They had developed an assured academic habitus that the vast majority of Northern students were still struggling to acquire. As Jude, a white, working-class History student at Southern, commented:

> If I'm struggling with something, or needed some advice on anything I doubt I would go to anyone here. But that's partly because of my personality, um, I was brought up in a context of individuals, I'd always been taught that the only person who can help you is yourself.

The same resilient independence was also evident in what Jamie said:

> My time at school was entirely down to me and if I didn't do anything it didn't get done. It wasn't going to happen. No one expected that much of me. But here there are loads of people who have had a much more structured education. It's not forced on them but you know they're expected to do this or that in certain ways and that just wasn't the case for me.
>
> (Jamie, white working-class Law student, Southern)

All the working-class students at Southern displayed self-regulation in learning (Vermunt, 1998) that came from their decision, often from an early age, to 'go it alone' as strongly academically inclined learners. This was far less often the case at Northern. Four of the Northern students complained at length about the low levels of commitment to academic work at Northern:

> The majority of the people on the course never wanted to do it, a good majority, and there are people now who don't even attend, I know one particular person and he has not, he's been here a few hours all year.
>
> (Laura, white working-class Law student at Northern)

Mary, another white working-class Law student at Northern, talked negatively about what she sees as pervasive instrumental attitudes to knowledge and learning:

> The amount of people who think that they can just look at their notes and understand it and not come to seminars is unreal. They are not going to understand it by just reading about it, it's impossible . . . there are a couple who I talk to and I've actually said to them a few times, why are you even here? Because they're just not bothered at all and they're like, 'oh I don't know, I just thought I'd come here'. I said, 'do you actually want anything out of it'? And they're like 'yeah a degree' and like well. I don't know, they just don't seem to really care and you just don't think they are ever going to be actually able to come out with anything worthwhile.

Here we see another stark contrast between Northern and Southern. Northern's broad spectrum of learners did not exist at Southern where nearly everyone was seen to be studious. The data evokes Phil Brown's study of working-class secondary school boys (1987). The Southern students resemble Brown's academically inclined students who are getting into learning rather than just trying to get through; the committed learners who were excited about, and engrossed in their learning. However, at Northern a majority of the working-class students talk in terms of 'getting through' the learning experience rather than getting into it:

> To be honest, this is my fourth year of study and I'm sick and I want it over and done with, do you know what I mean. I want it finished. Now I just want it out of the way and finish my degree.
>
> (Adam, white working-class History student, Northern)

The next section focuses more specifically on the learning contexts in the two institutions, examining the students' learning experiences in detail.

## The impact of two very different learning contexts

In Southern, 93 per cent of students rated the intellectual challenge as high compared to just 39 per cent at Northern. Similarly, there were wide differences in the level of academic support students perceived. Some 41 per cent of Southern students rated academic support as high, while in Northern the figure was 10 per cent. Relatedly, the questionnaire responses revealed that 82 per cent of Southern students had regular one-to-one support while the figure for Northern at 15 per cent was much lower. These are glaring disparities but perhaps unsurprising when contextualised within Roger Brown's (2012) statistics on University spending per student. In 2010/11 spending per head was over £60,000 at Southern, at Northern it was under £10,000. I have written elsewhere, with colleagues (Reay *et al.*, 2010), of the polarisation between institutions caused by their widely differing levels of resources and personnel. These generated starkly different institutional habitus (Reay *et al.*, 2001) that privileged those students at the elite university who are already advantaged, while disadvantaging those working-class students at the new university who needed the most support in developing confident and entitled learner identities.

In the quote below Jude puts some flesh on the statistics on academic challenge and outlines the repercussions for his learner identity at Southern, and the ways in which academic challenges, aligned with intensive interaction with lecturers and tutors, generate intellectual growth:

> The first four supervisions I'd say were nerve-wracking. Anxious. I was anxious. And it's still just feels, well not so much now but, the first two terms felt like I was preparing for an exam before each supervision . . . You know, I tidy up everything and my heart was pounding. And now I'm a lot more relaxed about it and I've started to enjoy them. You know, I actually engage with the material and things. It just, it took me quite a long time I think.
>
> (Jude, a white, working-class History student, Southern)

Jude's heightened sense of anxiety – you can almost hear the adrenalin pumping – was in sharp contrast to Northern where there was less evidence of challenging experiences or regular supervision sessions with staff:

> I would have preferred more classroom contact, maybe that's because I don't particularly like just total independent learning, I like feedback and maybe that's because I'm not err, I wasn't fully, how can I put it? I was worried about

> my ability to do work on my own, whether I was going in the right or the wrong direction, I wasn't sure and I find that I would like more contact with lecturers within the module. I find that a lecture and a seminar isn't enough.
> (Arthur, white working-class History student, Northern)

However, compounding such institutional influences, the students' complex and often over-loaded lives at Northern meant neither were students in a position to challenge themselves academically. While a significant number of our Southern case study students were on course for first class degrees, the students at Northern were juggling so many conflicting commitments they were often having to settle for less:

> This year I was quite happy with a 2:2 and then to sort of develop on that next year and put a bit more effort in because if I'm honest I haven't put the effort that I would normally put in because of all my other commitments,
> (Barbara, white working-class History student, Northern)

And:

> It's been terrible, it's clouding my degree a little bit because there comes a time like Christmas, like the holidays when your family needs money, extra money, it's always at the time of an exam and I'm always ending up working leading up to my exams, so it's impeding my studies a bit.
> (Arthur, white working-class History student, Northern)

Both Arthur and Barbara, as student parents with young children were particularly disadvantaged. As Barbara, reflecting on a year in which one of her four children had been seriously ill, commented:

> I think I am going through this in a daze at the minute. I can't believe I'm doing it, but I think it's important to do it and I've just got to keep on and there has been a couple of rough times this year and hopefully next year it will settle down a bit . . . I mean nothing worse can be thrown at me surely. I mean I've had a pretty bad year really, but it's just one of those things isn't it so we've got to get on with it.

Rachel Brooks (2015) found that the new university she researched lacked any dedicated childcare facilities or information packs, and no members of staff were employed with the specific remit of providing services to mature students with children. While Northern did acknowledge the special needs of student parents, any commitment it professed had not impacted materially on either Barbara or Arthur's situation. Both felt isolated and unsupported in their efforts to function well as both students and parents.

These students display a great deal of fortitude and resilience as learners but against enormous odds. So Barbara, quoted earlier, has been coping over the year with the death of her sister, the recurrent illness of one of her 4 young children, and a broken wrist. In such circumstances studying inevitably becomes a marginal activity unlike the top priority it represents at Southern. But concerns around the impossibility of 'fitting it all in' were not just voiced by the student parents:

> When I had my two jobs I felt like I was paying too much attention to one job or too much attention to the other job and I just didn't feel like I was focusing on the university at all. I felt like I was just squeezing it in when I could
>
> (Deborah, white working-class Engineering student, Northern)

Students at Northern are governed by expediency and 'the logic of necessity' (Bourdieu, 1984) in which their learner identities are constantly at risk of being subsumed by their responsibilities and commitments as workers and family members. The negative impact of competing priorities of work, family and study is highlighted in Kylie's story of being able to give up work on receipt of a small inheritance from her grandfather:

> I was working so many hours and I got quite low grades . . . then I got an inheritance from my granddad so if it hadn't been for that I'd still be working full-time hours. I mean my marks went right up because I used to get like 40s, 50s and stuff like that and all my marks last semester were firsts.
>
> (Kylie, white working-class History student, Northern)

As Kylie goes on to point out, there is a clear connection between competing demands such as work and family commitments and realising one's academic potential:

Simply giving up my job, because I was doing 36 hours a week and being a full-time student, it's impossible. I just wasn't going to reach my potential.

Northern University did not have the personnel and resources to regularly put students in challenging learning situations such as the regular one to two or one to three supervisory sessions provided at Southern. As is clear from the statistics on university income levels, cited earlier, it is far poorer and less resourced than Southern (Brown, 2012). It is unsurprising then that there were enormous disparities in the levels and quality of support for learning across the two institutions. In Southern with its very regular tutorials and supervisions students could make clear connections between regular guidance and improvement in learning skills. So for Jim detailed feedback has enhanced his awareness of what a good essay should look like:

> My current supervisor and my supervisor last term both made me quite aware of how detailed the essay was, how it conformed to their ideas and how the question should have been answered. So, because of that I was far more aware of whether it was a success or not.
> (Jim, white working-class History student, Southern)

Less support is possible at overstretched institutions like Northern, as Barbara makes clear when explaining that her third year lecturers are too busy to provide the level of support that she feels she needs:

> I think that if I'd had the lecturers I've got now I'd just have packed it in. I don't think I could have kept going. I was quite close to leaving as it was so I think if I'd had them I think they would have tipped me over the edge.

Support for learning has an enormous impact on the extent to which working-class students can develop positive learner identities. Paradoxically it is in Northern, with a critical mass of students with negative experiences of schooling, and consequently fragile and unconfident learner identities, where the relative lack of resources means that students have to operate largely as independent learners:

> At the beginning of the year they gave you like little assessments and when it became clear that you couldn't spend a couple of hours doing it, you had to spend more time and prepare more carefully and that no-one is going to teach you how to do it, you just basically had to learn the hard way.
> (Adam, white working-class History student, Northern)

As Adam's words indicate they are largely left to their own resources. This was very definitely not the case at Southern. Jamie was identified by his college tutor at the end of year one with the same difficulties as Adam in handling assignments. However, unlike Adam, he is not left 'to learn the hard way'. Rather the university found him a local poet whom they paid to provide him with six individual tuition sessions to work on his essay writing skills.

The interplay between incentives of the field together with an already highly motivated academic habitus meant being a student in Southern became the individual's main source of identity to the extent that being a student often filled the whole of the individual's life with studying as an all-consuming preoccupation. Southern students had both the dispositions and advantageous field conditions to totally immerse themselves in the field. This was rarely the case for Northern students.

The situation for students in these two universities exemplifies a growing divide in UK universities between those institutions where students have parents who are able to subsidise their living costs so that students can actually be students, and those universities where a majority have competing demands that make being a student a marginal activity. Southern exemplifies the few elite HEIs at the privileged core of the HE field. While the originary habitus of all the working-class students was largely incongruent with the social conditions of the HE field, the working-class Southern students, with their high levels of academic capital, were for the most part able to adapt successfully to the new field's logic of practice (Bourdieu, 1990a). They, unlike most of the Northern students, developed a feel for 'the academic game' (Bourdieu, 1990b: 66) that reinforced and extended their sense of themselves as successful academic learners.

## Conclusion

Growing inequalities in HE become very apparent when we focus on two institutions at polar extremes in the wider field of higher education, with Southern at the very centre of power and distinction within the field, and Northern at the edges with far less access to either power or distinction. In particular, the consequences for working-class students have been highlighted. Northern working-class students constitute the marginal within a marginal section of the HE field, struggling to achieve a degree of fit with a new unfamiliar field. Yet, they comprise by far the largest working-class constituency within HE. While universities like Northern now admit almost 50 per cent of their intake from the working-classes, universities such as Southern admit only 10 per cent (Havergal, 2016) And, with new austere times for young people in the UK, Southern working-class students are becoming a shrinking and endangered species (Koppel, 2014).

Despite the many sacrifices the working-class Northern students had made to gain a position in the field, they remained peripheral within it. Habitus was more durable and resistant to change than was the case in Southern where the working-class students' habitus was more closely aligned with the academic culture of the HE field. They were the group best equipped with 'affinities and convergences' (Grenfell, 2007: 138) in relation to the new field. However, this is not simply an instance of habitus transformation in one sector of the field and 'a habitus of recalcitrance' (Skeggs, 2004: 89) in another. The incentives of the field, the paucity and richness of the capitals underpinning them, and the disparate ways in which they operated in different sections of the field were pivotal to whether working-class habitus was able to adapt and develop new dispositions. The relative insulation of the elite centre of the HE field allowed for a degree of immersion and commitment that was not possible for the Northern students, while Southern's resources of social, economic, cultural, and symbolic capitals provided possibilities of capital acquisition that were largely absent in Northern.

The data reveals the powerful influences of habitus, of students' prior learning experiences and dispositions, but also the dynamic interplay between these and the field of higher education. Key to the possibilities of success is the degree of proximity to the field's axes of power and distinction, but also the range and quantity of capitals accessible to students from their specific position in the field. Of particular importance is the extent to which academic fields are insulated and independent of other fields that hold the potential for making competing demands of students, and the protective qualities of dominant cultural capital. These all conspire to enable our Southern students to position themselves in the HE field as 'good learners'; those who most approximate to 'the ideal learner'. Four of our nine Southern students achieved first class degrees compared with only one student in Northern. These are the working-class students who have developed almost superhuman levels of motivation, resilience, and determination, sometimes at the cost of peer group approval in the schools they had attended. They have managed to achieve considerable success as learners and acquire the self-confidence and self-regulation that accompanies academic success against the odds. And the teaching methods, academic support systems, and resources at Southern all reinforce and nurture this developing sense of 'mastery' in relation to knowledge. In contrast, at Northern students are far more likely to be exhausted from parenting and part-time work, distracted by financial, health, and family problems and lack the confidence and self-esteem to be able to construct themselves as successful learners. They are jostling competing demands that impinge on and undermine the potential of adapting and integrating into the field of HE; that a number succeed is a testament to their resilience and determination in a less conducive and comparatively under-resourced academic environment.

## References

Archer, L. Hutchings, M., and Ross, A. (Ed.). (2003). *Higher Education and Social Class: issues of exclusion and inclusion.* London: Routledge/Falmer.

Blanden, J., and Machin, S. (2004). 'Educational inequality and the expansion of UK higher education. *Scottish Journal of Political Economy, 51*(2), 230–245.

Bourdieu. (1983a). The genesis of the concepts of habitus and of field. *Sociocriticism, 2*(2), 11–24.

Bourdieu, P. (1983b). The field of cultural production or: The economic world reversed. *Poetics 12(4–5)*, 311–356.

Bourdieu, P. (1984). *Distinction: A social critique of the judgement of taste.* London: Routledge.

Bourdieu, P. (1990a). *The logic of practice.* Stanford: Stanford University Press.

Bourdieu, P. (1990b). *Homo academicus.* Cambridge: Polity Press.

Bourdieu, P., and Wacquant. L. (1992). *An Invitation to Reflexive Sociology.* Chicago: University of Chicago Press.

Brooks, R. (2015). Social and spatial disparities in emotional responses to education: feelings of 'guilt' among student-parents *British Educational Research Journal, 41*(3), 505–519.

Bradley, H., and Ingram, N. (2012). Banking on the future: choices, aspirations and economic hardship in working-class student experience. In W. Atkinson, S. Roberts, and

M. Savage, (Eds.), *Class inequality in austerity Britain: Power, difference and suffering.* Basingstoke, UK: Palgrave Macmillan, 51–69.

Brown, P., Hesketh, A., and Wiliams, S. (2003). Employability in a knowledge-driven economy. *Journal of Education and Work, 16*(2), 107–126.

Brown, R. (2012). Figures reveal deep inequalities between rich and poor universities the gap in income and resources between universities is even greater than that between public and state schools. *The Guardian.* September 24th. Retrieved November 27, 2016 from www.theguardian.com/education/2012/sep/24/university-inequality-income-resources-unfair

Brown, R. (2013) *Everything for sale? The Marketization of UK Higher Education.* London: Routledge.

Clarke, S., Mountford-Zimders, A.M., and Francis, B. (2015). Risk, choice and social disadvantage: Young people's decision-making in a marketised higher education system. *Sociological Research Online, 20*(3), 9. Retrieved from www.socresonline.org.uk/20/3/9.html

Davey, G. (2009) Using Bourdieu's concept of habitus to explore narratives of transition. *European Educational Research Journal, 8*(2), 276–284.

Gorard,S., Smith, E., May, H., Thomas., L., Adnett, N., and Slack, K. (2006). *Review of Widening Participation Research: addressing barriers to participation in higher education.* HEFCE: Bristol.

Havergal, C. (2016). Elite universities 'going backwards' on widening access. *Times Higher Education* February 18th 2016. Retrieved February 16, 2016 from www.timeshigher education.com/news/elite-universities-going-backwards-widening-access

Higher Education Funding Council for England. [HEFCE] (2005). *Higher education admissions: assessment of bias.* Bristol: Higher Education Funding Council for England.

Koppel, G. (2014). Why is Oxbridge taking fewer state school students? *The Guardian.* Retrieved November 27, 2016 from www.theguardian.com/education/2014/may/27/oxbridge-state-school-numbers-falling

Lave, J., and Wenger, E. (1991). *Situated learning.* Cambridge: Cambridge University Press.

Leathwood, C., and O' Connell, P. (2003). "It's a struggle": The construction of the 'new student' in higher education. *Journal of Education Policy, 18*(6), 597–615.

McDonough, P., and Fann, A. (2007). The study of Inequality. In P. Gumport. (ed) *Sociology of higher education,* Baltimore: John Hopkins University.

Modood, T., and Shiner, M. (1994). *Ethnic minorities and higher education.* London: Policy Studies Institute/Universities and Colleges Admissions Services.

Naidoo, R. (2004). Fields and institutional strategies: Bourdieu on the relationship between higher education, inequality and society. *British Journal of Sociology of Education 25*(4), 457–471.

Office for National Statistics [ONS]. (2013). *Full Report – Graduates in the UK Labour Market* 2013. ONS: London.

Reay, D, Crozier, G., and Clayton. J. (2010). "Fitting in" or "standing out': working-class students in UK higher education. *British Educational Research Journal, 36*(1), 107–124.

Reay, D., Crozier, G., and Clayton. J. (2009). Strangers in paradise: Working class students in elite universities. *Sociology, 43*(6), 1103–1121.

Reay, D., David, M., and Ball, S.J. (2005). *Degrees of choice.* Stoke-on-Trent and Sterling, USA: Trentham Books.

Reay, D., Ball, S., and David. M. (2001). Making a difference?: institutional habituses and higher education choice. *Sociological Research Online, 5*(4), U126-U142.

Skeggs, B. (1994). Situating the production of feminist ethnography. In M. Maynard, and J. Purvis, (Eds.), *Researching women's lives from a feminist perspective*, London and Philadelphia: Taylor & Francis, 72–92.

Skeggs, B. (2004). Exchange, value and affect: Bourdieu and 'the self'. In B. Skeggs, and L. Adkins (Eds.), *Feminists after bourdieu*. London: Blackwells, 75–95.

Stahl, G. (2015). *Identity, neoliberalism and aspiration, educating white working-class boys*. London: Routledge.

The Sutton Trust. (2000). *Entry to leading universities*. London: Sutton Trust.

The Sutton Trust. (2004). *Missing 3000*. London: Sutton Trust.

The Sutton Trust. (2007). *University admissions by individual schools* London: Sutton Trust.

Tinto, V. (1993). *Leaving college: Rethinking the causes and cures of student attrition.* 2nd edition. Chicago: University of Chicago Press.

Tinto, V. (1996). Reconstructing the first year at college. *Planning for Higher Education, 25*(1), 1–6.

Thomas, L., and Quinn, J. (2007). *First generation entry into higher education*. Maidenhead: Open University Press.

Ward, M.R.M. (2014) "I am a geek, I am": Academic achievement and the performance of a studious working-class masculinity. *Gender and Education*, 26(7), 709–725.

Ward, M.R.M. (2015). *From labouring to learning*. Basingstoke: Palgrave MacMillan.

Wilkins, A., and Burke, P. (2015), Widening participation in higher education: the role of professional and social class identities and commitments. *British Journal of Sociology of Education, 36*(3), 434–452.

# Chapter 6

# How to win at being a student

*Matthew Cheeseman*

## Introduction

The majority of research into undergraduate student life in the UK stems from Sociology, although it is couched within the boundaries of a number of disciplines, from Human Geography to Sports Studies. Such research typically derives its theoretical orientation from Pierre Bourdieu, who provides the conceptual means by which writers describe student culture. In discussions of older students (Lusk, 2008) and students who live at home (Holdsworth, 2006; 2009) Bourdieu is used to refer to a 'master/mainstreamed' culture (Lusk, 2008: 109) defined by residence and location and focused on socialising. A national, mainstream student habitus is perceived by non-traditional students, despite (or indeed because of) Widening Participation (WP) initiatives; this influences the stereotype of the 'typical student' defined (in part) by the media (Holdsworth, 2006). In 2005, when I began my ethnographic fieldwork investigating the 'mainstream' student culture at the University of Sheffield (2011), the literature on what the 'mainstream' habitus was, or who traditional students were, was scarce (Lusk, 2008), as it had been in the late 1990s (Silver and Silver, 1997).

My research focused on non-international undergraduate students aged between 17 and 20 at the time of their first year of study, living away from parents or family in full-time education at the University of Sheffield. HE is an important industry in Sheffield, which is also home to Sheffield Hallam University, a former polytechnic college. This is seen by some as less prestigious than the University of Sheffield, a member of the elite Russell Group (Naidoo and Jamieson, 2005). Since older students, those from a racial minority and/or from poorer backgrounds tend to go to less prestigious institutions (Reay *et al.*, 2001; Brennan and Osborne, 2008; Allen and Ainley, 2010), the University of Sheffield might expect to receive a smaller proportion of these students than less-prestigious, newer universities such as Sheffield Hallam University, just as the University of Sheffield might expect to host proportionally more mobile students, moving to Sheffield and often living in university accommodation. Where data is available, it is noted that 18 per cent of students for the years 2000 and 2004 were drawn from disadvantaged social classes (Mathers, 2005: 376–386).

I sought to describe and understand the construction of the 'typical' student experience as it was imagined and sometimes experienced by students at the University of Sheffield. This chapter refers to those experiences which were thought of as 'typical' or 'mainstream' by many students, who may not have experienced or enacted them at all times.[1] My data emphasised the centrality of masculine behaviours to the construction of this 'typical student'. These behaviours were engaged with by both men and women (often critically) and my discussion of them should not in any way be taken as a valorisation, but rather as an evocation of the performances and idealisations of being a 'typical' student, as seen by students, many of whom only engaged in such behaviours occasionally, and often only in their first year of study.

I undertook ethnography between October 2005 and July 2010, in a variety of situations and locations in Sheffield. Ethnography is often described as a means of appreciating the difference between what people say and what people do (Atkinson and Hammersley, 1994). I engaged in planned fieldwork sessions with two groups from a hall of residence. The first was the portering and security staff. The second was a large group of approximately twenty students, easily divided into two gendered groups. The fieldwork consisted of a year of residence with these groups followed by semi-regular meetings and interviews up to the graduation of most of these students in July 2008, through the typical 3-year undergraduate degree. I then continued my research in other capacities as I began to write up. Informed consent was obtained in all cases and all names and situations have been anonymised.

My ethnographic strategies ranged from passive and exploratory ('just being there' and reacting to situations) to planned and exploratory (going to a specific place and/or time to see what happened) to targeted (working with a specific group/ situation to inquire about a certain topic). To record and document my experiences in the field I made and collected an assortment of field texts in a range of media which included diary entries, letters, emails, notes, documents, photographs, video and the internet. I also carried out 69 formal semi-structured interviews with groups or, more commonly, single participants. I interviewed students, porters and security staff, community forums, police officers, shop owners, bar owners, bar workers and various University staff. In all cases I notated comments, using quotation marks to indicate a verbatim transcription. In addition to these interviews I conducted 23 recorded interviews with 28 participants. These ranged in length from 30 minutes to 3 hours, with the average time being about one hour. They were generally informal and semi-structured around a few questions. I coded all my data by hand, inducing themes and thinking about them in respect to the literature.

## Studentland

My ethnography was orientated towards understanding the distinctive means by which students identified as a group outside of the official university agenda of learning and teaching. It became apparent through my research process that this mainstream culture was situated in student residences. Moving to Sheffield implied a complete reformation of a student's social network, substituting their previous domestic situation, for a collection of other students living in specially designed student accommodation. Mobility thus *limits* the student's social environment by removing various former social networks (family, friends, etc.) and replacing them with students alone. As a result of this the experience of going to Sheffield, and by implication, all mobile students, is immersive and intensive. This is key to understanding the central territory of studentland (Chatterton and Hollands, 2003) and the source of anxiety that non-mobile students have in accessing this territory and having a 'typical experience'. In terms of the life course, a mobile student's social environment is never likely to be as particular or well-defined again (Kenyon, 2000).

Mobility dictates two key principles upon which elite Higher Education Institutions (HEIs), like the University of Sheffield, market student life. The first is a students' ability to make friends, the second is a student's ability to maximise pleasure. These are dominant elements of the mediated university experience, often expressed in terms of hedonism, one of the important ways in which elite universities are both thought of and marketed (Quinn, 2007). Alcohol, youth culture and 'independence' thus intersect with discourses on mobility and residence, defining, in their own way, the mediated 'student experience', whether it is actually experienced or not.

Both Chatterton (1999) and Holdsworth (2006, 2009) identify the 'residential tradition' of HE in England and Wales as the framework for developing the physical spaces that support the habitus of student life. Chatterton (1999: 129), whose work on the 'exclusive geographies' of University of Bristol undergraduate students informed his later thinking on the night-time economy, suggests student venues and houses weaving 'distinctive time-space patterns through certain areas of the city', patterns that are embedded and subsumed in the night-time economy and the student housing market. Experiencing the infrastructure that supports this often means following a particular spatial and temporal trajectory, from, on a typical night out, home to pub to Students' Union (SU)[2] to night club to fast food outlet to home. In the wake of expansion, Chatterton hypothesised

> [C]lass-based strategies will evolve to maintain the value of a university experience. Bourdieu and Passeron (1979) describe this process as 'creative redefinition' in which the middle- and upper-classes are likely to colonise the residential student experience at Britain's older universities as a strategy to distance themselves from a less socially valuable stay-at-home university experience.
>
> (Chatterton 1999: 131)

My previous work (Cheeseman, 2010) indicated that a residential, traditional student drinking culture was firmly in place at the University of Gloucestershire, a non-elite university,[3] indicating that Chatterton's hypothesis relied more on student mobility than academic prestige. I found two distinct alcohol cultures distinguished by four factors: temporality, levels of consumption/bingeing, participation in drinking routines and social class. The first culture was composed of middle-class, mobile traditional students who binged to very high levels on a Monday and/or Wednesday while participating in drinking routines such as 'predrinking', 'fancy dress', 'drinking games', 'shot-slamming' and 'torpedoes'.[4] The second culture (who drank on Friday and/or Saturday) tended not to live in student accommodation and consumed and binged less than the mid-week students. All indications suggested that student drinking on Friday/Saturday was part of the general weekend alcohol culture of the local town. Mobility and participation in sport were the variables which placed students in the Monday and/or Wednesday culture, the student nights.

Broadly speaking, this temporal pattern was confirmed during my research in Sheffield. I found that friendship was enacted between accommodation and the student-orientated night-time economy. Friendship, that perennial marker of the student experience, was performed in a monetised environment twice over, in bedrooms and on dancefloors. The commercialisation of both of these sites from the early 1990s on foregrounded the commodification and individuation associated with the introduction of fees. In this paper I briefly describe the commercialisation of residence, discuss its role in forming friendship groups before detailing the night-time economy and its centrality to the contemporary experience of friendship. I go on to characterise engagement with the night-time economy as obligatory for anyone negotiating the mainstream of student culture before concluding with some of the exclusions this necessitates.

## Bedrooms and dancefloors

Harold Silver (2004: 131) describes the 1980s as a time which saw a shift from the provision of 'residence' to 'accommodation', where 'the planning of student residence partly as control, partly as a function of liberal education . . . disappeared' Silver characterises this as the 'abandonment of a tradition' marked by three features: (a) the absence of residence from any discussion of what a university is, (b) the rise of private student accommodation providers such as Unite from the mid-1990s, and (c) Public-Private Partnership (PPP) of universities with private companies in constructing and managing student residences.[5] In Sheffield, this has seen the end of 'traditional' halls of residence where students lived communally, sharing facilities such as showers, kitchens, and social space, and the construction of a student village, where all shared facilities are centralised and students live in apartment blocks. This cost £158.7 million and was funded by £17 million of equity and £141.8 million of debt in a PPP deal between the University of Sheffield, Catalyst Higher Education (Sheffield) Plc, Catalyst Lend Lease Holdings Ltd and HSBC Infrastructure Fund Management Ltd. This occurred halfway through my fieldwork and I was able to see the change from one system (Silver's 'residence') to another ('accommodation') and how that increased the marketisation of student life.[6]

My fieldwork indicated that in Sheffield, as elsewhere (Chatterton and Hollands, 2003), the central student ritual of 'going out' had been formalised into a commercial weekly calendar. This can be clearly seen in the student press from the mid-1990s on, approximating the development of the consumerist framework in HE. This formalisation is based around venues offering what are referred to as 'nights', themed entertainments run by promoters and designed to attract customers. They are targeted to young people, while simultaneously responding to fashions and tastes. The night-time economy thus encourages the performance of 'going out' by providing a stage on which the consumers 'perform' (as per Goffman, 1959; 1963). This is the key definition of what 'going out' means, above all else, it is a performance hosted by the theatres of the night-time economy. When young people go out the audience is made up by the actors themselves, performing together in small troupes. The night-time economy is, essentially, a collection of stages helping and encouraging these troupes all improvise the same play. Its performance is mediated by the consumption of alcohol, soaked up by the 'actors' like applause.

For the students of both the University of Sheffield and the University of Gloucestershire, student nights were never staged on Friday or Saturday (outside SUs) as the night-time economy can rely on non-students to perform for higher prices at weekends. My fieldwork suggested going out has a basic plot which begins in *definition* and ends in *dissolution*. The former does not simply mean sober, and the latter intoxicated. The terms are used generally, and ambiguously, to describe the style, state and general tone of the performance. In definition the two extremes are comparable to the Apollonian/Dionysian dichotomy. One defines, decides, projects, looks, controls, and excludes while the other dissolves, breaks free, and runs out of control. Neither state is definitive, but both work in a dialectic: *definition* always having a touch of *dissolution* and vice versa.

Winlow and Hall (2006) believe that contemporary youth no longer form and experience relationships in the reflexive late modern manner that Giddens (1991, 1992) and Beck (1992) describe. Instead they suggest that friendship has been subsumed and that youth, including students, are increasingly instrumental in their choice of friends, befitting the atomising and competitive pressures of market forces which have shaped the night-time economy as a site to exchange friendship and identity. My fieldwork only partially concurs with this, and in fact supports Brooks' (2007) limited study of friendship at HEIs. In general Sheffield students have, as Brooks suggested, two groups of friends, 'the people they live with' whose relationships resemble the 'the transformation of intimacy' that Giddens (1990: 123) discusses, although with much less individuation, and 'the people they know from elsewhere' whose relationships largely accord to Bauman's (2003) description of casual, causal instrumental ties. For convenience, I have called the first group 'families' as they are arbitrary (largely formed by the process of residence allocation) and often long-standing (in the case of many of my collaborators) and the second group 'acquaintances'. These terms and concepts are understandable to students, although not all students would use them or apply them to their own situation.

Because the night-time economy serves different groups of students, the nascent family suggested by residence architecture becomes its initial customer base. 'Going out' does not form families, despite its rhetoric, it cements them in an efficient ritual of bonding. In anthropological terms, going out is a group ritual, a 'formalised, symbolic performance', 'action intended for an audience' and 'acted in a manner to be seen or heard and 'read' by others; therefore, it is also a text, a dramatic text' (Quantz, 1999: 506). To begin the process of family formation all a student needs to do is be willing to 'go out' with one's neighbours, typically the first acquaintances one makes in Freshers' Week.[7] A student's residence-based friends typically becomes their oldest friends at university. As '[s]eeing friends means going out, and going out means seeing friends' (Winlow and Hall, 2006: 57), the business of making friends at the University of Sheffield was also the business of making places. Friendship, for the contemporary student, is as much a spatial as a temporal bond. Family friendships may develop the intensity of reflexive pure relationships, in the corridors and rooms of the residence, but this is an intensification of bonds forged out in the night-time economy, which is dominated, temporally and spatially by the SU.[8]

Student families are inexorably linked with the passage from the residence to the nightclubs of the SU, a journey made countless times, week in, week out, as experience is racked up, night after night, in accordance with the constant reflexive dictates to 'make memories'. Thus families develop over the student's university career, from first to third, in a temporal and spatial dialogue with the study-bedroom and the night-time economy, from the exploratory to the familiar. They are at their most fluid in the first year, where they can always admit new acquaintances, because at their core is a stable residential unit: the group that lives together and goes out together.

Moving into private housing at the beginning of the second year is thus a crucial transition for any family. The larger community of the residence falls away and the family is defined further by the architecture of the private house, and contextualised among other families caught in the same process. However, the key point here is that the decision on who to live with in the second year is actually made either side of Christmas in the student's first year of university. Although there is a glut of student housing in Sheffield, the pressures of both tradition and the market urge students to sign up to contracts as soon as possible, to secure 'good houses' with 'good locations'. As a result there is a huge amount of continuity between the first and second years within University of Sheffield student culture, which, in terms of social network formation, only highlights the importance of the architecture of the University residences in suggesting the boundary of the initial family. Gendered families are thus the norm, but even students who live in mixed-gender corridors or flats in University accommodation tend to form gendered families, and certainly further define them on gender lines when choosing second year accommodation. As I found, this is partly because students tend to avoid living with anyone they are sexually or romantically attached to, and also because the night-time economy stratifies, divides, and sexualises men and women.

The transition to third year accommodation allows students their first real opportunity to spatially break away from friendship decisions made close to the beginning of the first year. In the majority of cases the lease is renewed, the family is retained and relationships remain, but in some instances it is broken, often as part of a student's attempt to 'unlearn the rules' of the first year of university. The students who found happy families enjoy intense relationships that validate friendship. However, the process of simultaneously making friends and making places in the night-time economy effectively means that individuality, and to some extent, identity is ceded to the group, especially when it concerns 'going out'. This is well illustrated by the following quotation by a third year student in a 'family' group:

> I 'have' to go out tonight unfortunately. This is due to severe pressure . . . for me to not let the side down and also the fact that I lost a best of three on Pro Evo[9] to Lawrence. Since the beginning of last year, a stupid rule has been carved into 946's[10] rules that if someone doesn't want to go out and others do, they have to play one of those people on Pro Evo and if they lose they have to go out. Regardless of what others say, I didn't really want to go out tonight, compared to other occasions where I did all along. As a result, I have a disgusting morning to look forward to tomorrow, as I have lectures at 10 am . . . not mint. I will be there though, even if I'm not there in mind.

Having a family and subsuming personal identity to the group is something that many students find deeply enervating and satisfying. It is the central experience of being a mobile student and is often unlike anything students have experienced before. Indeed, it is unlike anything they have experienced before or will again, as the mechanism of friendship is unlike that experienced outside of the mobile student experience. Key to this is the role architecture plays in limiting the 'diversity of possibilities' (Giddens, 1991: 87) that friends are selected from. This is encouraged by the theatres of the night-time economy which, by necessity, speak to groups. As one must be in a group to go out, Winlow and Hall (2006: 93) have accused young people of selecting their friends 'as a means of facilitating the "right" type of cultural engagement' in the night-time economy. The difference is that mobile students do not have a free choice in selecting their friends, as they do not control the processes of room allocation.

This automated, random procedure, significantly broadens the potential of friendship beyond a self-selection on the basis of the night-time economy. As an example, one of the students I interviewed confessed to me that he 'couldn't stand anyone Black or Indian or anything' before coming to University. He explained to me this was because he came from a 'bad background' and then told me that going out with an Asian student who lived on the same corridor as him had changed his mind, not only about the Asian student, but about all those from ethnic minorities. Of course, going out remains the key activity in this process, and I doubt whether the student would have had a similar experience had the Asian student refused to participate in going out.

As I have illustrated in the previous section, families cement themselves in the journey towards dissolution, which equips students with skills, confidence, and experience, forming the 'memories' that enable young people to engage with mainstream discourse on university experience.

## I bet you don't look good on the dancefloor

In Sheffield at least, if a student was not willing to 'go out' then a student forfeited their full exchange value on the social field. This was not an exercise in distin-guishing between minority and majority cultures, for the culture that engages in going out is diverse and composed of various sexualities, ethnicities, and classes: everyone who has been touched by the supple and persistent massage/message of youth consumerism, which orientates all towards the nightclub floor.

The student phrase 'being good at life' illustrates this well. It is often said ironically in relation to a sensibility of loss over the subjunctive potential of education. When comparing themselves to students who were successful at their studies, or when just deciding to go out rather than work, students sometimes commented 'at least I win at life'. The definition of 'life' is of course inter-action with the night-time economy, and the implication is that students who do not choose to immerse themselves in this world are not properly alive. Of course there are many reasons why students may not go out (typically personal choice, cultural background or religious belief). As a result of this choice, however, they are not afforded the same social potential as others claim. They simply do not exist as 'students' in the general, mainstream sense of the word. The night-time economy becomes, in effect, a social field related to education totally distinct in its concerns.

There is no better way to completely kill a nascent acquaintance relationship then to answer the ubiquitous student question, 'Did you go out last night?' with 'I don't go out', or even worse 'I don't like going out, I prefer working'. Such answers are effectively saying 'I don't belong here'. It is perfectly acceptable to say 'I had to work', or 'I stayed in and watched a DVD', for those answers maintain the importance and centrality of going out. Because making friends is making places, admitting to not liking going out is tantamount to saying, 'I don't want to have a social connection with you'. I interviewed one student who, on the first weekend in halls, declined an invitation to go out, saying they did not like to do that sort of thing. As a consequence, he overheard the people around him telling others that he was 'a bit quiet'. In his perception, this resulted in many people not getting to know him within his student accommodation.

Since a family is a group of students who live and perform together, and the night-time economy is structured around interaction via such friendship groups, this is where mobile, residential students have a distinct advantage over students who live at home, who are effectively denied the advantages of 'protected trading' in the night-time economy that the family provide. In terms of social capital, the family can thus be interpreted as a bank, into which students deposit their social capital at the beginning of university. In return the family keeps their capital safe, protecting it from the sometimes exhausting and alienating process of exchanging cultural capital in studentland, and only gambling it as a group. This can turn going out into a form of group play whereby families are set in performative competition against each other.

This encourages a form of aggressive speculation in the cultural capital of dissolution, which I call 'banter' after the student use of the term, where it is frequently evoked to describe a humorous discourse associated with hegemonic masculinised behaviours which have been investigated in HE context by a number of researchers on lad culture (Dempster, 2009, 2011; NUS, 2013; Phipps and Young, 2015). In the broader sense that I am deploying it, as a form of cultural capital, banter is complicated. It is performative and harbours many of the features of Bakhtin's (1968) carnivalesque, especially in its disregard for authority, its preoccupation with all things bodily, and its fascination with the earthy and the base. It lacks, however, any utopian sense of a repressed class united by their common humanity, and is instead, profoundly competitive, befitting a neoliberal environment. As such it is heavily mediated, especially in social media. However, contested, the raw and aggressive performances of banter enacted by (both men and women) in the night-time economy are important to student culture and its understanding of friendship. Leaving further exposition of banter to a future work, I consider instead the obligatory joys of the night-time economy to students at the University of Sheffield.

## Pressing throng

Youth consumerism has long recognised and marketed the subjunctive, symbolic potential of the dreamspace that nightclubbing creates. For students this potential is tangible, despite, or even because of the aggressive jousting of banter and the sheer bodily violence of binge-drinking. For every pool of vomit there is a kiss. Memories *are* made. Going out, although riven with individualism, instrumentalism, and consumerism, also presents itself as the solution to these problems, for it imagines community, indeed suggests it in the 'pressing throng' (Bakhtin, 1968: 255). While there are no strangers in student life, as everyone has the shared identity of being 'one who studies', this potential unity, this subjunctive group potential, is only ever experienced as a felt state, in performance. This is the visionary centre of student life.

None of this, of course, is to say that there are not alternative ways to 'becoming a student', but rather to suggest that all of them engage in the night-time economy.

For students the pervasive and persuasive depth of the night-time economy is both a cause for celebration and also the root of a sensibility of loss over the subjunctive potential of education: a coming to terms with the prominence claimed by the night-time economy in student life. It is both grim admission of its limitations in terms of education and identity, and joyous, boozy trickster-like celebration of those very limitations: *Fuck it maaaaan!* Either way, going out becomes the only way to become a student, even if a student never goes out.

This was brought home in a discussion I had with a group of student activists who rejected the alcohol culture. Some were abstainers, but all of them, including those who did on occasion go out, felt an extreme amount of pressure from attempting to 'stand in opposition' to the mainstream culture. An older woman, a mentor to some of the activists, was present for the discussion, she had been a student in the 1950s. I asked her what role alcohol played in her experience of university, and she replied none, she could not remember alcohol ever featuring in either her or her friends' time at university. This may not have been unusual for a female student in the 1950s, yet there was a noted silence when she said this, as all the contemporary students, including myself, came to terms with the gulf that had just opened up in the room. Someone commented that such a state of affairs would be 'unimaginable' today.

Yet there are many outsiders to this model, all of which, I contend, have been deprived of representation by the dominance of the night-time economy, as witnessed in Somer Finlay and Richard Jenkins' (2008: 17) report on the sense of community at the University. There are references to nights 'overcome by alcoholism and infantile regression' and 'a masculinised culture of abuse and drinking'. As I have argued, while it is possible to avoid this culture, students must define themselves in opposition to it. While some form families according to specialist interests, ethnic or religious lines, others never do. One student from an ethnic and religious minority led what she described as a double life, engaging in the night-time economy in Sheffield, and hiding this from her real family outside of Sheffield. She imagined she'd meet others 'like her' (in terms of religion and ethnicity) at university, but never did, so she joined what she saw as the mainstream of student culture.

For the majority of students diversity is experienced as negotiating binaries accommodated by 'staying in' and 'going out'. Prominent to home students[11] is the north/side divide, which, contextualised in Sheffield, casts northerners (both men and women) as stereotypically masculinised and southerners as cautious and (particularly for men) feminised. There is also the private/state school binary, much commented on by students ('coming to Sheffield meant that I met people who'd gone to a private school'). Indeed it is a credit to the unitary nature of Sheffield student culture that the University is notable for its lack of a 'rah scene'[12] (see chapter by Mountford in this volume). The point is, for the majority of students, the role of the night-time economy in student life is not questioned. It is simply accepted as 'normal'.

## This is normal

Aside from divided and disparate individuals and minorities, there are two large blocks of students in the city of Sheffield that do not engage, or 'trade' with the University of Sheffield focused night-time economy. Both to some extent, constitute the cultural other: international students, and students that attend Sheffield Hallam University. Before discussing these groups, however, I shall briefly consider non-student 'locals', with whom there is little friction, especially in comparison to the *passim* references to student-bashing found in the student press of the 1970s and 1980s. This is partly because of HE expansion and lifelong education, and partly because the night-time economy has consolidated going out at the centre of many people's lives, whether they are in education or not (Winlow and Hall, 2006). There is thus more general cultural agreement between students and non-students. In some cases the universalities of youth culture has made it impossible to tell a student from a local, and in situations where it would be obvious, the temporal and spatial stratifications of the night-time economy keep groups apart. Recent research (Ward, 2015) indicates that this is not the case across all areas of the UK, where locality and heritage play a part on attitudes towards students by non-students.

International students, especially those from Asia, were often thought of by home students as not engaging with the night-time economy, or rather not engaging with the night-time economy servicing the mainstream experience. As a result these students were often invisible to the home students. The International Students' Cultural Evening illustrates this well. A big event in the University of Sheffield's calendar, this is when the student national societies compete in a variety show, putting on skits,[13] dances and musical performances. In 2007 the variety evening fell on St Patrick's Day, which the night-time economy has developed, since the 1990s, as a day devoted to alcohol consumption. This created the wonderful scene of the Octagon, the largest University venue, full of International students performing what amounted to a traditional student revue-style show, with very few home students in attendance. They were outside, weaving in and out of the SU bars, wearing foam promotional hats and occasionally vomiting pints of Guinness into the gutter.

International students, especially Asian students have commented that socialising with home students is an either or situation. During my fieldwork a student from Hong Kong told me that two things happen to students who go abroad, either they spend all their time on the internet or they 'go native' and spend their time out drinking. Perhaps this was a scare story: I did not encounter many international students during my fieldwork, especially Asian students from this second group.[14]

While the bulk of undergraduate international students are from Asia, some are from Sheffield's participation in the Erasmus Programme (an HE exchange programme for both undergraduates and teachers). These students are not as alienated by the centrality of the night-time economy to mainstream UK student culture as Asian international students are, as they share the orientation to Western youth culture that permeates it. However, all of the Erasmus students I interviewed couldn't understand elements of going out as performed by home students. As one commented 'Why the chanting? Why standing and dancing on chairs? Not in France'. Others were perplexed by fancy dress: 'It is so strange! Everyday I see costumes in Bar One. I don't like it, Halloween is okay, but every night?' A German student put this down to English 'eccentricity'. He was particularly struck by the aggressiveness of the drinking culture, the excess in the street and the absence of socialising before and after lectures (as I have said, mobile home students tend to form friendships based on residence).

The other group of outsider students are those that attend Sheffield Hallam University. There is little crossover between the two groups in the day, aside from annual competitive sport competitions. During the night, however, these students meet when engaging in the night time economy, especially in the streets between nightclubs, as these are largely segregated (in that Hallam students do not tend to visit the other university's SU and vice versa, and the nightclubs in town hold 'Hallam' or 'Sheff Uni' events on different nights in order to cater to each group). As these groups of students only meet in sports competitions or in the streets and interstices of the night time economy, interaction between the two is strongly characterised by banter, typically in the form of football-style chants:

> During Freshers' Week my flat mates and I attended the community bar crawl. We reached the pub (alcohol prevents me from knowing which one) to chants of 'I'd rather go to Hallam than Ranmoor' and subsequently joined in the halls banter. 'Hallam or Uni' is often the opening line to a stranger on a night out and the direction of the conversation is dictated by the answer they provide.
>
> (Purkis, 2008, p. 15)

As indicated, anti-Hallam chanting is quite intimately connected to the student time cycle, often heard in Intro Week and during the first term, sung on bar crawls and in nightclubs, taught by second and third year students to first years, who are being initiated into the aggressive aspects of student life. This does, on occasion, spill over into physical violence at Varsity events and also in the night-time economy, when banter becomes 'ostensive' (Anderson, 2010). Friction between the universities is centred on chanting, which typically comments on four subjects: sexuality, intelligence, wealth, and arrogance. Sheffield students, particularly women, are portrayed as ugly, sexually inexperienced and arrogant, while Hallam students (particularly women), are portrayed as sexually attractive but permissive, stupid, and poor.

The chants themselves are a sub-genre[15] of blason-populaire, a genre that 'present[s] a stereotype of a particular group or region' (Widdowson, 1981: 36). Joanne Luhrs (née Green) describes chants as 'An expression of one group's outlook and self-image, often involving the implied simultaneous detraction and/or detriment of another (rival) group' (Green and Widdowson, 2003: 9). As a form chants are (obviously) repetitious and highly formalised, and as such are an eminently suitable way of thinking about how a group performs, imagines and projects its own identity (Noyes, 1995). Hallam has an integrative chant, *Boing Boing Sheffield Hallam*, while University of Sheffield had a series of integrative chants for each hall of residence. I collected one divisive Hallam chant, *I'd rather be a poly than a cunt*, which is typically countered by University of Sheffield students with *I'd rather be a cunt than unemployed*. In contrast I collected fifteen examples of divisive chants by University students, a selection of which are listed here:

> *I go somewhere you don't go! Uni! Uni!*
> *I go somewhere you don't go! Uni-ver-si-ty!*

> *Give us an E ... E! Give us an E ... E! Give us an E ... E! What do you get? Into Hallam!*

> *Your dad works for my dad, La la, la la,*
> *Your dad works for my dad, La la la la la.*

> *Today was going to be the day when you finally learn your ABC,*

> *By now, you should have somehow found a way to count up to three, I don't believe that anybody could be as dumb as you,*
> *But you are from Hallam.*

> *Your sister is your mother, Your father is your brother, You're fucking one another, The Hallam family,*
> *Der der der der [clap clap]*
> *The Hallam family.*

This is, of course, a folk commentary on the differential status of both Universities resulting from Hallam's origin as a pre-1992 polytechnic, although, many Sheffield students are not aware of this and simply believe that they are 'the better university'. This stratification explains the preponderance of anti-Hallam chants as all are adaptations of those used at football matches (Luhrs, 2007) where fans typically taunt each other over their lack of intelligence, wealth, and morality, sexual or otherwise (Widdowson, 1981; Luhrs, 2007). Perhaps, due to the persistence of the perceived stratification of the HE system, Hallam students are left with a poverty of response from the chanting lexicon. This perfectly demonstrates the highly competitive, instrumental and banter-sodden atmosphere of HE, where students are desperate for identity and find it at the expense of any sense of solidarity. Certainly, the mapping of football chants and other examples of *blason populaire* onto the stratified HE landscape of pre- and post- 1992 universities is by no means unique to Sheffield and has been recorded between many other HEIs (e.g. the University of Nottingham and Nottingham Trent University).

## Conclusion

Friendship is deeply entrenched in the making friends making places relationship of student accommodation to the night-time economy, for mainstream students at least. This is not, of course, to deny the positive potential of such friendships, only to describe how they are both enacted and imagined. The majority of my participants were delighted by their time at university and the friends they made. In terms of the way the University of Sheffield was structured, the accommodation services and the SU 'provide' and 'service' student families (in their attention to student flats and nightclubs). It is the regular subsumption of individuality in the social banking of living and performing together that is, for many, the defining experience of mobility.

It is worth highlighting the importance of local factors. In Sheffield, the Union's dominance in the local night-time economy disguises division, which is more temporally and spatially distinct at other HEIs, where the gulf between mobile, non-mobile and minority students is obvious (Cheeseman, 2010). While this has prevented an overt 'rah' scene developing at Sheffield, it has hidden stratification and competition, and is in danger of alienating 'invisible' international students from the home student culture.

To avoid such stratifications, and enhance other influences on university friendship I suggest that horizontal connections need to be established between students in separate academic departments. Such a conclusion was a suggestion of the report into student community (Finlay and Jenkins, 2008) and could be manifested in compulsory, cross-discipline 'orientation' modules, introductions to both HE and the history and culture of the University of Sheffield and the city of Sheffield. This could explicitly target the role of international students, and could be undertaken in conjunction with Sheffield Hallam University, relying on the stated aim of both HEIs to work together as closely as possible. Such occasions could also equip students with the intellectual tools to interrogate youth culture, neoliberal pleasure and the night-time economy, perhaps by allowing students to conceptualise student culture and their position within it.

As I have suggested, the interplay between architecture and the social processes of friendship is real and could, if desired, be empirically assessed in a study of social networks. The establishment of these social networks used to be managed in the larger hall environment via the process of allocation. Accommodation blocks could, for example, be loosely structured according to language-use, interest in drama, or music, which may encourage community development beyond the flat (and beyond the night-time economy). Above all, greater attention should be spent on family formation, with prospective students entering into the process. Indeed, pre-arrival is the time to appeal to students' subjunctive desire to engage in the potential of education. It is this desire that is washed in waves of gradual ridicule and receding promise by the tides of the night-time economy.

# Notes

1  For a discussion of the problems of applying the term mainstream to student culture, see my PhD thesis (Cheeseman, 2011). Indeed, for further discussion of pretty much anything in this chapter, see my PhD thesis.

2  A student run representational organisation common to the majority of UK HEIs. Depending on size SUs also provide a range of social, commercial, and support services to students.

3  Sheffield Hallam University was established in 1992, and the University of Gloucestershire in 2001 as a result of previous legislation passed in 1992. Although they are significant differences between them they would both be deemed 'post-1992 universities'.

4  'Pre-drinking' refers to the practice of consuming alcohol at home before visiting licensed establishments, 'fancy dress' to the wearing of themed costume, 'drinking games' to ludic group play designed to facilitate the consumption of alcohol via schemes of reward and punishment, 'shot-slamming' to the rapid drinking of spirit measures and 'torpedoes' to the rapid drinking of bottled alcoholic drinks made possible by the positioning of a straw to act as an extra-oral air conduit.

5  PPPs are a result of neoliberal Private Finance Initiatives whereby private money is used to build public (or in this case university) infrastructure. In the University of Sheffield's case this has seen Bovis Lend Lease build (and collect the rents from) the Endcliffe Student Village. These apartments are run in competition with other student accommodation providers in the city.

6  See Cheeseman, M. (2017). On going out and the experience of students. In J. Burkett (ed.), *Students in Britain and Ireland*. London: Palgrave Macmillan.

7  An introductory week held before the first semester of the academic year starts. For students it is a time to go out, make new friendships and reinvigorate old ones.

8  The importance of the SU to the University of Sheffield's student night-time economy cannot be overestimated, but this is the result of some thirty years of dedicated management by full-time professional staff. The centrality of SUs to student night-time economies at other institutions is not always comparable.

9  *Pro Evolution Soccer*, a computer game.

10  The number of the house in which the family reside.

11  The phrase 'home student' refers to a United Kingdom (UK) national in HE. A home student is the opposite of an international student, which refers to a student not from the UK.

12  Rah being the name by which wealthy, privately educated students are known, so-called from the sound of their accents.

13  Short comedic sketches.

14  Although after my fieldwork had ended I attended a karaoke bar to witness a large gilded room full of partying Asian students arranged around tables covered with alcohol bottles as a long-haired student sang sweet songs to a giant, human-size teddy bear. It was excellent fun, but quite distinct from the mainstream experience.

15  In fact, 'football chants' have been described as a 'sub-genre' of blason populaire (Luhrs, 2007, p. 14), which makes university chants a sub-sub-genre.

# References

Allen, M., and Ainley, P. (2010). *Lost generation? New strategies for youth and education*. London: Continuum Publishing Corporation.

Anderson, R. (2010). *Community of practice: language and identity amongst Sheffield students*, Unpublished MA dissertation. Sheffield: University of Sheffield.

Atkinson, P., and Hammersley, M. (1994). Ethnography and participant observation, In N.K. Denzkin, and Y.S. Lincoln (Eds) *Handbook of qualitative research*. Thousand Oaks: Sage Publications, 248–261.

Bakhtin, M.M. (1968). *Rabelais and his world*. Cambridge, MA: MIT Press.

Bauman, Z. (2003). *Liquid love: On the frailty of human bonds*. Cambridge: Polity.

Beck, U. (1992). *Risk society: Towards a new modernity*. London: Sage.

Brennan, J., and Osborne, M. (2008). Higher education's many diversities: Of students, institutions and experiences; and outcomes? *Research Papers in Education*, *23*(1): 179–190.

Brooks, R. (2007). Friends, peers and higher education. *British Journal of Sociology of Education*, *28*(6), 683–707.

Chatterton, P. (1999). University students and city centres—the formation of exclusive geographies: The case of Bristol, UK. *Geoforum*, *30*(2), 117–133.

Chatterton, P., and Hollands, R. (2003). *Urban nightscapes: Youth cultures, pleasure spaces and corporate power*. London: Routledge.

Cheeseman, M. (2010). *An analysis of the undergraduate alcohol culture at the University of Gloucestershire with particular reference to traditional and non-traditional students*. Unpublished MSc dissertation. Gloucester: University of Gloucestershire.

Cheeseman, M. (2011). *The pleasures of being a student at the University of Sheffield*, Unpublished PhD thesis. Sheffield: University of Sheffield.

Dempster, S. (2009). Having the balls, having it all? Sport and constructions of undergraduate laddishness. *Gender and Education*, *21*(5), 481–500.

Dempster, S. (2011). I drink, therefore I'm man: Gender discourses, alcohol and the construction of British undergraduate masculinities. *Gender and Education*, *23*(5), 635–653.

Finlay, S., and Jenkins, R. (2008). Perceptions and experience of student community at the University of Sheffield. Sheffield: Student Services.

Giddens, A. (1990). *The consequences of modernity*. Cambridge: Polity.

Giddens, A. (1991). *Modernity and self-identity: Self and society in the late modern age*. Cambridge: Polity.

Giddens, A. (1992). *The transformation of intimacy: Sexuality, love and eroticism in modern societies*. Cambridge: Polity Press in association with Basil Blackwell.

Goffman, E. (1959). *The presentation of self in everyday life*. Garden City: Doubleday.

Goffman, E. (1963). *Behavior in public places: Notes on the social organization of gatherings*. New York: Free Press.

Green, J., and Widdowson, J.D.A. (2003). *Traditional English language genres: Continuity and change, 1950–2000*. Sheffield: University of Sheffield, NATCECT.

Holdsworth, C. (2006). 'Don't you think you're missing out, living at home?' Student experiences and residential transitions. *The Sociological Review*, *54*(3), 495–519.

Holdsworth, C. (2009). Going away to uni: Mobility, modernity, and independence of English higher education students. *Environment and Planning A*, *41*(8), 1849–1864.

Kenyon, E. (2000). Time, temporality and the dynamics of community. *Time & Society*, *9*(1), 21–41.

Luhrs, J. (2007). *Football chants and the continuity of the* blason populaire *tradition*, Unpublished PhD thesis. Sheffield: University of Sheffield.

Lusk, C.I. (2008). *The social construction of the mature student experience*. Unpublished PhD thesis, St Andrews: University of St Andrews.

Mathers, H. (2005). *Steel city scholars: The centenary history of the University of Sheffield*. London: James & James.

Naidoo, R., and Jamieson, I. (2005). Empowering participants or corroding learning? Towards a research agenda on the impact of student consumerism in higher education. *Journal of Education Policy, 20*(3), 267–281.

Noyes, D. (1995). Group. *The Journal of American Folklore, 108*(430), 449–478.

NUS. (2013). *That's what she said: Women students' experiences of 'lad culture' in higher education*. London: NUS.

Phipps, A., and Young, I. (2015). Neoliberalisation and 'lad cultures' in higher education'. *Sociology, 49*(2), 305–322.

Purkis, E. (2008). All together now. *Sheffield Steel Press, 120*, 15.

Quantz, R. A. (1999). School ritual as performance: A reconstruction of Durkheim's and Turner's uses of ritual. *Educational Theory, 49*(4), 493–513.

Quinn, J. (2007). Welcome to the pleasure dome: women taking pleasure in the university. In P. Cotterill, S. Jackson, G. Letherby (Eds.), *Challenges and negotiations for women in higher education*. Dordrecht: Springer, 117–129.

Reay, D., Davies, J., David, M., and Ball, S.J. (2001). Choices of degree or degrees of choice? Class, 'race' and the higher education choice process. *Sociology, 35*(4), 855–874.

Silver, H. (2004). Residence and accommodation in higher education: Abandoning a tradition. *Journal of Educational Administration & History, 36*(1), 123–133.

Silver, H. and Silver, P. (1997). *Students: Changing roles, changing lives*. Buckingham: Society for Research into Higher Education and Open University Press.

Ward, M.R.M. (2015). *From labouring to learning, working-class masculinities, education and de-industrialization*. Basingstoke: Palgrave Macmillan.

Widdowson, J. (1981). Language, tradition and regional identity: *blason populaire* and social control. In A.E. Green (Ed.), *Language, culture and tradition: papers on language and folklore presented at the annual conference of the British Sociological Association*. Leeds and Sheffield: CECTAL, 33–46.

Winlow, S., and Hall, S. (2006). *Violent night: Urban leisure and contemporary culture*. Oxford: Berg.

Chapter 7

# Social class, ethnicity, and the process of 'fitting in'

*Berenice Scandone*

## Introduction

In this chapter, I will draw on the experiences of young British-born women of Bangladeshi heritage to explore some of the multiple ways in which social class intersects with ethnicity in shaping how students 'get on' in higher education. Previous research has revealed how, despite expanding access, minority ethnic students' experiences of higher education and related 'gains' appear to be qualitatively distinct from those of their white, middle-class counterparts (Shiner and Modood, 1994; Modood and Acland, 1998; Runnymede Trust, 2010, 2012; Boliver, 2013; Alexander and Arday, 2015). Compared to the latter, working-class students and those of all minority ethnic backgrounds but Chinese are largely over-represented in the generally less prestigious post '92 universities, have lower retention rates, and tend to graduate with lower grades. Leaving aside the 'racial' discrimination that is known to exist in the labour market (Mirza, 1992; Botcherby, 2006; Ahmed and Dale, 2008), this in itself represents a powerful barrier in terms of employment. In addition, one's perceived (lack of) 'success' at university is likely to have a lasting impact on individual and collective identities, as it contributes to structure interpretations of what 'people like us' do (Bourdieu, 1984; Reay *et al.*, 2009a). That is to say, the systematic encounter of more difficulties in education can lead those who share a given class or ethnic background to see themselves as incapable of achieving within that field, and to dismiss it as 'not for them'. When structural and cultural processes at work in excluding minority ethnic and working-class students from the academic and social environment of prestigious universities, and in constructing them as 'underachievers', are not explicitly recognised, they can in fact easily be overlooked and internalised as a sense of self (Bourdieu, 1984). This, in turn, can generate practices of auto-exclusion from higher education and especially from top-ranking institutions. In the light of these considerations, the quest to expose the structures and dynamics underlying minority ethnic students' experiences in this area becomes ever more pressing.

Women of Bangladeshi ethnicity, in particular, have long been considered as 'problematic' due to their especially low levels of participation in education and the labour market (Bhopal, 1997; Ahmad, 2007; Ahmed and Dale, 2008). The last 20 years, however, have seen the number of those moving into university and employment increasing substantially. While a break-down by gender of data is not available for the 1991 Census, statistics show that between 1991 and 2011 the proportion of Bangladeshis aged 16+ holding degree level qualifications has risen from 5 per cent to 20 per cent, with women accounting for around 8 per cent (ONS, 2011a, ONS, 2011b; Lymperopoulou and Parameshwaran, 2015). In what follows, I will engage with the viewpoints of some of these young women who have entered higher education, often belonging to the first generation to do so, in the attempt to uncover structural and cultural influences informing their experiences. The current study will first be located within a larger body of literature that applies a Bourdieusian framework of analysis to the understanding of social inequalities within higher education, and the specific merits of such an approach in directing attention to the structural conditionings that come to bear on students' practices will be considered. I will then provide a broad overview of the research context and methodology, which draws heavily on Bourdieu's conceptual 'toolbox' and on notions of intersectionality (Horvat, 2002; Brah and Phoenix, 2004). Discussion of findings will mainly revolve around participants' perceptions of 'fitting in' at the institutions attended, touching on some of the most common issues confronted at both a social and academic level. Specific focus will be placed on the role that is played in this sense by class and 'race'/ethnicity, and on resulting inequalities.

## Explaining differential experiences of higher education

Since the turn of the century, unequal access and experiences of higher education have been investigated by a growing number of studies from a Bourdieusian class perspective (Reay *et al.*, 2001a, 2001b, 2009a, 2009b; Ball *et al.*, 2002a, 2002b; Archer *et al.*, 2007; Abrahams and Ingram, 2013). This literature has importantly highlighted how, contrary to what is implied by myths of merito-cracy and equal opportunity, university 'choices' and concrete experiences are still substantially linked to students' socio-economic background, and to the economic, social and cultural capital that this gives access to. Considerations of affordability, family care and work commitments, capacity to navigate the education system, and perceptions of 'fitting in' at specific institutional environments, all enter into play in shaping decisions of whether and where to go to university, and whether to continue towards graduation (Archer and Hutchings, 2000; Reay *et al.*, 2001a, 2001b; Ball *et al.*, 2002a, 2002b;). Furthermore, they impinge on students' ability to achieve high grades as well as to participate in social and extra-curricular activities, functioning as both objective and 'internalised' constraints (Reay *et al.*, 2009a; Abrahams and Ingram, 2013; Bathmaker *et al.*, 2013). In other words, these elements do not only act as concrete limitations on one's capacity to do something, but they also produce an anticipation of one's limits, either at a conscious or subconscious level, which can lead to the avoidance of people, places and activities that become perceived as 'not for the likes of us' (Bourdieu, 1984; Archer *et al.*, 2007; Reay *et al.*, 2001a, 2009a). The relatively few studies that have extended this theoretical framework to the higher education experiences of minority ethnic students have mainly focused on 'choice' of institution, and have revealed the working of similar processes revolving primarily around class (Reay *et al.*, 2001b; Ball *et al.*, 2002b). Adding to this, they have shown how, while by no means the only consideration, perceived lack of 'ethnic mix' and 'white predominance' within a given university's student population appeared to discourage some students of minority ethnic background from applying, as this tended to produce an anticipation of being regarded as 'other' as opposed to 'fitting in'.

As some of this research has evidenced, another essential way in which social class affects the experience of university is through the dynamics of 'habitus', which has been defined by Bourdieu (1977: 72) as: '[a] system(s) of durable, transposable dispositions, structured structures predisposed to function as structuring structures'. Habitus can therefore be seen as a matrix of perception, which builds on subsequent individual and collective 'classed' – and, I suggest, 'racialised' (Horvat, 2002; Archer and Francis 2006; 2007) – experiences, and engenders practices in line with that pre-reflexive understanding. Like individuals, higher education institutions too have a habitus, which mainly includes 'curriculum offer, organisational practices, and less tangible, but equally important, cultural and expressive characteristics' (Reay *et al.*, 2009a: 3), and of which academic status is an important aspect. Bourdieu argues that when habitus encounters a field of which it is not the product, as happens to working-class students in top-ranking universities, it finds itself like 'a fish out of water', which leads to one becoming more self-aware (Bourdieu, 1990). This can in turn generate what Bourdieu (1999: 511) defines as a 'cleft habitus', that is: 'a habitus divided against itself, in constant negotiation with itself and its ambivalences'. Other studies have brought to light a more nuanced situation, with the students' habituses responding in different ways to the newly encountered context, and performing a varied range of adaptations to the institutional environment ranging from detachment to immersion (Reay *et al.*, 2009a; 2009b; Ingram, 2011; Abrahams and Ingram, 2013). In their articles on the experiences of working-class students, in particular, Reay *et al.* (2009a, 2009b), highlight how there is no 'easy fit' between social identities, dispositions towards learning (learner identities) and different institutional habituses. Some of the students in predominantly working-class institutions, characterised by a 'laid back' approach to study, felt in fact like they 'fitted in' socially but not academically, while most of those in high-status, predominantly middle-class institutions, experienced the 'paradox of fitting in in terms of learner orientations' (Reay *et al.*, 2009a:11). Both social and learner identities are moreover modified, reinforced or transformed through the experience of university. As these studies also point out, however, even where students appear to be able to 'successfully' adapt to the university environment, this involves nonetheless considerable distress.

Some research has also been done which looks more specifically at how students from a minority ethnic background in general, and South Asian women in particular, 'get on' in university (Modood and Acland, 1998; Osler, 1999; Tyers *et al.*, 2004; Tyrer and Ahmad, 2006; Bagguley and Hussain, 2007; Dhanda, 2010). The issues emerged have mainly to do with scarcity of finances, perceived lack of academic support and of attention to ethnic diversity within curriculum and practices, feelings of social isolation and with more or less direct experiences of racism and Islamophobia. While some of these aspects can be traced back to students' class background, it is clear that 'race' and ethnicity also play a major role in shaping higher education experiences. Apart from explicit 'racial' discrimination and harassment, which do not seem to be as common but still exist, all of these studies mention students' sense of isolation and their concerns for the lack of diversity in institutional culture and social networks as recurring themes in participants' accounts. In this respect, the substantial under-representation of minority ethnic academic staff appears to feed into the mono-culturalism and institutional racism prevailing in university environments, while stripping students of the benefits of a more diverse range of perspectives and of important role models (Andrews, 2015; Shilliam, 2015). South Asian Muslim women, moreover, have long been depicted as being prevented from fully participating in 'modern' British society, including education and the labour market, by 'traditional' patriarchal family and community norms (Bhopal, 1997; Ahmad, 2007; Ahmed and Dale, 2008). Despite growing research challenging such stereotypes by emphasising diversity and 'agency' within their lived experiences (Ahmad, 2001; Tyrer and Ahmad, 2006; Mellor, 2012), Muslim women still tend to be depicted by media portraits and common-sense assumptions as either 'victims' or 'rebels', and their appearance and behaviour have increasingly come under public scrutiny as symbols of 'oppression' and 'extremism' (Navarro, 2010; Janmohamed, 2014a, 2014b; Iqbal, 2015; Waheed, 2015). As will emerge from reported findings, while these die-hard stereotypes are far from representative of the young girls I interviewed, they can nonetheless have important consequences in terms of their involvement in the university's social environment.

## Research context and methodology

The present study focuses on the experiences of 21 British-born young women of Bangladeshi ethnicity, who at the time of this research were undertaking undergraduate studies at a range of different universities in London. London is home to around 58 per cent of the UK Bangladeshi population, which is highly concentrated in specific areas (ONS, 2011c). 19 per cent of the total live in the Eastern borough of Tower Hamlets, where they account for 32 per cent of residents (ONS, 2011c). This is one of the most deprived local authorities in England, and a traditional area of settlement for Bangladeshi immigrants, with most of them coming from the rural district of Sylhet (Department for Communities and Local Government 2009, 2010; ONS, 2011c). Although unintentionally, this residential pattern was also manifested in my sample, where most participants originally came from Tower Hamlets. Some of them had then moved with their parents to Outer London boroughs, especially those of Redbridge and Barking and Dagenham, reflecting the tendency for upwardly mobile minority ethnic families to move from the inner city to the suburbs in search for better housing and schooling opportunities, and for a 'safer' neighbourhood environment (Butler and Hamnett, 2011).

The universities attended by the young women who took part in this study are very different from one another in terms of ranking, educational curriculum and practices, student intake, social environment, and all of those elements which can be seen as constituting their institutional habitus (Reay *et al.*, 2009a). Such diversity afforded the opportunity to gather a range of perspectives on the 'fit' between individual and institutional habitus at different levels (social and academic), and to explore in this way the array of structural and cultural aspects that enter into play in shaping these perceptions. All of these universities are located in London. While this was a consequence of my 'recruitment strategy', it was interesting to note that most interviewees had only applied to institutions within the city, reflecting what is already indicated by other studies (Runnymede Trust, 2010). The few exceptions were represented by applications to Oxbridge and other Russell Group universities[1] outside of London. However, since those who applied to these universities had very high A-level grades and some of the most prestigious Russell Group universities are in London, they finally ended up remaining here, as this allowed them to attend the 'best' institution they could access with those grades.

Blueville, High Valley, Western, Greenshore, and Bayside (pseudonyms) are all Russell Group universities, Riverdale is an 'old' university but not part of the Russell Group, and Melrose, Woodgate, and King George are all ex-polytechnics. High Valley, Western, and Blueville, in particular, are among the country's highest ranking institutions, while Melrose and Woodgate are among the lowest (The Complete University Guide, 2016). All of the Russell Group universities, except for Bayside, have very high minimum A-levels entry standards, a sizeable international student body, and a UK-domiciled minority ethnic constituency which in the year 2013/14 accounted for about 20–25 per cent of the total of those studying at undergraduate level (University of Oxford, 2015). While also being part of the Russell Group of Universities, Bayside represents an exception in terms of both entry standards, which are somewhat more 'relaxed', and of UK-domiciled minority ethnic students' intake. Being the only Russell Group university to be located in an inner city area, Bayside is 'local' to a considerable minority ethnic population, which is mirrored in the student composition. Here, in 2013/14, UK-domiciled ethnic minorities represented around 45 per cent of undergraduate students, with a large proportion of South Asians (approximately 30 per cent of UK-domiciled students and 20 per cent of the total) (University of Oxford, 2015). Riverdale has similar entry standards to those of Bayside, and, according to the university's statistics, UK-domiciled students of minority ethnic background accounted in 2013/14 for around 30 per cent of the total number of undergraduates.

At the other end of the spectrum, King George, Woodgate, and Melrose all have a substantial percentage of UK-domiciled ethnic minority students, ranging from approximately 40 to 50 per cent of the total in 2008/09, and not as many international students. Woodgate's and King George's student bodies, in particular, are among the most diverse in the UK, with a proportion of South Asians which is one of the highest (21 per cent and 28 per cent respectively of the undergraduates total) (The Complete University Guide, 2016).

In terms of family background, almost all of these young women's parents, except two of the mothers, were born in Bangladesh, and came to the UK at different points in their lives. Most fathers or stepfathers (15 out of 21) had jobs which could broadly be defined as working-class. It is however important to note that differences existed among these jobs not only in terms of earnings and status, but also and especially of the type and amount of related social and cultural capital, as this category included occupations as diverse as construction and factory workers, mini-cab drivers, chefs, tailors, shopkeepers, mentors, and tutors. One was unemployed, and four had what can instead be seen as 'typically' middle-class jobs, either as business owners or as professionals, which also appeared to differ from one another in terms of social and cultural capital. For example, between that held by a restaurant owner without formal qualifications and a doctor with both a Bangladeshi and a UK university degree. Most of the mothers (14) were housewives, with the exception of five who worked at different levels in the social and education sector (as childminder, primary school supervisor, teaching assistants and local government social worker), and of two who were company directors. Apart from those young women whose parents had middle-class jobs, they were all of the first generation to go to university, although some of them had older siblings and family members who went before them. This last aspect, like the age at which their parents came to the UK, and even subtle differences between their parents' jobs, were all significant elements in shaping participants' university experiences, but could not be discussed here for reasons of space.

What I intend to do, instead, is to provide a broad overview of such experiences, touching on mostly recurring themes. In doing so, I will apply a Bourdieusian lens to the analysis of characteristic features, in the hope to uncover underlying structures and processes at work in shaping stances and practices, and in (re)producing inequalities. As mentioned earlier, I consider this an imperative task at a time where, at least in a large part of policy and public discourse, the blame for minority ethnic 'underachievement' in education tends to be uncritically attributed to 'dysfunctional community cultures'. Contrary to this view, I contend that experiences of higher education can be more adequately seen as shaped by intersecting economic and cultural dynamics of power, which contribute to place students of working-class and minority ethnic backgrounds outside of dominant social fields. Particular attention will thus be paid to the multiple ways in which different dimensions of social identity such as class, 'race', and ethnicity inter-relate with, and qualify, one another, to produce differential positionings and experiences (Brah and Phoenix, 2004). In the context of this work, the use of

Bourdieu's conceptual toolbox is deliberately intended as a methodological approach which helps us to unpack intersectionality, recognising and more fully attending to the layering of class and 'race'/ethnicity in mediating agency (Horvat, 2002).

## Perceptions of 'fitting in'

### The role of multiple dimensions of social identity and habitus

Perceptions of 'fitting in' at particular institutional settings emerged as a major aspect affecting participants' higher education experiences. As pointed out by Ball *et al.* (2002b) in the above discussed study, such perceptions were largely related to the universities' 'ethnic mix'. Findings from this research, however, portray a slightly more complex picture of students' interpretations of the context, where class, religion, and habitus also enter into play in characterising 'ethnic mix' and 'fitting in'. In this respect, it is evident that what is defined by participants as a 'multicultural' environment, in which they feel 'comfortable', can vary substantially depending on their socio-economic background and past experiences of 'ethnic mix' in primary and secondary school.

The relevance held by multiple layers of social identity (social class, ethnicity, gender, religion, etc.) in defining students' position within a given context, as well as their understanding of this same context and related sense of belonging, is apparent when comparing the accounts of two young women, Sadia and Flora (pseudonyms), both attending top-ranking institutions, Greenshore and High Valley. Like most participants in this study, Sadia is Muslim, and comes from a working-class background. In the following quote, these elements can be seen as adding to her being of minority ethnic origins, and coming together to convey her sense of 'standing out':

> 'At first, I will be honest, it was quite difficult because Greenshore is still a very white middle-class institution and that is reflected in my course. [. . .] And then international students like even though there is a mix but they still come from, I mean they all went to private schools, British or American colleges, so you will see the kind of calibre within the course. [. . .] But then it's quite tragic the way I see it. Why should I be one of the few, one of the only within a course of 160 you know, to be the only person wearing a scarf or you know, just to be of that background?'
>
> (Sadia, working-class, Greenshore)

For Sadia, ethnicity, religion, and class all function to position her as 'other' with respect to the majority of students in her course. Therefore, even though there are other students who come from different ethnic backgrounds, her being working-class and Muslim still acts to confer distance. This resonates with the experiences of most other working-class young women in top-ranking universities, and allows in some cases for the development of a reflexive stance, where they become aware of how important their presence in predominantly white, middle-class environments is in challenging such 'exclusivity'. This is in fact what happened with Sadia, enabling her to become more resilient:

'And then I realised like, when I felt like I shouldn't be here or anything like that, I thought it's actually really important for us to be in the institution in order to change the institution. So I felt as it was more of a responsibility'.

Conversely, the description provided by Flora, who comes from a middle-class family and is the only non-Muslim in my sample, serves to illustrate how the obliteration of class and religious distinctions allows for an emphasis on common minority ethnic background. That is, shared cultural capital along the lines of class and religion, and a habitus in line with that of her institution and the majority of its student body, mean that Flora is not constantly reminded of her 'being different'. Unlike Sadia, her self-awareness in terms of these dimensions is thus weakened, enabling her to focus solely on ethnicity:

'It's really great, it's really a multicultural environment because there's so many international students so you never really feel, you probably, I think people who are from ethnic minorities or from abroad probably feel like they are more in the majority than the minority because there's so many of us at High Valley'.

(Flora, middle-class, High Valley)

Greenshore and High Valley have a very similar proportion of UK-domiciled minority ethnic students, accounting for around 25 per cent of those studying at undergraduate level. Adding to this minority ethnic presence, is that of international students, who make up about 25 per cent and 40 perc ent respectively of the total number of undergraduates. The socio-economic profile of this latter group is quite distinctively upper/middle-class (HEFCE, 2010). While Flora, who comes herself from a middle-class background, can thus largely identify with this presence, Sadia's possibility for identification is instead problematised by the markers of different socio-economic locations.

Another important element in producing different perceptions of the same environment is a students' habitus, intended as dispositions acquired through the integration of past experiences. Class and ethnicity undoubtedly play a major role in shaping habitus, as they substantially contribute to delineate the range of possible experiences. Findings from this study, however, show how even among students from similar ethnic and class backgrounds, exposure to different 'class and ethnic mixes', especially during secondary school, can have a considerable impact on attitudes. This is especially visible in Chandi's and Shay's narratives. In contrast to the former, who was brought up and schooled in Tower Hamlets, the latter had moved at a young age to an area with only a small number of South

Asian Muslims, and had been attending a secondary school where she was one of the very few Bangladeshi pupils. Even though they both go to the same university, Bayside, their perceptions and descriptions of such context appear to be very different:

> 'It's very multicultural so I like that. There's every sort of race, religion, culture all over and I mean, I like that. I'm learning more about other people, I'm learning more about me, there is so many languages and cultures to learn and I enjoy that'.
>
> (Chandi, working-class, Bayside)

> 'It's a bit dirty, yeah, not very diverse, yeah. It just felt like, because it's very Bengali centred around here so it wasn't, it was just like being at home, it wasn't something new. [. . .] I mean I'm not too fond of Bengali culture. So it gets a bit annoying when you are just surrounded by those cultures that you don't really fit into and I don't fit into the Bengali culture'.
>
> (Shay, working-class, Bayside)

UK-domiciled ethnic minorities represent around 45 per cent of Bayside's intake, with South Asians making up for approximately 20 per cent of the total. For Chandi, who has always attended schools where South Asian Muslims, and Bangladeshis in particular, were a large majority, this specific make-up is perceived as 'very multicultural'. Shay, on the other hand, whose secondary school experience has been characterised by engagement with pupils from other ethnicities and progressive dis-identification with her own, considers this same environment as 'not very diverse'. Interestingly, it is with students from her same ethnicity that she feels like she does not 'fit in'.

The four stories reported above are profoundly revealing of the role that is played by class and 'race'/ethnicity in shaping perceptions of 'fitting in' at given institutions. First, they show how these young women's considerations over the aspects that make them feel more or less 'at ease' within their universities' environment have much to do with the institution – or, as attested by other accounts, degree subject – socio-economic intake. Furthermore, they testify to the weight that class and ethnic identifications, and past schooling experiences, hold in generating differential appraisals of similar settings. Flora's and Sadia's distinct class positions, for example, respectively support and undermine their sense of 'fitting in', despite both their universities being characterised by a large minority ethnic presence. Shay and Chandi demonstrate in addition how such perceptions are not only affected by social identities, but also, significantly, by self-identifications and acquired cultural capital. In this respect, the experiences to which one is exposed both at school and outside, particularly during childhood and adolescence but also later in life, can be seen as especially crucial, because of how they influence access to different types of cultural capital and ideas of self.

### The impact of symbolic violence on 'choice' and self-perceptions

Participants' narratives also highlight the variety of preferences which can be expressed in terms of the university's ethnic composition, with some being more drawn to a setting characterised by a large number of ethnic minorities and 'familiarity', and others looking for 'something different' from what they are used to. Chandi and Kanta provide an example of this range of approaches:

> 'So I thought if I got to Western it would be full of sort of stuck up posh people that I wouldn't be able to get along with. But over here [at Bayside] is much more cultural, it's like you could get along with people, you could understand East London or London life so that's nice'.
>
> (Chandi, working-class, Bayside)

> 'I think it's because I've always been living in Tower Hamlets, I've always been in the same community surrounded by the same sort of people. So I think part of it was to have University as an option to expose myself to a different, not even to a different lifestyle but to different types of people and to really experience University in a different way'.
>
> (Kanta, working-class, Western)

As emerges from Chandi's account, prevailing class and ethnic composition almost appear to overlap in the understandings that some of these young women offer of the university climate, with middle- / upper-'classness' and whiteness being perceived as strictly entrenched. However, it must also be recognised that, despite anticipations of not 'fitting in' at the institution of their choice, almost all participants opted to apply for the most prestigious London universities they could access with their grades.

Chandi is the only one to talk about her decision not to apply to a more prestigious institution, despite having the grades to potentially do so, as an active 'choice'. As her further elaboration reveals, however, this 'choice' is in effect underlaid by the workings of symbolic violence, which constructs predominantly white middle-class universities as the domain of 'ambitious' students, and consequently dismisses minority ethnic and working-class students who do not fit into that environment as simply 'not ambitious enough':

> 'This was my first choice. I didn't bother applying for Blueville or Western because even though I did get really good A-level results I feel like Blueville or Western wouldn't take me for some reason. I guess I wasn't ambitious enough. But I thought Bayside would take me so.'
>
> (Chandi, working-class, Bayside)

It is in this taken-for-grantedness that the symbolic power of dominant attributions of value relative to institutions and their intake asserts itself fully, by concealing the hierarchies of inequality that both sustain and result from them

(Bourdieu, 1984; Robbins, 1991). The equation of locality and large minority ethnic presence with low educational standards represents in this sense a relevant example. The ambiguity expressed by Farhan in relation to Woodgate, where she is currently studying, testifies to the pervasiveness of this conception, and shows how unsettling it can be for students especially as they start university:

> Farhan: 'I didn't want to come to Woodgate only because it's no good for me, and when I started uni Woodgate didn't really have a great reputation. [. . .] But when I got into Woodgate, I got to settle down and everything, it was a lot more different. I didn't realise that it was better for me to come here than to have gone all the way to Oakley in terms of everything. [. . .] I feel more comfortable than I think I would have in any other place [. . .]'.
>
> Berenice: 'Right, in what sense do you feel like you would be more comfortable here rather than any other uni?'
>
> Farhan: 'I would have to say because of the people. Because where I come from, whether it's been school, college, even where I live, it's always filled with ethnic minorities. So I can get a link, I can communicate or I gain an instant bond. [. . .] A lot of people have this image of Woodgate so it's like I'd rather not come in. [. . .] Because it's a local uni, everyone local goes there so therefore it's not as great because only local people come here. They're not very clever, they're not very intelligent, they just got here for the sake of getting here because they couldn't get anywhere else'.

Throughout her reflection, Farhan brings up the dissonance between Woodgate's negative reputation and the positive experience she had of the university. This reputation informed her view of Woodgate and its students to the point that she 'didn't want to come'. Yet, when finally going, she found herself feeling 'more comfortable [here] than [she] would have in any other place'. This dilemma, of 'fitting in' at universities that are commonly considered of lesser value, was experienced by many of those young women whose grades at A-levels prevented them from accessing more prestigious institutions. Where these stereotypes go unchallenged, they can have a detrimental impact on students' confidence, and on the images they hold of themselves as learners.

## Academic experience

As we have seen, research focusing on the difficulties experienced by students from diverse minority ethnic backgrounds in relation to 'educational achievement' has revealed that main concerns have to do with the extra burden imposed by limited finances, and with a perceived lack of support from teaching staff (Tyers et al., 2004; Bagguley and Hussain, 2007; Dhanda, 2010). The widespread reference to the impact of restricted economic resources among minority ethnic students is strictly related to prevailing working-class background among this population (Clark and Drinkwater, 2007). Other studies have clarified the relation between financial constraints and lower academic attainment, showing how these considerably affect the amount and quality of time which can effectively be spent on studying, which also resonates with my participants' accounts (Reay *et al.*, 2009a; Bradley and Ingram, 2012).

Perceived lack of academic support is another issue which tends to be reported more by students of minority ethnic origins than by their White British peers (Dhanda, 2010). While the relationship here might seem less straightforward, I propose the adoption of Bourdieu's concept of habitus as a useful tool through which to aid explanation. Habitus is especially helpful as it allows to place the attention on the links between one's past and current learning environments, and to interpret students' 'easiness' with certain approaches as structured by previous exposure to similar expectations. In the following excerpts, Labiba and Kanta, two working-class young women who have attended secondary school together, and are studying at the top-ranking university Western, reflect over the teaching and assistance received now and back then, providing an example of these links. Kanta additionally makes explicit the lower likelihood for her as a Bangladeshi of being exposed to challenging modes of learning, because of living in a borough like Tower Hamlets where schools have a predominantly working-class, minority ethnic intake.

'I think it's really, I mean it's a big jump between school and university, a big jump. [. . .] Because obviously your first term, there is this kind of, you know, just throw you in so they don't kind of, there's no support available to help you settle in if that makes sense. I think they just kind of like expect you to do all these essays, all these like so many readings, and just expect you to know things rather than supporting you, understanding, helping you'.

(Labiba, working-class, Western)

'I think the learning I got at my school was fantastic, but I think, compared to some other schools in Tower Hamlets. But even then I would say there was an element of spoon feeding for instance and lack of critical thinking at my school which I perhaps would have got if I wasn't a Bengali, which would have meant I would probably live somewhere else and I would have received a certain type of education'.

(Kanta, working-class, Western)

Such connection is even more evident when we compare the above accounts with that of Flora, who has been privately schooled throughout her life and is now enrolled at another prestigious university:

'So our school did exams every year rather than just SATs, so it means I was really used to doing exams. Also, because it was a private school, you were always expected to perform well. We were used to working hard, like what to us was working normally to someone else would be working hard. So I'm used to kind of working, and I was used to my level of knowledge being at quite a high standard even without me realising just because of the school'.

(Flora, middle-class, High Valley)

Once we take this perspective, it can be seen how difficulties with the considerable workload and mainly individual mode of learning which is expected of students at university, and feelings of 'not being supported enough', can be traced back to dispositions acquired throughout primary and secondary school. Where we consider that a higher proportion of minority ethnic students live in fairly deprived areas compared to White British, which as noted by Kanta in the above quotation also means receiving a different type of education, it is therefore not so surprising that they tend to report these problems more often. This 'mismatch' between acquired dispositions and institutional environment, or between individuals' learner and institutional habitus (Reay *et al.*, 2009a; 2009b), is especially evident in high-ranking and elite universities, where the majority of students traditionally come from middle- and upper-class backgrounds and will most likely have had different schooling standards. While some interviewees had developed a reflexive viewpoint, which allowed them to recognise this nexus, for some this appeared to generate feelings of pressure and insecurity.

## Social experience

For the young women who took part in this research, class, 'race'/ethnicity, and importantly religion, also appeared to substantially shape their experiences of university in terms of relations with other students, friendship networks and social activities they got involved in. This happened in more or less obvious ways, as these dimensions of social identity interacted with one another to produce different outcomes, with cultural capital and habitus being especially important elements in defining social identity in the first place. In particular, as will emerge more clearly from the following accounts, the environment where one has been living throughout his/her life, and previous schooling, seem to have a crucial influence on the degree to which he/she is accustomed to relating with people from different socio-economic backgrounds. Furthermore, findings suggest that it is mainly through cultural capital that class and ethnic distinctions take place, especially with regards to lifestyles, beliefs, and values.

When asked about their relationships with people from different ethnicities, all participants stated that neither ethnicity nor religion were important to them. Yet, for most of them, their actual friendship networks did not include anyone from a White British background, and close friendships were mainly formed with other Muslims. Leena's and Jamila's observations, reported below, show how even 'ethnically mixed' institutions like Bayside can have low levels of 'ethnic mixing' (see also Hollingworth and Mansaray, 2012). Rather than this being an active 'choice', it appears to be linked to different lifestyles and opportunities for socialising, as well as to processes of 'othering', of which these young women are very aware. In this respect, being Muslim stands out as an especially relevant aspect in characterising social experiences:

> 'It just sort of happened. [. . .] During Fresher's week, and you know, the other parties that there are on campus, and so they tend to . . . and also most

[White students] live out of, they live on campus so outside, so they have that kind of friendship where they are seeing each other and they party or they are living together [. . .]. Whereas most of, well actually all of my friends, we live at home, and we don't really party like that or drink so we don't have that kind of exposure in that sense'.

(Jamila, working-class, Bayside)

'I think people tend to gravitate towards that they feel comfortable with. So if I see like someone that's my face and culture I'd probably gravitate towards them, it's more safe I guess, and comfortable, so I think that's why everyone tends to stick together. [. . .] Like I know that especially wearing the headscarf like you come across like: 'Oh she's practicing, she's religious, she might not be like us'. There's that whole divide thing, so I think that might affect my uni life'.

(Leena, working-class, Bayside)

Those participants who came from a middle-class background, on the other hand, seemed more confident than others in forming friendships with White British students. This appears to be best attributable to habitus as a whole, including the 'imprinting' of past experiences, as both Shirina and Flora have been schooled in a non-Bengali Muslim environment, with a large number of White British pupils. Rani, instead, who also comes from a middle-class background but has been living in Bangladesh for most of her schooling years, and was home-schooled when in UK, has mainly made friends with international students. Nevertheless, it is significant that even Shirina and Flora's closest friends are mostly Asian. As Shirina herself is keen to tell me, this provides her with a sense of 'community', with whom she could relate in terms of common issues:

'I love Bangla Society because it's basically people that I can relate to. Because at my school there wasn't as many Bengalis, so like I didn't have anyone in my culture who had the same issues like curfew, staying in London, not going out late. [. . .] So at Bangla Society I have a whole family of friends that can relate to me, so if we do socials we ensure that it ends at 9, not like at 12, so that everyone can get home on time because everyone is in the same boat [. . .] and yeah, I love it'.

(Shirina, middle-class, Blueville)

One of the main ways in which social class intersected with ethnicity in qualifying interviewees' social experiences was therefore by affecting the ethnic and class composition of their social networks, and especially by facilitating or hindering the formation of friendships with White British middle-class students. For the young women interviewed, in specific, it seemed to be the case that friendships were either formed with other minority ethnic students from different class backgrounds, or, especially for middle-class students, with others from the same class background including White British. This is especially important to where we consider the resulting differential in the capacity to access dominant social and cultural capital, which puts working-class minority ethnic students at a disadvantage in the higher education and labour market field.

As argued earlier, moreover, participants' narratives often referred to perceptions of (not) 'fitting in' at particular institutional environments, which was strongly related to the predominant class and ethnic composition of the university and course of studies attended, and mainly found expression in feelings of difference or similarity of mind-set. This is illustrated for instance in the following quotes from Sadia and Labiba, respectively studying Geography at Greenshore and Sociology at Western, where they reflect on the social environment of the course they are enrolled at:

> 'It's not even just the privileges, it's the mind-set, I wouldn't necessarily agree with them. Like, I don't know, I know someone who would be very like: 'Colonialism was okay, it was right'. [. . .] Or like they wouldn't think white supremacy exists when people of colour definitely know it exists. Those kind of differences, especially in mind-set and political views. Or like, you know, they're only in it for the money and, you know, that kind of lifestyle'.
>
> (Sadia, working-class, Greenshore)

> 'I mean in terms of my degree I think we're all pretty much the same, and even if we're not we're all pretty much like on the same wavelength I guess, if that makes sense, and it's more comfortable I guess. [. . .] Because we're pretty much split between quantitative and qualitative subjects. [. . .] Like social science type subjects, there's a lot more people like me, who have like very radical thoughts so it, the class system and left/right politics is very much, people who think like me. And they will talk to you like idiots, on the other side, but tend to be like white male, who tend to have very, like, right wing attitudes and from, you know, privileged backgrounds I guess'.
>
> (Labiba, working-class, Western)

What comes out from these accounts as being especially relevant is therefore the way in which other students approach issues of class and 'race'/ethnicity, more than their class and ethnic backgrounds *per se*, although the two are often related. Sadia's further elaboration provides in this respect an illuminating example:

> 'Sometimes I wish I went to another university which is Riverdale. [. . .] I have a lot of friends who study in both Greenshore and Riverdale, part of their kind of degree. And like they always mention how like Riverdale they'll only be questioned intellectually and people only look at your kind of the way in which you think, whereas in Greenshore people look at the way in which you are, the social group that you come from, where you live, how you, you know, what your parents do and whatnot, your background. [. . .]

And I think it's probably like, it comes from the selection process of the amount of people who are from private schools or from a white middle class background'.

These considerations serve to highlight how, while there is scope for attachments and belongings to be structured around either class or 'race'/ethnicity while cutting across the other, a strong influence is carried by the 'culture' which is dominant within certain institutions and subject areas, and by the type of capital which is mostly valued. This, in fact, can function to exacerbate social distinctions, hampering the establishment of relations across class and 'race' and contributing to mark not only certain universities but also certain degrees and areas of study as 'not for us'. For working-class and minority ethnic students, this means feeling excluded – and thus as attested by Sadia potentially being led to excluding oneself – from important fields of knowledge, experience, and interaction, which tend to remain a privilege of the white middle-classes. In this sense, the under-representation of ethnic minorities and the working-classes is both a symptom and a cause of a lack of inclusivity towards different lifestyles and systems of value.

## Conclusions

The above discussion has considered some of the overarching issues faced in higher education by the young British-born women of Bangladeshi heritage who participated in this study. Especially recurrent in their narratives of university experiences, both social and educational, were references to feelings of 'fitting in' or 'standing out' in particular settings, more or less positive comments on the support received from teaching staff, and concerns over the lack of 'ethnic mixing'. These findings are therefore broadly in line with those reported in previous research on minority ethnic university students (Osler, 1999; Tyers et al., 2004; Tyrer and Ahmad, 2006; Bagguley and Hussain, 2007; Dhanda, 2010), as well as further qualifying them. In presenting such findings, I have employed a Bourdieusian framework of analysis, and have heavily drawn, in particular, on his concepts of cultural capital and habitus. I have done so with the intention to provide more solid groundings to the broader understanding of the distinctive character that the interplay of class and 'race'/ethnicity confers to experiences of university, which the individual stories of the young women interviewed can help to illuminate.

In particular, this approach has allowed light to be shed on the dynamics underlying multiple (mis)alignments between students and the social and educational environment they find themselves in. Most of those I spoke with had applied for the 'best' possible universities in London they could hope to be accepted at, depending on the grades they had achieved during GCSEs and A-levels. They did so despite expecting a challenging environment, where they might not have easily 'fitted in', with some expressing the deliberate will to tackle perceptions of top-ranking institutions being exclusively for the white middle-class. However, it also needs to be recognised that symbolic violence constructing universities with a large number of ethnic minorities as holding lower standards, and predominantly white middle-class institutions as for the 'bright and talented' still has a profound impact on students' self-perception and experiences. As we have seen, one of these young women decided not to apply for a more prestigious university despite having the grades to potentially do so because she felt 'she wasn't ambitious enough'. While it was her anticipation of feeling excluded from that world rather than lack of ambition that made her opt for a more 'ethnically mixed' university, therefore, she had internalised a specific (dominant) discourse, which functioned to conceal underlying structures of exclusion while placing the blame on the individual. In addition, the majority of them either did not have the grades to apply to 'better' universities, or had the application for their 'first choice' rejected. For these students, symbolic violence meant they had to come to terms with the lower status attributed to their university and, consequently, to them as learners. Finally, those that managed to access prestigious institutions encountered a number of issues relating to both social and educational aspects of 'fitting in'. In making sense of these issues, it is useful to think about the mis-match between students', institutions' and subject areas' habitus and valued cultural capital (Reay *et al.*, 2009a), all of which are classed and racialised – as well as gendered, although there was no space to discuss this in the context of the present chapter. In this light, the influence of class and 'race'/ethnicity in shaping experiences can be seen as especially revealing itself through the ways in which these dimensions of social identity, in their various manifestations, are perceived and received in 'dominant' settings.

## Note

1   The Russell Group is an organisation that represents 24 top-ranking, research intensive UK universities, with a widespread reputation for academic excellence

## References

Abrahams, J., and Ingram, N. (2013). The chameleon habitus: exploring local students' negotiations of multiple fields. *Sociological Research Online*, *18*(4), 21.

Ahmad, F. (2001). Modern traditions? British Muslim women and academic achievement. *Gender and Education*, *13*(2), 137.

Ahmad, F. (2007). Muslim women's experiences of higher education in Britain. *American Journal of Islamic Social Sciences*, *24*(3), 46.

Ahmed, S., and Dale, A. (2008). Pakistani and Bangladeshi women's labour market participation'. *Cathie March Centre for Census and Survey Research CCSR Working Paper*.

Alexander, C., and Arday, J. (2015). *Aiming Higher. Race, inequality and diversity in the academy*. Runnymede: London.

Andrews, K. (2015). The black studies movement in Britain: Addressing the crisis in British academia and social life. In T. Runnymede (Ed.), *Aiming higher. race, inequality and diversity in the academy*. London: Runnymede.

Archer, L., and Francis, B. (2006). Challenging classes? Exploring the role of social class within the identities and achievement of British Chinese pupils. *Sociology*, *40*(1), 29–49.

Archer, L., and Francis, B. (2007). *Understanding minority ethnic achievement: Race, gender, class and 'success'*. London: Routledge.

Archer, L., Hollingworth, S., and Halsall, A. (2007). "University's not for me – I'm a Nike person": Urban, working-class young people's negotiations of style', identity and educational engagement. *Sociology, 41*(2), 219–237.

Archer, L., and Hutchings, M. (2000). 'Bettering yourself'? Discourses of risk, cost and benefit in ethnically diverse, young working-class non-participants' constructions of higher education. *British Journal of Sociology of Education, 21*(4), 555–574.

Ball, S. J., Davies, J., David, M., and Reay, D. (2002a). 'Classification' and 'judgement': Social class and the 'cognitive structures' of choice of higher education. *British Journal of Sociology of Education, 23*(1), 51–72.

Ball, S. J., Reay, D., and David, M. (2002b). 'Ethnic choosing': Minority ethnic students, social class and higher education choice. *Race, Ethnicity and Education, 5*(4), 333–357.

Bagguley, P., and Hussain, Y. (2007). *The role of higher education in providing opportunities for South Asian women (Vol. 2058)*. Policy Press.

Basit, T.N. (2012) 'My parents have stressed that since I was a kid': Young minority ethnic British citizens and the phenomenon of aspirational capital. *Education, Citizenship and Social Justice, 7*(2), 129–143.

Bathmaker, A.M., Ingram, N., and Waller, R. (2013). Higher education, social class and the mobilisation of capitals: Recognising and playing the game. *British Journal of Sociology of Education, 34*(5–6), 723–743.

Bhopal, K. (1997). *Gender, "race," and patriarchy: A study of South Asian women*. Aldershot: Ashgate.

Boliver, V. (2013). How fair is access to more prestigious UK universities?. *The British journal of sociology, 64*(2), 344–364.

Botcherby, S. (2006). *Pakistani, Bangladeshi and black caribbean women and employment survey: aspirations, experiences and choices*.

Bourdieu, P. (1977). *Outline of a theory of practice* (Vol. 16). Cambridge: University of Cambridge press.

Bourdieu, P. (1984). *Distinction: A social critique of the judgement of taste*. Boston: Harvard University Press.

Bourdieu, P. (1990). *In other words: Essays towards a reflexive sociology*. Cambridge: Polity.

Bourdieu, P. (1999). The contradictions of inheritance. In P. Bourdieu (Ed.), *Weight of the World: Social Suffering in Contemporary Society*. Cambridge: Polity Press, 517–551.

Bradley, H., and Ingram, N. (2012). Banking on the future: Choices, aspirations and economic hardship in working-class student experience. In W. Atkinson, S. Roberts and M. Savage (Eds.), *Class inequalities in Austerity Britain*. Basingstoke: Palgrave Macmillan.

Brah, A., and Phoenix, A. (2004). Ain't I a woman? Revisiting intersectionality. *Journal of International Women's Studies, 5*(3), 75–86.

Butler, T., and Hamnett, C. (2011). *Ethnicity, class and aspiration: understanding London's new East End*. London: Policy Press.

Centre on Dynamics of Ethnicity. (2014). Addressing ethnic inequalities in social mobility. *Research findings from the CoDE and Cumberland Lodge Policy Workshop*. Retrieved November 27, 2016 from www.ethnicity.ac.uk/medialibrary/briefings/policy/code-social-mobility-briefing-Jun2014.pdf

Clark, K., and Drinkwater, S. (2007). *Ethnic minorities in the labour market: dynamics and diversity*. London: Policy Press.

Department for Communities and Local Government. (2009). *The Bangladeshi Muslim Community in England. Understanding Muslim Ethnic Communities.* Retrieved November 27, 2016 from www.swadhinata.org.uk/document/Bangladeshi_Muslim.pdf

Department for Communities and Local Government. (2010). English indices of deprivation 2010. Retrieved November 27, 2016 from www.gov.uk/government/statistics/english-indices-of-deprivation-2010

Dhanda, M. (2010). *Understanding disparities in student attainment: black and minority ethnic students' experience.* Wolverhampton: University of Wolverhampton.

Hollingworth, S., and Mansaray, A. (2012). Conviviality under the cosmopolitan canopy? Social mixing and friendships in an urban secondary school. *Sociological Research Online, 17*(3), 2.

Horvat, E.M. (2002). The interactive effects of race and class in educational research: Theoretical insights from the work of Pierre Bourdieu. *Penn GSE Perspectives on Urban Education, 2*(1), 1–25.

Ingram, N. (2011). Within school and beyond the gate: The complexities of being educationally successful and working class. *Sociology, 45*(2), 287–302.

Iqbal, S. (2015). I'm a Muslim woman Mr. Cameron: Here's what your radicalisation speech means to me. *The Guardian,* 2015.

Janmohamed, S. (2014a). Muslim women don't need the West's version of feminism, OK? *The Telegraph,* 2014.

Janmohamed, S. (2014b). Muslim women's bodies – the hottest property in 2014. *The Telegraph,* 2014.

Lymperopoulou, K., and Parameshwaran, M. (2015). 'Is there an ethnic group educational gap?' In S. Jivraj, and L. Simpson (Eds.), *Ethnic identity and inequalities in Britain,* Bristol: Policy Press, 181–198.

Mellor, J. (2012). British Muslim women, peer relationships and educational trajectories: Reflections on Muslim Stereotypes in Western Settings. In T. Lovat (Ed), *Women in Islam: Reflections on historical and contemporary research.* Springer: Amsterdam. 197–212.

Mirza, H.S. (1992). *Young, female and black.* London: Routledge.

Modood, T. (2004). Capitals, ethnic identity and educational qualifications. *Cultural Trends, 13*(2), 87–105.

Modood, T., and Acland, T. (1998). *Race and higher education.* London: Policy Studies Institute.

Modood, T., and Shiner, M. (1994). *Ethnic minorities and higher education.* London: Policy Studies.

Navarro, L. (2010). Islamophobia and sexism: Muslim women in the western mass media. *Human Architecture: Journal of the Sociology of Self-Knowledge, 8*(2), 10.

Noden, P., Shiner, M., and Modood, T. (2014) *Black and minority ethnic access to higher education: a reassessment.* Retrieved November 27, 2014 from www.lse.ac.uk/news AndMedia/PDF/NuffieldBriefing.pdf

Office for National Statistics. (2011a). *2011 Census: CT0247 Ethnic groups by highest level of qualification by age by sex – National to local authority.* Retrieved November 27, 2016 from http://webarchive.nationalarchives.gov.uk/20160105160709/http://www.ons. gov.uk/ons/about-ons/business-transparency/freedom-of-information/what-can-i-request/published-ad-hoc-data/census/ethnicity–identity–language-and-religion–eilr-/index.html

Office for National Statistics. (2011b). *2011 Census: DC2101EW Ethnic group by sex by age.* London: Office for National Statistics.

Office for National Statistics. (2011c). *2011 Census: KS201UK Ethnic group, local authorities in the United Kingdom*. London: Office for National Statistics.

Reay, D., Crozier, G., and Clayton, J. (2009a). 'Fitting in' or 'standing out': working-class students in UK higher education. *British Educational Research Journal, 36*(1), 107–124.

Reay, D., Crozier, G., and Clayton, J. (2009b). 'Strangers in paradise'? Working-class students in elite universities. *Sociology, 43*(6), 1103–1121.

Reay, D., David, M., and Ball, S. (2001a). Making a difference? Institutional habituses and higher education choice. *Sociology, 35(4)*, 855–874.

Reay, D., Davies, J., David, M., and Ball, S.J. (2001b). Choices of degree or degrees of choice? Class, 'race' and the higher education choice process. *Sociology, 35*(4), 855–874.

Robbins, D. (1991). *The work of pierre bourdieu: Recognizing society*. Milton Keynes: Open University Press.

Runnymede Trust. (2010). *Ethnicity and participation in higher education*. London: Runnymede Trust.

Runnymede Trust. (2012). *Briefing on ethnicity and educational attainment*. London: Runnymede Trust.

Shah, B., Dwyer, C., and Modood, T. (2010). Explaining educational achievement and career aspirations among young British Pakistanis: Mobilizing 'ethnic capital'? *Sociology, 44*(6), 1109–1127.

Shilliam, R. (2015). Black academia: The doors have been opened but the architecture remains the same. In T. Runnymede (Ed.), *Aiming higher: Race, inequality and diversity in the academy*. London: Runnymede Trust.

Shiner, M., and Modood, T. (2002). Help or hindrance? Higher education and the route to ethnic equality. *British Journal of Sociology of Education, 23*(2), 209–232.

The Complete University Guide. (2016). *University profiles*. Retrieved from www.thecompleteuniversityguide.co.uk/universities.

Tyers, C., Modood, T., and Hillage, J. (2004). *Why the difference? a closer look at higher education minority ethnic students and graduates*. Nottingham: DfES Publications.

Tyrer, D., and Ahmad, F. (2006). Muslim women and higher education: Identities, experiences and prospects. *A Summary Report, Liverpool John Moores University and European Social Fund, Liverpool*. Liverpool: Liverpool John Moore.

University of Oxford. (2015). *Equality Report, 2014/15* Retrieved from www.admin.ox.ac.uk/eop/policy/data/report/

Waheed, A. (2015). Sex, divorce and infidelity: Meet the Muslim women bloggers tackling taboos. *The Telegraph*, 2015.

# Chapter 8

# The 'Jack Wills brigade'

## Brands, embodiment, and class identities in higher education

*Vicky Mountford*

## Introduction

> *Jack Wills creates fabulously British clothes for the university crowd. Drawing inspiration from Britain's rich history and culture, juxtaposed with a heavy dose of the hedonistic university lifestyle, we create authentic and relevant clothing for today.*[1]

While this is not a piece about Jack Wills, the clothing brand, nor a deconstruction of student fashions or brands *per se*, this slogan prefaces a chapter focusing on the complex interplay of sociocultural codes negotiated in the ways in which student (class) identities are performed and (re)constructed in their everyday university experiences. The role of clothing and the symbolic associations in the embodiment of different brands and manners of dressing presents a noteworthy means of distinction and differentiation in and between different students. The significance of the terms used in the Jack Wills slogan above such as the 'hedonistic university lifestyle' of 'the [British] university crowd' and the reference to authenticity is remarkable as these very notions factor in the ways many students differentiate between ideas of studenthood and relationships to the identity category 'student'. In this chapter I focus on the way in which the British 'university crowd' is interpreted, what signifiers are used as codes and how ultimately subtle and yet powerful distinctions around clothing denote who stands inside or outside of that crowd; who get its right and what it feels like to get it wrong. As such I highlight some of the ways in which differential access to capital affects and restricts means of claiming the identity 'student'; what the conditions of membership to studenthood involve and how the formation of and relationship to the identity of 'student' is negotiated in and through student experiences in the everyday.

This chapter highlights the subtleties of the 'fit and misfit' (Bradley, 2012); the experiences of 'fitting in' and 'standing out' (see Reay *et al.*, 2010); and the complex negotiations of class identities within higher education. The research analysis emphasises the visual and sociocultural means of distinction (Bourdieu, 1984) in the everyday experiences of undergraduates in two English universities.

As such this research joins a significant body of work focusing on undergraduate student experience (see Wakeling this volume for a discussion of post-graduate student identities) most of which has concentrated particularly on experiences of (dis)advantage and/or exclusion within and between different higher education institutions (HEIs) (Archer *et al.*, 2003; Longden, 2004; Redmond, 2006; Waller, 2006; Greenbank, 2007; Crozier *et al.*, 2008; Clayton *et al.*, 2009; Reay *et al.*, 2009; 2010; Taylor and Scurry, 2011; Bradley and Ingram, 2012; Bathmaker *et al.*, 2013; 2016). The research analyses and context in which the study discussed here took place continues to bear relevance and provoke considerations in an educational landscape wherein the proliferations of foci on 'student experience' arguably risks ongoing (mis)recognition of the persistence and pervasiveness of class in the lives of university students; and differential access to the resources needed for success and accrual of capital (Abrahams and Ingram, 2013; Bathmaker *et al.*, 2013). By critically examining government rhetoric we can begin to understand how class is muted and becomes something of an unspeakable term – the 'c' word (Sveinsson, 2009). The undergraduate students' experience and identities explored in this chapter also further highlight a reluctance to explicitly discuss or name class. Instead other class terms and use of sociocultural codes or markers to make distinctions with different 'types' of students offer insights into the way in which class *works* in Higher Education (HE).

## Research context and methodology

As Diane Reay's work (2001: 333) emphasises, 'working class relationships to education cannot be understood in isolation from middle-class subjectivities'. 'Unconscious aspects of class that implicate both middle-class and working-class subjectivities' (Gillies, 2005: 837) are important also to this research, which seeks to problematise the normativity of middle-class students and their experiences. This research is concerned with exploring how privilege is maintained and challenged, and how privileged identities are performed, recognised, upheld and/or challenged; and it holds such discussions in contrast to the discourses of meritocracy surrounding HE. Furthermore, as Archer (2003: 14) argues, 'any analysis of class inequalities in relation to higher education must take into account not only people's shifting class identities but also the role of the educational institution itself in creating and perpetuating class inequalities'. This chapter draws on qualitative data from an ESRC-funded PhD research study conducted using 18 in-depth, semi-structured interviews and two focus groups involving predominantly White, British undergraduate students (one identified as British-Chinese) mixed gendered sample (16 female, 11 male), which took place between 2009 and 2010. This study was conducted with self-identified working- and middle-class students from two closely situated universities of differing status, to explore a variety of experiential factors of their everyday practices of university life. The two institutions involved included one Russell group[2] and one post-1992 institution situated in the north of England. Although the area is quite distinctive in terms of its history, the names of the institutions are referred to simply as OLD and NEW throughout this chapter on the basis that the analyses could be equally valid to any English university at the time, no less the many examples of university cities encompassing similar examples of institutional pairings (e.g. the Paired Peers project,[3] including the chapter by Bradley and Waller in this volume, and Bathmaker *et al.*, 2016).

The focus on appearance and branded clothing in this chapter is just one aspect of embodiment repeatedly highlighted throughout the research as markers of distinction and signs of student identity and belonging in their various forms (e.g. Mountford, 2014; Addison and Mountford, 2015). As part of this analysis, attention to 'the body' requires understanding of the ways in which the body provides the means to bridge individual and social dimensions (Shilling, 2007: 3) which 'erupts onto the surface . . . (manifested via forms of marking, decoration and dress) . . . enabling individuals to recognise others as participants in a common culture' (Durkheim, 1995 [1912]: 125) – or culturally different. Archer *et al.* (2007: 219), in their study on practices of taste and style in the educational field, argue that 'young people seek to generate worth and value through their investments in style'. While the subjects of their research are working-class and of school age, their work is similar to this aspect of the research in the recognition that the practice of style and use of particular brands within the educational field, is one way in which class identities are performed. Further, it follows that certain practices necessarily implicate exclusions that are present in this research context also.

Bourdieu's work and his concept of habitus as embodiment – the social incorporated into the body, 'of power as subtly inculcated through the body' (Adkins, 2004: 5) offers enormous potential for theorizing social class. For example, Moi (1991: 1019) praises Bourdieu's '*microtheory* of social power' for the ability to 'link the humdrum detail of everyday life to a more general analysis of power'. For Moi, the fact that Bourdieu finds seemingly banal, everyday practices analytically interesting, is a great advancement in the study of social life. Such championing of the everyday concerns and experiences as worthy areas of analysis is incredibly valuable in this research. Bourdieu's work allows analysis of everyday life in which the *process* of class and performance of class identities occur and thus, allows study of the minutiae of everyday experiences that contribute to student life. One of the most compelling aspects of Bourdieu's work, especially *Distinction* (Bourdieu, 1984), was its focus on the middle-classes; it is a work that takes as its central aim to explore the ways in which privilege is sustained and replicated across all areas of social life and thus the ways in which social inequality perpetuates. That aim is also very close to that of this research. Using Bourdieu's work, or in Moi's terms 'appropriating Bourdieu' therefore is especially useful, theoretically and conceptually, in research aimed at exploring the perpetuation of privilege and operations of class and class identities in higher education.

Bourdieu (1998) highlighted that class is 'something to be done' just as identities are. Talking to students and analysing their accounts of personal experiences, relationships and interactions with others and various student spaces and places, their motivations and expectations, choices and sense of value, alongside their personal circumstances, offers a way of seeing how class and class identities are continually 'being done'. While the academy is said to define and regulate what a student is (Morley, 1997), how such definitions are taken up, resisted or challenged is likely only to be enriched from the accounts of undergraduate students themselves. What is important here then are the often emotional and 'moral aspects of the experience of class and the concerns that people have regarding their class position and how others view them' (Sayer, 2005: 947). Although the way that power works through these positional views is such that 'what gets to count as tasteful is simply that which is claimed as their own by middle-class people' (Lawler, 2008: 126). Class judgements are interconnected with emotions, morality, and taste, and analysing the judgements people make in the everyday involves grasping the processes and the spaces within which normativity is established, via the making of class judgments.

There is a relative lack of sociological attention to middle-class 'emotional responses to social class inequalities' (Reay, 2005: 919) and thus research of this kind needs to be sensitive to the psycho-social and emotional dimensions of class, researching this with students from a variety of social backgrounds. Class is 'experienced in multiple, divergent ways according to a range of factors' (Woodin, 2005: 1014); it is as Kuhn (1995: 117) says, not 'just about the way you talk or dress . . . or how much money you make doing it . . . Class is something beneath your clothes, under your skin, in your reflexes, in your psyche, at the very core of your being'. Building on this notion, Reay (2005: 911) adds, in 'contemporary British society social class is not only etched into our culture, it is still deeply etched into our psyches, despite class awareness and class consciousness being seen as a "thing of the past"'. Class is not something that is always consciously considered in the everyday – it forms our unconscious as well as often being emotionally mediated. Therefore, although research participants may not actively and consciously construct their lives and opinions about others in class terms, it is possible to infer from their accounts of everyday HE experience, the way that class operates in HE. This chapter is an exploration of these nuanced operations of class in the everyday – through the naming and reframing of class in everyday colloquialisms and the means in which distinctions are visually (re)constructed. The way the students position themselves against others and experience their everyday encounters with university life provides insight into the implications of getting it right and getting it wrong.

## The 'Jack Wills brigade'; introducing the 'rah'

One of the most common ways in which participants talked about class and normative student identities was in relation to the figure of the 'rah'. The circulation of the term 'rah' and its particular usages demonstrates some of the ways in which class 'circulates socially while being unnamed' (Lawler, 2008: 126); or rather in a sense, 'renamed'. Very simply put, a 'rah' is a classifying term and signifies a status system. Its currency is largely pejorative as a term for a person or persons seen to be embodying a particular (young, white, upper-middle-class) student identity and is implicit in the operation of class fractions and struggles to claim legitimacy within HE. The term 'rah' therefore becomes a blanket term for 'posh people' and all that they are imagined by other students to represent. The application and use of the term 'rah' is demonstrative of the culturally specific processes of boundary formation involved in class distinctions and moreover, is demonstrative of the displacement and individualisation of distinction making. A meritocratic discourse operates in this context to position students as having achieved their (HE/class) status via hard work; an imperative of individualistic subjectivities to claim entitlement via having achieved such positions and not merely having them bestowed upon them. As such, the naming of the 'rah' and the position taking, in relation to these figures, is demonstrative of performative statements that suggest what student normativity consists of. In many interesting ways discourses of meritocracy that circulate in (higher) education run through the many expressions of the figure of the 'rah' and within these spaces notions of taste and authenticity in/of identity performance are highlighted in the everyday distinctions between student social groups and what studenthood entails.

The students in the research discuss the 'rah' in relation to a number of areas of student life including residential and leisure spaces, studying and finance, making friends and 'fitting in' and most frequently, in the naming and making of distinctions between students and the notion of 'studenthood' in the everyday of 'student experience'. The term 'rah' was used interestingly as a means to differentiate between the two institutions used in this research with OLD University being 'more rah' or having proportionally lots more 'rahs' according to the vast majority of students in the research but in particular those from NEW University. See the chapter by Cheeseman in this volume for a further discussion of this phenomenon. The term 'rah', was also often alluded with the term 'typical student', particularly with local students who considered their relational atypical student status often 'between the two worlds' (Holdsworth, 2009: 235) of the 'local' and the 'university'. Despite some differentiation over the proportion of 'rahs' in different university populations and some minor variations of what constituted a 'rah' identity; it was apparent that this identity was one that was conferred rather than claimed and was often used a blanket term for a number of (distasteful) sociocultural factors.

The questions posed to the undergraduate students centred on asking them to identify any common student 'looks'; and what people tended to wear and how they dressed for university. Participants almost always immediately involved identifying 'rahs' and the clothing brands they wore.

> ... so you've got your, like, 'rahs' if you like; so you've kind of got like the Jack Wills brigade who all wear the same kind of tracksuit bottoms and stuff...
> (Tim,[4] 21, middle-class, OLD University)

There is like, in a way, a student 'look' but it's very like stereotypical of like-private school people . . . you can tell 'rahs' a mile off . . . (laughs) it's like, they all wear like Jack Wills and like Abercrombie and Fitch and stuff like that, – which I really like personally. So, like before I came here I was like, you know – but they wear it like, religiously! They have like, they're quite lazy in the way they dress like, they'll have like tracksuits with Ugg boots – you know, like Jack Wills tracksuit with like a hoody or something . . . and they do genuinely have an impression that they're better than you and that's just like, that's just from, you know, like, seeing them. And you know, I speak to a few of them and they are – like, they're still kind of, you know, high and mighty and up themselves . . . cause they're all really rich you know, 'rahs', and they have a tracksuit on with like, big Prada earrings and like [a] Chanel bag or . . . but like, I think they're doing it as a statement – you know like wearing what they wear as a statement with like, you know, like they're doing it a bit subtly like I think it's a bit conscious really . . . they think they look cool.

(Faye, 18, middle-class, OLD University)

Several noteworthy themes appear in Faye's expression of a particular 'university crowd' here and are in common with others that run through many of the students who took part in this research, albeit in different and interesting ways. The 'rah' descriptions entail signifiers of wealth such as private schooling and (often designer or luxury) branded clothing; particular accents and ways of talking (usually distinctive received pronunciation or 'Queen's English); cultural expressions and codes including (bad) manners; superiority; and ostentatious behaviour and spending. Tim's comments confirm that 'Jack Wills' in particular has become something of a 'rah' emblem, certainly in OLD University at least. The brands themselves, their noticeable display and knowledge of their material value are frequently commented on when 'rahs' are being discussed. In the naming of branded clothing as distinctive to a 'type' of student, the symbolic and material associations with particular branded items intersect and mark out sociocultural codes and distinction. Furthermore, in Faye's dialogue and with Tim's (and many others) the suggestion that Jack Wills is 'all they wear' is significant to the extent that this portrays a sense of bad taste, but more so deliberateness and pretention, an outward performance, is being constructed. The comment that Faye makes regarding being 'lazy in the way they dress' has further significance; the typical attire referred to is lounge-wear and leisure-wear; yet these items are often juxtaposed with visible luxury designer accessories conventionally out of place in leisure/lounge-wear occasions. That the ostentatious display of expensive branded goods and leisure wear coupled with a messy and unkempt appearance conveys a particular type of studenthood is interesting; interpreted by research participants as depicting a sense of contrived nonchalance, part of the 'hedonistic lifestyle' they lead rather than the studious approach of meritocratic success. As Charys explains below

> ... you always see them outside the library like smoking and just acting cool ... just really, really scruffy like student-like – trying to live up to some sort of expectation of what a student should be like – and they go to like lectures in their pyjama bottoms and ... like 'oh I've been up all night like partying' – that kind of impression they wanna give – so they're standing outside the library and like trying to give the impression of 'oh I've just rolled out of bed' but you can tell that they've spent probably quite a lot of time getting like that.
>
> (Charys, 21, working-middle-class, OLD University)

The sense of inauthenticity was also prominent in dialogues wherein the material value of this particular look was embedded in the comments about the pretentiousness of the 'rah'; in these dialogues the pretension was more focused towards the notion of a 'penniless student' (with several uses of the word 'tramp') but made inauthentic by the visual, branded displays to subvert this association.

> ... what it seems to me is that someone who looks like a tramp but has got money to look like that! (laughs)
>
> (Siobhan, 18, working-class, OLD University)

> It just seems to be the students who are more funded by the parents maybe so obviously like if you're getting the government grants and stuff it's like – it works out like six grand a year or something like that and with six grand a year you can't really afford to buy brands like Jack Wills which is like £90 for a t-shirt, so it seems to be more like the richer students generally who get that kind of look.
>
> (Nadine, 20, middle-class, NEW University)

What Nadine and Siobhan highlight here is a tendency for some participants to comment on the material affordability of this look but it is deemed inauthentic because they are, as in Charys' words, 'trying to live up to some sort of expectation of what a student *should* be like'. The repeated mention of 'tramp' in many descriptions is significant because this goes beyond the standard limits of leisurewear; the affordability of the brands the messiness hits on another issue of affordability in the sense of what is deemed appropriate social attire and the notion of affordability in terms of the judgements of others. The idea of maintaining respectability visually, through appearance, has historical gendered and classed legacies, whereby cleanliness and tidiness are central. The look and appearance of the students being discussed, offend such cultural norms of respectability as in Skeggs' (1997) analysis of working-class women's 'respectability' but in an important departure from the subjects of Skeggs' (1997) research, these ('rah'/'typical') students *are* able to 'convert their competencies into a form of authority, into symbolic capital' and increase their cultural capital beyond the local level, although their performances are field/context specific. The performance is (penniless/typical) 'student'; as (middle-class) students within higher education; judgements of them as 'tramps', rather than 'penniless students' will not stick.

The adoption of this 'look' of contrived nonchalance and hedonism and the 'penniless student' is interpreted as a temporary and purposeful measure, which they can afford to change and adapt at their will; an inauthentic depiction of what a 'student' is imagined to be. Such experimentation is part of what Lury (1998: 1–2) terms 'prosthetic culture', whereupon individuals are engaged in 'strategic-decision making' that have implications for 'recognitions of belonging, collective identification and exclusion'. The 'tendency towards experimentation' is something that Lury suggests has become a social and cultural norm in Western societies and it certainly fits with the picture that has been drawn of the 'typical students' or 'rahs' identified by the research participants in this study. The concept of 'mimesis' is central to Lury's argument, which is 'to become and behave like something else'; it is a relation of 'making oneself similar to the environment' (Lury, 1998: 5). In this culture, she further adds:

> ... the subject as individual passes beyond the mirror stage of self-knowledge, of reflection of self, into that of self-extension ... The prosthesis – and it may be perceptual or mechanical – is what makes this self-extension possible. In adopting/adapting a prosthesis, the person creates (or is created by) a self-identity that is no longer defined by the edict 'I think, therefore I am'; rather, he or she is constituted in the relation 'I can, therefore I am'.
>
> (Lury, 1998: 3)

By adopting the prosthesis then, the self-extension is achieved via appropriation of classed, cultural signifiers that can be dis-assembled and re-assembled at will. However, what is important to highlight here is the notion of 'I can therefore I am'. It warrants posing the question of *who* 'can' and likewise who 'cannot'. As the following section will show, who *can* prostheticise 'student' or perhaps, 'rah' or indeed a different 'type' of student is not always a straight-forward matter of choice. Rather the ability to 'create' this identity involves a complex negotiation of (classed) signifiers and capital.

## The student 'look'; getting it 'right' or 'wrong'

The identity category of 'student' involves claiming and conferring membership and therefore a sense of belonging to the collective. However, different relationships to student normativity suggest such identification is problematic and often only attainable for certain classed actors. The branded clothing and particular unkempt style of wearing it is associated as an embodiment via prosthesis of 'rah', or 'studenthood' more broadly, as different degrees of taste or affordability restrict or give access to the means to construct a particular student identity. As Nadine says above, it is only the 'richer students' who have access to this look; only they can afford to buy the expensive, branded goods that make up the look. The issue of who is able to propertise/prostheticise the student look is clearly central to 'recognitions of belonging, collective identification and exclusion' (Lury, 1998: 1–2).

There appears to be a distinct preoccupation with authenticity of identity in the distinctions that the students make. This relates in part to the conceptualising of identity as being related to a true, inner self that structures Western notions of identity (Elias, 1994). What has also been highlighted, however, is the notion of authenticity in terms of fashion and appearance – of wearing or assembling a look in such a way that performs a contrived performance, a 'cynical performer' (Goffman, 1959) seeking to 'pull the proverbial wool over our eyes'. However, what has also surfaced from the research dialogues and the theoretical work undertaken by authors such as Skeggs (2004) and Chaney (2002), are strong suggestions that visual identities and fashions are being selectively adapted and meanings played around with in these HE contexts. Chaney's (2002: 80) argument that 'the languages of social life will be increasingly ironicised' where the 'semiotics of social identity . . . will be increasingly accepted as relative' are appropriate here. This 'ironic consciousness creates opportunities to subvert traditional associations' (Chaney, 2002: 80) contributing to ongoing (re)constructions of (privileged) class identities:

> . . . there is a process of extreme sensitivity to, and yet comparative distance to, stylistic norms in everyday life. Although fashionable codes are capable of infinite gradations and internal differentiations within any particular group, it has been assumed that the demands of fashionable conformity work to create some sort of uniform. The very attractiveness of the metaphor of uniform and its implied expectations of conformity should not, however, blind us to the way that the relativism of fashion both individualises as well as communalises.
>
> (Chaney, 2002: 80)

The student 'uniform' relies on shared recognition or shared meanings of the value of particular signifiers. The ability to take on this uniform also relies on affordability, in the sense of the risk of being (mis)read, as well as being able to have the economic resources to invest and convert to cultural and symbolic competencies. As Faye indicated earlier, for some it is not the [Jack Wills] brand *per se*, but the association of 'rahs' with this brand within university and this style that changes ways of thinking about how students dress and perform their [class] identities. For example most students indicated a change in their 'look' since starting university:

> . . . it's weird because after a while you can't really tell who's who 'cause people like start to imitate them and like wear the same kind of things to maybe like erm . . . update their social status . . . Kind of like – well no one would ever like put on the accent or like act the way they are, but like the dress definitely – they kind of like set the kind of standard of like, what you

should wear and what you shouldn't wear really . . . I tend to shop in nicer places than I did before because erm everyone kind of sets a higher standard over here than they did back home, do you know what I mean? (laughs) . . . [students] conform to the style but don't necessarily like copy, they kind of like take their own take on that style . . . so it's kind of like you take your inspiration (laughs) from rahs and then make it your own.

(Charys, 21, working-middle-class, OLD University)

. . . like the Canterbury tracksuit that they [wear] . . . Like, I've got one and lots of people have and would just wear that to the gym and that's like considered like, even when it's uni, like just the trousers or something and like that's considered to be . . . I dunno, fashionable I guess . . . but if you were to turn up in like a tracksuit from Primark – or something – I don't think that would really have the same effect . . . .

(Elspeth, 21, middle-class, NEW University)

Charys in particular here denotes a sense of the 'chameleon habitus' outlined by Abrahams and Ingram (2013); the adaptation occurring between the working-class home field and the middle-class university field is one of the habitus negotiating new cultural capital', moving within social space. Elspeth mentions another brand here that was frequently mentioned by NEW university students (as well as Jack Wills); with both her and Charys speaking to the sense of adapting their style, being mindful of the social status and effects of brands. That wearing Primark[5] wouldn't 'have the same effect' is key in understanding *who* is able to take up this 'student' look and how exclusions operate. In this sense, brands act as symbolic markers; while the meanings accorded to them can be often locally constructed and understood, they can also be 'manipulations of symbolic prestige in the judgements of significant others and as such be continually drawing boundaries between what is and how it could be otherwise' (Chaney, 2002: 82).

Even those who attempt to take on the student look may be at risk of getting it wrong if they do not have access to the brands, or 'symbolic markers' that typify affiliation with the student community or indeed to mark out as 'other' and risk drawing associations of being a 'chav' (or 'charver'/'charva' in the north east of England – the disenfranchised white poor – see Nayak, 2003; Tyler, 2008), the wrong kind of working-class, a stranger to the university environment. The price of the brand is clearly implicated in their value. High stocks of economic capital are converted to cultural capital; as Elspeth says, brands like Primark won't have the same effect as the more acceptable student brands such as Jack Wills and Canterbury she herself refers to. The latter brands are laden with symbolic prestige. Getting this 'right', she implies is part of student identity. Interestingly, Colin provides an example of an experience he has of wearing the 'wrong' brand:

. . . two days ago in university I decided to wear tracksuit bottoms . . . they're just 'Adidas' ones with stripes down the side and the instant reaction I got when I walked in the class – well first of all, it's not like me to dress like that ... I usually dress quite smartly erm just because of my part-time job normally. But erm, it was like, 'Colin, what are you doing, you look like a charva?!'; 'cause I was speaking to Mandy and John about it and I was like, 'Hold on; all the other boys on campus wear tracksuit bottoms, yet do they look like charvas? No. So do I look like a charva?', and they were like, 'Well, yeah, you do' ... it made me think because it's not Canterbury then maybe yeah or Kryki or something like that (it's another sports brand that they wear); could [it] be that or ...? ... It had me thinking like, is it me?! Like, do they know that I'm from like a rougher background and it makes them associate something or, I dunno, but it made me think...

(Colin, 22, working-class, NEW University)

The branding differentiation between a pair of seemingly similar items of clothing (tracksuit bottoms; leisure-wear) are interpreted very differently and the class associations between the 'Adidas' brand and the 'Canterbury' or 'Kryki' are made abundantly clear. On the day that Colin hasn't dressed for work and has 'dressed down' in more of a relaxed leisure (one may say 'student') style, his performance is denigrated with the association of 'charva' (or 'charver', 'chav') rather than as 'student'. He gets the 'student look' wrong, seemingly marked out via clothing brands. His misrecognition of the significance of brands is part of the way that exclusion works. Student fashion here then, provides a 'means of affiliation that differentiates those who do recognise the prestigious object from those who do not' (Chaney, 2002: 78). Different brands work as prestigious objects in the two institutions, with Canterbury and Kryki being more prevalent in NEW and Jack Wills in OLD. However, Colin also includes a point that needs further consideration. He ponders whether their judgement of him is sanctioned by their knowledge of his having come from a 'rougher' background. It is not that the prestige awarded to different brands exists independently of the person, but that the association of the brand and the wearer work in a combinatory form and are inherently complex and dynamic. The significance of the brand is relative to the wearer and the context and thus is part of the complex negotiation around meaning involved and visual identities. Colin's use of 'Adidas' leisure clothing is a cultural capital he employs in his student attire but it is not symbolically recognised as student and is instead read as classed; as 'chav' in the sub-field of HE. What is of further significance in the 'dressing down' of the student look is captured here in Colin's normal manner of dress being dictated by his work commitments. Colin worked long and frequent hours in a shop (admitting to often full-time hours of over 40 hours per week), which required him to 'look smart-ish' and wear black trousers. While perhaps not considered excessively 'smart', the contrasting 'dressing down' of wearing sportswear in a seemingly 'wrong' brand here is compelling.

The conditions under which different students experience their time studying at university enable and restrict their access to the resource of 'choice' to perform student identity visually, in the ways discussed above. Undertaking paid employment during term-time, has the effect of exclusion from taking up this student 'look', as dressing so 'shoddily' (Craig) or like a 'tramp' (Siobhan) is incompatible with the required standards of dress for most workplaces. Five of the students worked part-time on a regular basis (all working-class students) said that their choice of attire for university was influenced by their need to work before/after being in university. Like Colin, for most this meant at least wearing black trousers or skirts that could be easily adapted to suit working environments such as various retail outlets and offices. The '[e]xclusionary processes' operating in HE that Reay (2007: 196) states involves, 'far more working-class than middle-class students talking about undertaking paid employment in both term time and the vacations', which in this context also suggest this is also experienced as potentially limiting in terms of freedom of clothing choice.

The take-up of paid employment during term-time then, suggests that far more working-class students are excluded from being able to take up this student 'look' and thus the visual, symbolic associations of this 'student' identity. Often students are materially constrained both through the necessity to work alongside studying to finance themselves and through their lack of access to economic capital needed to convert to cultural capital, via embodiment of the student look.

## Summary: student fashions and identities

The visual aspects of identity discussed in this chapter present fascinating distinctions between the students in this research and point to complex everyday experiences of studenthood and claims to student identity. As Chaney (2002: 81) states:

> ... concern with fashion for everyday life lies in the opportunities it provides for more complex vocabularies of social identity ... fashion is better understood as semiotics of inclusion and affiliation that has provided the basis for new modes of social grouping called lifestyles (Chaney 1996) ... If lifestyles are concerned with the representation of identity then a theme of dramatisation of the self should not be puzzling.

A number of ways in which student fashions or 'looks' were discussed by the participants involved referencing 'rahs'; a conferred identity for seemingly easily recognisable (upper-middle-class) students often referred to as a sub-group of the student population. Through each of the dialogues about visual identity, there are examples of the ongoing conversion of economic capital into cultural and symbolic capital; the 'rah' display is certainly only affordable to wealthy students and yet there exists a complex struggle over the legitimacy of these student looks and the particular capitals involved in everyday exchanges. Much of the data refers to the figure of the 'rah' and relates to the different interpretations of the 'look' they are seen to embody; prostheticising and perhaps ironicising aspects of what they assume a student 'should be', because they can. This access to 'others' culture as a resource in their own making', according to Skeggs (2004: 177) is 'central to how the middle-class is formed' and within these relationships of entitlement and exclusion, '*new forms of exploitation are shaped*'.[6] While the image and representations of 'rahs' were repeatedly denigrated, the brands and styles are also posited as being extremely influential, creating trends that are imitated by other students. This suggests that there are complex negotiations of meaning circulating whereby the style, the brand and the (classed) body are implicated in the making of distinctions. Further, while it is not possible to provide an analysis of the motivations behind the wearing of some of the widely named brands in the research dialogues (the Jack Wills branding prefacing this chapter may simply be coincidental and is one of many highlighted), this brief analysis highlights the significance of these particular brands in everyday identity performances of 'student'. The perceived 'cynical performers' purposefully styling 'student' highlight meritocratic understandings of studenthood; however, access to the propertising of a student look (in various degrees of exaggeration) is not an option available to all. Using brands in practices of style and identity performances, raises issues of equity within the student experience; the exclusivity of particular brands and the material investments required to participate in these performances, highlight ways in which power and privilege operate to exclude those more restricted financially. These visual markers of belonging to sub-groups or to the category 'student' are part of the way that class works in HE and through which power and privilege operate in the everyday, seemingly banal aspects of student experience.

## Notes

1   See: www.carnaby.co.uk/store/jack-wills [Accessed 28th November 2016]
2   The Russell Group was formed in 1994 with 17 universities and currently includes 24 that are research-intensive and 'world-class' institutions. Many of these institutions are closely situated to a post-1992 institution as well as those involved in this research study.
3   www.bristol.ac.uk/spais/research/paired-peers/about/[Accessed 28th November 2016]
4   All names used throughout are pseudonyms
5   A well-known high street brand that markets itself on providing low cost or affordable clothes and goods.
6   Emphasis in the original.

## References

Abrahams, J., and Ingram, N. (2013). The chameleon habitus: Local students' negotiations of a multiple fields. *Sociological Review Online*, *18*(4), 21, www.socresonline.org.uk/18/4/21.html

Addison, M., and Mountford, V.G. (2015). Talking the talk and fitting In: Troubling the Practices of Speaking 'What You Are Worth' in Higher Education in the UK. *Sociological Research Online*, *20*(2), 4 www.socresonline.org.uk/20/2/4.html

Adkins, L. (2004). Reflexivity: Freedom or habit of gender? In L. Adkins and B. Skeggs (Eds), *Feminism after bourdieu*, Oxford; Malden: Blackwell Publishing, 191–210.

Archer, L. (2003). Social class and higher education. In L. Archer, M. Hutchings, and A. Ross (Eds.), *Higher education and social class: Issues of exclusion and inclusion*. London: RoutledgeFalmer, 5–21.

Archer, L., Hutchings, M., and Ross, A. (Eds). (2003). *Higher education and social class: Issues of exclusion and inclusion*. London: RoutledgeFalmer.

Archer, L., Hollingworth, S., and Halsall, A., (2007). "University's not for Me – I'm a Nike Person": Urban, working-cass young people's negotiations of 'style', identity and educational engagement. *Sociology*, *41*(2), 219–237.

Bathmaker, A.M., Ingram, N., Abrahams, J., Hoare, A., Waller, R., and Bradley, H. (2016). *Higher education, social class and social mobility: the degree generation*. London: Palgrave.

Bathmaker, A.M., Ingram, N., and Waller, R. (2013). Higher education, social class and the mobilisation of capitals. *British Journal Sociology of Education*, *34*(5–6), 723–743.

Bourdieu, P. (1984). *Distinction: A social critique on the judgement of taste*. London: Routledge.

Bourdieu, P. (1998). *Practical reason: On the theory of action*. Cambridge: Polity.

Bradley, H. (2012). Feeling classed and the feelings of class: Perceptions of 'fit' and 'misfit' among first-year university students. *British Sociological Association Annual Conference*, Leeds, Leeds University. 11th–13th April.

Chaney, D. (2002). *Cultural change and everyday life*. Basingstoke: Palgrave Macmillan.

Clayton, J., Crozier, G., and Reay, D. (2009). Home and away: Risk, familiarity and the multiple geographies of the higher education experience. *International Studies in Sociology of Education*, *19*(3), 157–174.

Crozier, G., Reay, D., and Clayton, J. (2008). Different strokes for different folks: Diverse students in diverse institutions – experiences of higher education. *Research Papers in Education*, *23*(2), 167–177.

Durkheim, E. (1995 [1912]). *The elementary forms of religious life*. New York: The Free Press.

Elias, N. (1994 [1939]). *The civilizing process*. Jephcott, E. (trans.). Oxford: Blackwell.

Gillies, V. (2005). Raising the 'meritocracy: Parenting and the individualization of social class. *Sociology*, *39*, 835–852.

Goffman, E. (1959). *The presentation of self in everyday life*. London: Penguin.

Greenbank, P. (2007). Higher education and the graduate labour market: The 'class factor'. *Tertiary Education and Management*, *13*(4), 365–376.

Holdsworth, C. (2009). 'Between two worlds: Local students in higher education and "Scouse" student identities. *Population, Space and Place*, *15*(3), 225–237.

Kuhn, A. (1995). *Family secrets: Acts of memory and imagination*. London: Verso.

Lawler, S. (2008). *Identity: Sociological perspectives*. Cambridge: Polity Press.

Longden, B. (2004). Interpreting student early departure from higher education through the lens of cultural capital. *Tertiary Education and Management*, *10*(2), 121–138.

Lury, C. (1998). *Prosthetic culture: Photography, memory, identity*. Abingdon: Routledge.

Moi, T. (1991). Appropriating Bourdieu: Feminist theory and Pierre Bourdieu's sociology of culture. *New Literary History*, *22*(4), 1017–1049.

Morley, L. (1997). Change and equity in higher education. *British Journal of Sociology of Education*, *18*(2), 231–242.

Mountford, V.G. (2014). Rules of engagement beyond the gates: Negotiating and capitalising on student 'experience'. In Y. Taylor (Ed.), *The Entrepreneurial University: Engaging Publics, Intersecting Impact*. Basingstoke; Palgrave Macmillan, 61–81.

Nayak, A. (2003). Last of the 'real geordies? White masculinities and the subcultural responses to deindustrialisation. *Environment and Planning D: Society and Space, 21*, 7–25.

Reay, D. (2001). Finding or losing yourself? working-class relationships to education. *Journal of Education Policy, 16*(4), 333–346.

Reay, D. (2005). Beyond consciousness? the psychic landscape of class. *Sociology, 39*(5), 911–928.

Reay, D. (2007). An insoluble problem: Social class and English higher education. In R. Teese,, S. Lamb, and M. Duru-Ballet (Eds.), *International studies in educational inequality, theory and policy volume 1: Educational Inequality: Persistence and change*. Dordrecht: Springer, 191–204.

Reay, D., Crozier, G., and Clayton, J. (2009). Strangers in paradise: Working-class students in elite universities. *Sociology, 43*(6), 1103–1121.

Reay, D., Crozier, G., and Clayton, J. (2010). 'Fitting in' or 'standing out': Working-class students in UK higher education. *British Educational Research Journal, 36*(1), 107–124.

Reay, D., David, M.E., and Ball, S. (2005). *Degrees of choice: Social class, race and gender in higher education*. Stoke on Trent: Trentham Books.

Redmond, P. (2006). Outcasts on the inside: Graduates, employability and widening participation. *Tertiary Education and Management, 12*(6), 119–135.

Sayer, A. (2005) Class, moral worth and recognition. *Sociology, 39*(5), 947–963.

Shilling, C. (Ed.) (2007). *Embodying sociology: Retrospect, progress and prospects*. Oxford: Blackwell Publishing/The Sociological Review.

Skeggs, B. (1997). *Formations of class and gender, becoming respectable*. London: Sage.

Skeggs, B. (2004). *Class, self, culture*. London: Routledge.

Sveinsson, K.P. (2009). *Introduction: The white working class and multiculturalism: Is there space for a progressive Agenda? Who cares about the white working class?* London: Runneymede Trust, 3–7.

Taylor, Y., and Scurry, T. (2011). Intersections, division, and distinctions: Exploring widening participation and international students' experiences of higher education in the UK. *European Societies, 13*(4), 583–606.

Tyler, I. (2008) "Chav Mum Chav Scum": Class disgust in contemporary Britain. *Feminist Media Studies, 8*(1), 17–34.

Waller, R. (2006). "I don't feel like 'a student', I feel like 'me!'": The over-simplification of mature learners' experience(s). *Research in Post-compulsory Education, 11*(1), 115–130.

Woodin, T. (2005). Muddying the waters: Changes in class and identity in a working-class cultural organization. *Sociology, 39*(5), 1001–1018.

# Part III

# Getting out: social class and graduate destinations

# Higher education and the myths of graduate employability

*Gerbrand Tholen and Phillip Brown*

## Introduction

The relationship between Higher Education (HE) and labour market has never been so contested as in the last decade. There are continuous and sharpened debates about whether the UK labour market can keep up with the growth of HE in creating 'graduate level' jobs. In addition, considerable political heat has been generated over who should pay for HE, as the earning prospects of many graduates have been below expectations (Tholen, 2014a).

Although these concerns are not necessarily novel, understanding the changing relationship between higher education and labour market in post-recession Britain, should be of central importance to sociologists of education. The role universities are expected to play in improving the employability of graduates and delivering intergenerational social mobility is in need of further sociological investigation. In contributing to a better sociological explanation of the changing relationship between higher education and the labour market, this chapter examines to what extent the increased reliance on universities to deliver graduate employability is congruent with current labour market realities.

We argue that the policy drive to reform higher education as a means of improving graduate employability and narrowing social inequalities, is difficult to reconcile with today's labour market. There is also little evidence on graduate incomes to support exaggerated claims of a significant 'graduate premium', as many graduates will not earn enough to repay their loans adding to the financial burden confronting future generations of graduates.[1]

We argue that the role of a graduate credential within the labour market is misunderstood. The employability skills that are becoming part of the formal curriculum in many universities bear little relationship to the way employers recruit for 'graduate' jobs. As a result, reliance on graduate employability to compensate for the increasing insecurity students face and to ameliorate the unequal nature of labour market access and outcome, is ultimately flawed. In order to show this, the chapter starts off with a critical review of the existing literature on graduate employability and then moves into an overview of some of the evidence on graduate employment. The chapter ends with a discussion of the limitations of the recent employability-focused drive to improve labour market outcomes for graduates.

## Graduate employability

From September 2012, universities in England have been allowed to charge tuition fees of up to £9,000 per year and the majority now do so. As maximum fees for courses are the norm, university education has effectively been made a private good. With this comes a transformed understanding of the aims of HE. Former Minister of State for Universities and Science, David Willetts, predicted that students would behave more like 'customers' and expect greater value for money as universities 'have to tell those customers what they are offering' (BBC, 2011). Since the introduction of £9,000 fees, the Higher Education Funding Council for England (HEFCE) demands that HEFCE-funded institutions provide increased and enhanced information for prospective students in order to choose the right course at the right institution.

This demand for greater transparency in respect to what students will receive at universities has also been extended to the future employability of students. Universities are expected to improve graduate employable either through increasing the 'quality' of their courses, or by providing students with so-called employability skills (understood as transferable skills needed by an individual to secure future employment opportunities) (see: HEFCE, 2010). Universities also need to publish information on the employability of their graduates in the form of 'employability statements' explaining how they promote student job prospects. The Department for Business, Innovation and Skills explains:

> It is a top concern for business that students should leave university better equipped with a wider range of employability skills. All universities should be expected to demonstrate how their institution prepares its students for employment, including through training in modern workplace skills such as team working, business awareness, and communication skills. This information should help students choose courses that offer the greatest returns in terms of graduate opportunity.
>
> (BIS, 2009, p. 8).

Universities to a large extent have assimilated the discourse of employability and implemented measures to enhance student employment. Through embedding employability and/or enterprise and entrepreneurship education in subject curricula, universities aim to provide students with practical knowledge and skills deemed desired by employers. Work-based learning has also been introduced to provide student with work experiences and extra-curricular awards and recognition schemes aim to widen the student experience.

Furthermore, how well universities perform in making their students employable is monitored and measured internally as well as externally. Graduation rates for individual universities are published annually (e.g. HESA, 2015; O'Leary, 2015; Page, 2014). Other league tables include graduate starting salaries by institution (and subject) as evidence of how successful universities are in increasing student employability. Global rankings also measure how universities perform on graduate employability worldwide, based on surveys of international recruiters (e.g. Emerging, 2015), highlighting internationalisation of student recruitment and global institutional branding.

The reframing of the purpose of a university education also reflects the concerns of students and families in a context of increasing labour market competition. Current and prospective students are now positioned as HE consumers, encouraged to take full account of future employability before 'investing' in a university education. UK students believe that the main responsibility for preparing them for life after university lies between the university and themselves (AGCAS, 2013). It is also accepted that a degree is not enough (Tomlinson, 2008) and extra-curricular experiences (alongside credentials) are needed in order to stand out from the crowd (Brown and Hesketh, 2004; Tholen, 2013).

## The problem of graduate employability

Employability has been conceptualised and measured in many different ways (Forrier and Sels, 2003). In most cases, it is construed to the likelihood of (continued) employment of the individual. To find employment, remain in employment or obtain new employment as, and when, required is thought to depend upon his or her human capital (e.g. skills, knowledge, abilities) (Hillage and Pollard, 1998; Thijssen et al., 2008). An employable person is portrayed as successful in reaching his or her goals within employment, via a competitive labour market. Investing in the right kind of human capital is therefore regarded as paramount (Confederation of British Industry, 2011). Much of the policy focus highlights the need for graduates to get marketable skills, but this includes a recognition that technical skills alone do not provide students with an adequate preparation for the labour market. The UK Commission for Employment and Skills (UKCES) (2010) states that there has been 'recognition that employers are looking for a broader set of generic employability skills (p. 6)' and these skills 'have been identified as a key element to ensuring that the employment and skills system is demand-led (p. 5)'. Examples are information and communication technology (ICT) and communication and interpersonal skills.

The concept of graduate employability has been subject to wide-ranging criticism. Numerous authors have criticised the use of the term employability and have pointed at flawed theoretical underpinnings (e.g. Tomlinson, 2010), reliance on educational signals (Harvey, 2001) or lack of attention to the subjective dimension (Holmes, 2001). Others have claimed that the discourse of employability conforms to a neoliberal view of market individualism (Brown and Hesketh, 2004; Boden and Nedeva, 2010).

These criticisms remain valid today. Notably, the tendency to accept employer accounts of skill requirements, despite a lack of specificity, as generic employability requirements are hard to establish. A study on employers' views on graduate employability reports that:

> employers expect graduates to have technical and discipline competences from their degrees but require graduates also to demonstrate a range of broader skills and attributes that include team-working, communication, leadership, critical thinking, problem solving and managerial abilities.
>
> (Lowden *et al.*, 2011: vi).

This does not mean that these skills are needed to perform the job advertised (James *et al.*, 2013). In other words, the supply of graduates may influence the demands of employers, regardless of job requirements. Employers may also not demand what universities teach. This is reflected in several empirical studies investigating employer skill requirements, demonstrating that hiring practices are not rewarding 'typical' graduate skills (Archer and Davidson, 2008; Wilton, 2011), nor are they merit-based (Jackson, 2007), making any university-labour market transition particularly complex.

This complexity poses a related problem for the proponents of reforming higher education to improve graduate employability which is the neglect of labour market context. This is because employability is framed as an individual phenomenon as opposed to a relational or social one. In the mainstream policy debate, as well as much of the management centred literature, employability is supply-sided issue and the result of *individual* factors such as skills, knowledge, experience and other personal attributes (e.g. personal competencies and character traits [Fugate *et al.*, 2004, Bridgestock, 2009]). Thijssen *et al.*, (2008) observe that many studies into employability ignore institutional and social context. Others argue for the inclusion of various factors with impact on labour market conditions and individual opportunities such as macroeconomic conditions, level of job vacancies, employer recruitment practices and government policy (McQuaid and Lindsay, 2005; Tholen, 2013).

Brown and Hesketh (2004), stress the importance of labour demand, introducing the notion of a 'duality of employability'. Here, employability cannot solely be defined in terms of individual skills or characteristics and whether one is able to fulfil the requirements of specific jobs (the absolute dimension). It also depends 'on how one stands relative to others within a hierarchy of job seekers' (Brown and Hesketh, 2004: 25). This relative dimension is becoming of increasing importance in the UK graduate labour market as the growth in the supply of graduates does not match the number of graduate level jobs. Brown and Hesketh argue this intensifies market competition and the struggle for positional advantage. This has led British students who aspire to 'fast-track' graduate jobs to seek new ways of distinguishing themselves from other students, which inevitably privilege those from middle- and upper-class backgrounds.

Cross-country studies on school-to-work transition also stress the importance of the national context such as labour market structure and institutions, as well as economic cycle, production regime and education system (e.g. Gangl, 2000; Wolbers, 2007) in shaping the relationship between education, employability and employment. In addition, labour market inequalities are mediated through structural features such as family influence, education system, recruitment and selection processes among others. Such factors are often ignored in policy debates on employability and higher education reform. This is because employability is treated as a decontextualised signifier in so far as it overlooks how structures such as gender, race, social class and disability interact with labour market opportunities (Morley, 2001: 132).

A third problem with the current employability agenda is that the perceived lack of labour market opportunities is treated as a case of market failure and has been given a market-driven solution. Student concerns about the future are interpreted as an educational issue in support of the view that universities should teach relevant skills. Greater transparency is being encouraged to ensure that students can make more informed market decisions, offering a solution to the difficulties recent graduates face in the labour market. However, although efforts to increase the quality of education are to be encouraged, the drive to make both students and HE providers solely responsible for improving labour market outcomes is disingenuous. Efforts to align learning experience with perceived employer demands underestimate the structural issues described earlier and, thus, masks structural inequalities in the graduate labour market. Next, we will outline some existing empirical evidence showing that many of today's concerns about the graduate labour market are structural and cannot be solved through consumerist solutions. This is why we argue that the promise of graduate employability is a myth.

## The state of the graduate labour market

There has been much debate within the realm of politics and the media on what is happening within the graduate labour market. For instance, reports on topics such as the role of internships in access to well-paid careers, the role of Higher Education in social mobility as well and existing skills gaps identified by employers cause many to reflect on the state of graduate employment. The majority of contributions in these debates are characterised by deep confusion and discontent about unexpected and disappointing labour market outcomes for graduates. The current misunderstanding is to a considerable extent, explained by an outdated understanding of the graduate labour market which is not in line with current labour market realities (Tholen, 2014a). The underlying assumption of the proponents of higher education for employability is that more informed educational choices, as well as the development of a set of practical skills, will enhance labour market outcomes for graduates. This supply side solution assumes the existence of a graduate labour market that rewards a growing number of labour market entrants with more relevant skills better attuned to what employers want, having invested in the right university courses. However, much of the existing evidence points towards the conclusion that 'improved' course selection and university experience is unlikely to lead to better outcomes for all graduates, as there are structural barriers that supply-side reforms cannot deal with.

## 1) Structural congestion

Congestion has been a structural feature of the graduate labour market for a considerable amount of time (Brown, 2013). Based on *The Skills and Employment Survey*, Felstead *et al.* (2002, 2007, 2013) observe a growth in demand for graduate qualification between 1986 and 2012, alongside an even stronger growth in the supply of graduates, leading to continuous over-qualification (ranging between roughly 20 and 30 per cent). Within the labour market for new graduates, skill mismatch is widespread.

It is clear that graduates do not exclusively work in what can be labelled 'graduate occupations'. Graduate share of employment has been increasing right the way down the occupational hierarchy, in particular, but not exclusively, in early career. For example, in 2013, of those in employment, 21.9 per cent of biology graduates, 20.9 per cent of English graduates, and 27.7 per cent of media graduates are working in retail, catering, waiting or as bar staff, 6 month after graduation (Higher Education Careers Service Unit, 2014: 17). There is an expectation that many of these will transfer into more relevant positions but past trends are no guarantee of future labour market outcomes. A large study of recent UK graduates found up to 40 per cent of those graduated in 2009 remained in non-graduate employment, 30 months after graduation (Purcell *et al.*, 2013). They also found a sharp increase in the share of graduates working in non-graduate jobs after graduation compared with a cohort that graduated in 1999.

The political and economic shock of the most recent recession masked the fact that some of the adverse conditions emerged before the recession and were exacerbated by it. This suggests that the improved labour market conditions following the recession are not likely to solve the issue of the oversupply of graduates. Providing students with graduate skills or ensuring that employability or entrepreneurship are covered in university degree programmes, will not fundamentally change the intensity of labour market competition. As education will not increase the number of good jobs, the role of education, whether attuned to employers or not, in solving this problem is limited (as is its ability to resolve issues of social mobility) (see Brown, 2013). Instead, intense competition for graduate level jobs will continue in the future. This not only pushes those without graduate qualifications down the occupational ladder, but also reinforces inequalities in labour market outcomes (Keep and Mayhew, 2010).

## 2) Deep-rooted inequalities

There remain stable and entrenched inequalities in access and progression within the graduate labour market. Class effects in the UK labour market are widespread and the graduate labour market presents no exceptions. Pathways of students from poor and working-class backgrounds tend to be more precarious than those from middle-class backgrounds (Bathmaker *et al.*, 2016; Ward, 2015). Students from socially disadvantaged backgrounds are less likely to gain access to more prestigious higher education institutions even after accounting for prior educational performance (Boliver, 2013; see also Boliver this volume). Furlong and Cartmel (2005) describe how early labour market experiences for working-class students often involves periods of unemployment and long periods in non-graduate employment.

Jacobs *et al.* (2015) recently found that the effects of parental education on entry into the higher-service class are significantly stronger in the United Kingdom compared with Germany. Others have pointed to the continuous struggle students from working-class backgrounds confront in entry to top professional jobs (e.g. Jacobs, 2003; Ashley and Empson, 2013; Friedman *et al.*, 2015). Examining a cohort of British children born in 1970, McKnight (2015) found that advantaged families effectively construct a 'glass floor' (Waller, 2011) to ensure their children succeed in the labour market irrespective of cognitive ability. The author argues that children from relatively high-income or social class backgrounds benefit from higher social and emotional skills as well as being more able to secure places in grammar or private secondary schools and are also more likely to attain a degree qualification. Access to these class-based resources remains crucial in the allocation of top jobs.

For particular ethnic minorities, the graduate labour market has shown further persistent barriers. Increased attainment over the past 20 years has not led to improved job outcomes (Sedghi, 2014). In fact, Rafferty (2012) found distinct ethnic penalties for several minority ethnic groups in terms of wage, unemployment, and over-qualification. Racial bias in recruitment, selection, and promotion decisions also seem to be hardwired in corporate environments (see Gorman, 2015).

Gender inequality in employment outcomes among (recent) UK graduates, including a gender pay gap, is substantial (Purcell *et al.*, 2013). Likewise, women continue to confront indirect but nevertheless insidious forms of exclusion within the graduate labour market. There remains prejudice against women in management or professional roles (Bolton and Muzio, 2007; Tomlinson *et al.*, 2013), and Smyth and Steinmetz (2008) found evidence of persistent gender segregation.

The inequalities described above based on class, ethnicity and gender, intersect and reinforce each other. Within a congested labour market, jobs are keenly contested. University credentials are rarely a sufficient source of labour market distinction. Not only are those from more privileged backgrounds more likely to enter elite universities, but they are also more likely to have access to the networks and cultural capital required for success in today's labour market. For instance, work experience opportunities are frequently unpaid and reports now appear of students having to pay for internships (Boffey, 2015; Greenslade, 2015).

### 3) Graduate wages

When we examine graduates earnings, there is little evidence to suggest that university education itself (including their employability initiatives) is able to secure high waged jobs. The relationship between Higher Education and labour market outcomes is far from straightforward. Although the average graduate premia, compared to non-graduates remain significant, earnings for graduates have dispersed over time. Tholen (2014a) shows that the growth in earning inequality within the graduate labour market is unlike the rest of the labour market. Between 1994 and 2011, the dispersion of wages between graduates was much faster than for non-graduates. Increasing dispersion in the returns on graduate education in the UK has also been detected by Green and Zhu (2010) over the period 1994 to 2006, when the numbers of graduating increased sharply. Brynin (2013) shows that due to the increase of graduates in the labour market, graduate-dense occupations no longer are necessarily well-paid.

There is an increasing overlap between wages for graduates and school-leavers. For those at the bottom of the wage distribution, learning has not led to earning (Brown et al., 2015). Mayhew and Holmes (2013) show that between 1994 and 2007, the UK graduate premium has fallen for all except those in the top 15 per cent. Wage differentials between graduates are substantial, therefore the use of average rates of returns for graduates and non-graduates is misleading.

Many graduates in a vast array of occupations have found that their university degrees have not increased their market power in influencing wage negotiation, even if it has helped them to find employment in competition with other labour market entrants. The reason is mass higher education has enabled employers to buy more skilled labour for less than has traditionally been the case. Higher education does not provide an elevated status on which graduates can symbolically influence their earnings, except for some graduates from globally elite universities or in specialist fields where there are genuine labour shortages. The growing earnings inequality within graduate occupations suggests that particular characteristics and (class) dispositions – only indirectly related to education – matter much more. Therefore, it is hard to see how reforming higher education for employability will lead to a narrowing of wage inequalities for graduates.

### 4) Graduates and skill use

We also know that skill utilisation is an issue within the graduate labour market. The jobs that graduates work in, do not always use the skill-set graduates bring into the job. Defining or measuring skill requirement in jobs is a difficult task. We've seen that there is compelling evidence that a growing number of graduates in the labour market are not utilising the skills they have acquired at university. Although there is a lack of data on skills utilisation within the graduate labour market, we know that a growing number of graduates are working in intermediate-level jobs, in which there is likely to be significant over-qualification.

Okay-Sommerville and Scholarios (2013) found that British graduates working in associate professional and technical occupations had a lower incidence of skill utilisation, as well as lower job control, opportunity for skills development, less job security and lower pay, compared to those in traditional graduate occupations.

Tholen *et al.* (2016) report on the work of residential estate agents – a non-graduate occupation which has experienced 'graduatisation'. Although a wide variety of (mainly soft) skills are deemed necessary, the role of higher education in both recruitment and labour process is limited. For more traditional graduate occupations the role of higher education for skill development may also have been overstated (Tholen, 2014b). Brinkley *et al.* (2009) estimate that merely a third of the UK workforce can be considered knowledge workers, who perform many 'knowledge tasks' as part of their job. Of these, 57 per cent were graduates, and 36 per cent reported that their jobs underutilised their skills and experience. For non-knowledge workers, reported skills underutilisation was higher, at 44 per cent. Although some may believe that graduates will 'upskill' non-graduate roles, there is little evidence this is necessarily happening (Chartered Institute of Personnel and Development, 2015). Therefore the reform of higher education aimed at improving graduate employability through developed skills viewed as more relevant to the workplace, ignores and realities of graduate employment and the problem of skills under-utilisation that result from a lack of employer demand.

## The limits of graduate employability

The labour market changes outlined above lead us to question whether university reforms will have a significant impact on improving graduate employability. Students are facing an increasingly congested graduate labour market in which workers are increasing unequally remunerated. This labour market still has persistent inequalities in class, gender, and ethnicity, and the skills and knowledge associated with HE are of declining importance for many of its constituents. The current emphasis on improving student employability skills within HE, will not be sufficient to solve the inherent inequalities and frictions that are deep-rooted within academic institutions.

The structural features of the post-recession graduate labour market outlined above are not only problematic for many students and graduates but also for policymakers and universities alike. All must accept that providing students with better labour market information or teaching them the skills employers may claim they want, cannot solve the shortage of traditional graduate positions nor growing wage inequality. Although some students may benefit from these initiatives and improve their labour market prospects, the graduate workforce as a whole cannot.

Although some weight was given to the reform of undergraduate and postgraduate programmes before the changes in fees (from the 1990s onwards), employability has become an even more forceful objective in the strategic plans of most English universities. This focus on employability skills is not politically neutral. The increased pressure on universities to ensure employability perpetuates a market-based solution and does not sufficiently address issues of fairness, affordability or labour market congestion. As others have described in detail, the employability discourse serves a neoliberal educational project (Boden and Nedeva, 2010) and may also aid social control (Coffield, 1999). Moreau and Leathwood (2006), for instance, have observed how the employability discourse has made the individual further responsible for low achievement and labour market failure by effectively removing structural and political explanations in understanding employment inequality. Wilton (2011) offers evidence to show that the development of employability skills at university had little impact on labour market disadvantage, particularly for females and ethnic minorities. The recent drive for further accountability and measurability of employability, has made HE even more complicit in covering up labour market realities. As labour market outcomes continue to widen for university graduates, it becomes more important to highlight the changing relationship between the skills associated with HE and the value of these within labour market recruitment and changes in the labour process as a whole. Without structural changes within employment and the wider economy, making students more job-ready, simply intensifies the competition for existing job openings.

Graduate over-qualification and labour market inequalities will not be addressed by giving students better information about university courses and teaching them employability skills. There is an urgent need to address structural inequalities within the graduate labour market which cannot be treated as a temporary form of market failure. The myth of graduate employability is rooted in the idea that the Higher Education sector can improve the labour market outcomes and opportunities of all it students. Yet employability is first and foremost determined by labour market conditions rather than the capabilities of individuals (Brown *et al.*, 2003: 110). But the employability agenda is not only destined to fail but involves a shift in focus from teaching academic disciplines to giving priority to a set of skills and competences which accord to the perceived 'needs' of employers.

## Note

1   Some predict that the majority of students will pay back relatively little to their future earning capacity, reducing the long-term sustainability of the whole funding regime (e.g. Higher Education Commission, 2014).

## References

AGCAS. (2013). Great expectations. How good are universities at making their graduates employable? AGCAS, Retrieved November 2, 2016 from www.agcas.org.uk/agcas_resources/540-Great-expectations-How-good-are-universities-at-making-their-students-more-employable

Archer, W., and Davison, J. (2008). *Graduate employability: The views of employers.* London: Council for Industry and Higher Education.

Ashley L. and Empson, L. (2013). Differentiation and discrimination: Understanding social class and social exclusion in leading law firms. *Human Relations*, *66*, 219–244.

BBC. (2011). Universities charging maximum fees could 'look silly'. *BBC*, 20th February 2011, Retrieved November 28, 2016 from www.bbc.co.uk/news/education-12518319

Department for Business, Innovation and Skills [BIS]. (2009). *Higher ambitions*. London: The Stationery Office.

Boden, R., and Nedeva, M. (2010). Employing discourse: Universities and graduate 'employability'. *Journal of Education Policy*, *25*(1), 37–54.

Boffey, D. (2015). Unpaid interns charged £300 for a job reference by thinktank, Guardian, 10th January. Retrieved November 2, 2016 from www.theguardian.com/education/2015/jan/10/thinktank-interns-charged-300-pounds-job-reference

Boliver, V. (2013). How fair is access to more prestigious UK universities? *British Journal of Sociology*, *64*(2), 344–364.

Bolton, S., and Muzio, D. (2007). "Can't live with 'em, can't live without Em": Gendered segmentation in the legal profession. *Sociology*, *41*(1), 29–45.

Bathmaker, A-M., Ingram, N., Abrahams, J., Hoare, T., Waller, R., and Bradley, H. (2016). *Higher education, social class and social mobility: The degree generation*. Basingstoke: Palgrave MacMillan.

Brown, P. (2013). Education, opportunity and the prospects for social mobility. *British Journal of Sociology of Education*, *34*(5), 678–700.

Brown, P., and Hesketh, A. (2004). *The mismanagement of talent: Employability and jobs in the knowledge economy*. Oxford: OUP.

Brown, P., Hesketh, A., and Williams, S. (2003). Employability in a knowledge-driven economy. *Journal of Education and Work*, *16*(2), 107–126.

Brown, P., Chueng, S.Y., and Lauder, H. (2015). Beyond a human capital approach to education and the labour market: The case for industrial policy. In D. Bailey, K. Cowling, and P.R. Tomlinson (Eds.), *New perspectives on industrial policy for modern Britain*. Oxford: Oxford University Press, 206–224.

Bridgestock, R. (2009). The graduate attributes we've overlooked: enhancing graduate employability through career management skills. *Higher Education Research & Development*, *28*(1), 31–44.

Brinkley, I., Theodoropoulou, S., and Mahdon.,M. (2009). *Knowledge Workers and Work*. London, The Work Foundation.

Brynin, M. (2013). Individual choice and risk: The case of higher education. *Sociology*, *47*(2), 284–300.

Confederation of British Industry [CBI]. (2011). Working towards your future: making the most of your time in higher education. CBI. Retrieved November 28, 2016 from www.cbi.org.uk/media/1121431/cbi_nus_employability_report_march_2011.pdf

Chartered Institute of Personnel and Development [CIPD]. (2015). *Over-qualification and skills mismatch in the graduate labour market*. London: CIPD. Retrieved November 28, 2016 from www.cipd.co.uk/binaries/over-qualification-and-skills-mismatch-graduate-labour-market.pdf

Coffield, F. (1999). Breaking the consensus: Lifelong learning as social control. *British Educational Research Journal*, *25*(4), 479–499.

Emerging. (2015). Global university employability ranking. Retrieved November 2, 2016 from http://emerging.fr/rank_en.html

Felstead, A., Gallie. D., and Green, F. (2002). *Work skills in Britain 1986–2001*. Nottingham: DfES.

Felstead, A., Gallie, D., Green.F., and Inanc., H. (2013). *Skills at work in Britain: First findings from the skills and employment survey*. London: Centre for Learning and Life Chances in Knowledge Economies and Societies, Institute of Education.

Felstead, A., Gallie, D., Green, F., and Zhou, Y. (2007). *Skills at Work 1986–2006*, SKOPE: Universities of Oxford and Warwick.

Forrier, A., and Sels, L. (2003). The concept employability: A complex mosaic. *International Journal of Human Resources Development and Management, 3*(2), 102–124.

Friedman, S., Laurison, D., and Miles, A. (2015). Breaking the 'class' ceiling? Social mobility into Britain's elite occupations. *The Sociological Review, 63*(2), 259–289.

Fugate, M., Kinicki, A., and Ashforth, B. (2004). Employability: a psycho-social construct, its dimensions and applications. *Journal of Vocational Behaviour, 65*(1), 14–38.

Furlong, A., and Cartmel, F. (2005). *Graduates from disadvantaged families: Early labour market experiences*. Bristol, The Policy Press.

Gangl, M. (2000). European perspectives on labour market entry: A matter of institutional linkages between training systems and labour markets? Mannheimer Zentrum für Europäische Sozialforschung (MZES) Working Paper 24. Mannheim: MZES.

Gorman, E. (2015). Getting ahead in professional organizations: individual qualities, socioeconomic background and organizational context. *Journal of Professions and Organization, 2*(2), 122–147.

Greenslade, R. (2015). Newsquest/Gannett plans to charge students to write for its titles, Guardian, Retrieved November 2, 2016 from www.theguardian.com/media/greenslade/2015/feb/10/newsquestgannett-plans-to-charge-students-to-write-for-its-titles

Green, F., and Zhu, Y. (2010). Overqualification, job dissatisfaction, and increasing dispersion in the returns to graduate education. *Oxford Economic Papers, 62*(4), 740–763.

Harvey, L. (2001). Defining and measuring employability. *Quality in Higher Education, 7*(2), 97–109.

The Higher Education Careers Service Unit [HECSU]. (2014). What do graduates do? HECSU. Retrieved from www.hecsu.ac.uk/assets/assets/documents/wdgd_september_2014.pdf

The Higher Education Funding Council for England [HEFCE]. (2010). 'Employability Statements' HEFCE, June 2010. Retrieved November 2, 2016 from www.hefce.ac.uk/pubs/year/2010/cl,122010/#d.en.62749

Higher Education Commission. (2014). 'Too good to fail: The financial sustainability of higher education in England'. Higher Education Commission. Retrieved November 2, 2016 from www.policyconnect.org.uk/hec/sites/site_hec/files/report/391/fieldreport download/hecommissionreport-toogoodtofail.pdf

Higher Education Statistics Agency. (HESA). (2015). *Destinations of leavers from higher education*. Cheltenham: HESA.

Hillage, J., and Pollard, E. (1998). *Employability: Developing a framework for policy analysis*, Research Brief RR85, Nottingham: Department for Education and Employment.

Holmes, L. (2001). Reconsidering graduate employability: The 'graduate identity' approach. *Quality in Higher Education, 7*(2), 111–119.

Jackson, M. (2007). How far merit selection? Social stratification and the labour market. *British Journal of Sociology, 58*(3), 367–390.

Jacob, M., Klein, M., and Ianelli, C. (2015). The impact of social origin on graduates' early occupational destinations—an anglo-german comparison. *European Sociological Review, 31*(4), 460–476.

Jacobs K. (2003). Class reproduction in professional recruitment: Examining the accounting profession. *Critical Perspectives on Accounting, 14*(5), 569–596.

James, S., Warhurst, C., Tholen, G., and Commander, J. (2013). What we know and what we need to know about graduate skills. *Work, Employment & Society, 27*(6), 952–963.

Keep, E., and Mayhew, K. (2010). Moving beyond skills as a social and economic panacea. *Work, Employment and Society, 24*(3), 656–577.

Lowden, K., Hall, S., Elliot, D., and Lewin, J. (2011). *Employer's perceptions of the employability skills of new graduates, University of Glasgow SCER Centre and Edge Foundation*. London: Edge Foundation.

Mayhew, K., and Holmes, C. (2013). The changing shape of the UK jobs market and the implications for the bottom half earners. Report on Symposium. Cardiff: WISERD. Retrieved November 2, 2016 from http://wiserd.ac.uk/files/5213/9565/7609/Evidence_Review_Paper_-_The_changing_shape_of_the_jobs_market_-_Ken_Mayhew.pdf

Mcknight, A. (2015). Downward mobility, opportunity hoarding and the 'glass floor'. Research Report. London: Social Mobility and Child Poverty Commission. Retrieved November 2, 2016 from www.gov.uk/government/uploads/system/uploads/attachment_data/file/447575/Downward_mobility_opportunity_hoarding_and_the_glass_floor.pdf

McQuaid, R.W., and Lindsay, C.D. (2005). The concept of employability. *Urban Studies, 42*(2), 197–219.

Moreau, M.P., and Leathwood, C. (2006). 'Graduates' employment and the discourse of employability: a critical analysis. *Journal of Education and Work, 19*(4), 305–324.

Morley, L. (2001). Producing new workers: Quality, equality and employability in higher education. *Quality in Higher Education, 7*(2), 131–138.

Okay-Somerville, B., and Scholarios, D. (2013). Shades of grey: Understanding job quality in emerging graduate occupations. *Human Relations, 66*(4), 555–585.

O'Leary. (2015). *The Times Good University Guide 2016*. London: Times Books.

Page, L. (2014). Guardian University Guide 2015: who came top for employability? The Guardian 7th June, 2014, Retrieved November 2, 2016 from www.theguardian.com/education/2014/jun/07/guardian-university-guide-employability-top-rankings

Purcell K., Elias P., Atfield G., Behle H., Ellison R., Luchinskaya D., Snape J., Conaghan, L., and Tzanakou, C. (2012). *Futuretrack Stage 4: Transitions into employment, further study and other outcomes*. Warwick: The Institute for Employment Research, University of Warwick.

Rafferty, A. (2012). Ethnic penalties in graduate level over-education, unemployment and wages: evidence from Britain. *Work Employment & Society, 26*(4), 987–1006.

Sedghi, A. (2014). Ethnic minorities face barriers to social mobility and job opportunities. Guardian 12th June. Retrieved November 2, 2016 from www.theguardian.com/education/2014/jun/12/ethnic-minorities-social-mobility-employment

Smyth, E., and Steinmetz, S. (2008). Field of study and gender segregation in European labour markets. *International Journal of Comparative Sociology, 49*(4–5), 257–281.

Tholen, G. (2013). The social construction of competition for graduate jobs: A comparison between Great Britain and the Netherlands'. *Sociology, 47*(2), 267–283.

Tholen, G. (2014a). *The changing nature of the graduate labour market: Media, policy and political discourses in the UK*. Basingstoke: Palgrave MacMillan.

Tholen, G. (2014b). The role of higher education within the labour market: Evidence from four skilled occupations. ESRC festival of Science, St. Anne's College. Oxford. 3rd November.

Tholen, G., James Relly, S., Warhurst, C., and Commander, J. (2016). Higher education, graduate skills and the skills of graduates: the case of graduates as residential sales estate agents. *British Educational Research Journal*, *42*(3), 508–523.

Tomlinson, M. (2008). "The degree is not enough": Students' perceptions of the role of higher education credentials for graduate work and employability. *British Journal of Sociology of Education*, *29*(1), 49–61.

Tomlinson, M. (2010). Investing in the self: structure, agency and identity in graduates' employability. *Education, Knowledge & Economy*, *4*(2), 73–88.

Tomlinson J., Muzio D., Sommerlad H., Webley L., and Duff, L. (2013). Structure, agency and career strategies of white women and black and minority ethnic individuals in the legal profession. *Human Relations*, *66*(2), 245–269.

Thijssen, J.G.L., Van der Heijden, B.I.J.M., and Rocco, T. (2008). Toward the employability link model: Current employment transition to future. *Human Resource Development Review*, 7, 165–183.

UK Commission for Employment and Skills [UKCES]. (2010). *Employability skills: A research and policy briefing*. London: UKCES.

Waller, R. (2011). The sociology of education. In B. Dufour, and W. Curtis (Eds.), *Studying Education: Key disciplines in Education Studies*. Maidenhead: Open University Press pp. 106–131.

Ward, M.R.M. (2015). *From labouring to learning, working-class masculinities, education and de-industrialization*. Basingstoke: Palgrave Macmillan.

Wilton, N. (2011). Do employability skills really matter in the graduate labour market? The case of business and management graduates. *Work, Employment and Society*, *25*(1), 85–100.

Wolbers, M.H.J. (2007). Patterns of labor market entry: A comparative perspective on school-to work transitions in 11 European countries. *Acta Sociologica*, *50*(3), 189–210.

# Chapter 10

# A glass half full?

## Social class and access to postgraduate study

*Paul Wakeling*

## Introduction – why be concerned about postgraduate study?

This chapter examines the relationship between social class and entry to postgraduate study in Britain. In the face of higher education's staggering growth in the last quarter century it is perhaps unsurprising that sociologists and higher education researchers have focussed their attention on access to first degrees. Extensive research in the UK and elsewhere has investigated entry to undergraduate study and its domination by the more advantaged social classes. Comparatively little attention has been paid to what happens after the first degree (Gorard *et al.*, 2007; Wakeling, 2010a; Wakeling and Kyriacou, 2010; McCulloch and Thomas, 2013; Moore *et al.*, 2013). Currently, there is a discernible turn in both policy and research towards the investigation of graduate outcomes, but even here the main object of interest is differences in the achievement of 'graduate-level' jobs across social class background. Until recently, there has been almost no consideration of access to postgraduate qualifications such as masters degrees, doctorates and professional diplomas, either in the UK or elsewhere.

Yet growth in postgraduate study has been no less meteoric than that for undergraduate qualifications. Numbers almost doubled in each decade between 1950 and 1990, after which they *quadrupled* in the decade to 2000 (Wakeling, 2009). In 2013/14, there were over one quarter of a million UK-domiciled postgraduate students studying in UK higher education institutions (source: Higher Education Statistics Agency, 2015a), meaning there are more postgraduates today than there were students in total on the eve of the *Robbins Report* of 1963 (Committee on Higher Education, 1963).[1]

The Postgraduate Initial Participation Rate, which measures the percentage of the English population aged 18–30 who have entered a postgraduate course, has hovered around one in ten between 2006/07 and 2013/14. The equivalent participation rate for undergraduate study was in the mid-forties percentage-wise during the same period (Department for Business, Innovation and Skills, 2015), meaning something like one in every four English graduates can be expected to continue to postgraduate study at some point. These patterns are not unique to

Britain (Morgan, 2014). Australia also saw staggering levels of expansion, with a 300 per cent increase between 1988 and 2007. In the USA, where postgraduate study has a longer pedigree and tertiary enrolment rates have historically been high, the system grew by about two-thirds between 1976 and 2006. Doctoral enrolments have expanded everywhere, increasing by two thirds in France, for example, between 1985 and 2007 (Wakeling, 2010a). So while there has been massification of initial entry to higher education, postgraduate enrolment rates have typically grown faster (European Commission *et al.*, 2007).

Despite the considerable growth in postgraduate enrolments, this level of education clearly remains a minority activity. Most graduates do not go on to do a postgraduate degree and among older workers, few hold such degrees.[2] Much postgraduate education is highly specialised, serving as preparation for certain occupations such as school teaching, scientific research or heritage management. Whereas the figure of the undergraduate student is commonplace in popular culture (think of UK comedy shows such as *The Young Ones*, *Fresh Meat* and *The Inbetweeners*, plus a whole raft of US 'college' movies), the postgraduate is not represented.[3] Postgraduate qualifications are nevertheless associated with positive outcomes. Holders of postgraduate degrees are less likely than first-degree graduates to be unemployed (HESA, 2015b); additionally they enjoy an earnings premium over first-degree graduates (Lindley and Machin, 2013). Moreover, doctoral degree holders form the cadre from which most of the future producers of new knowledge are drawn.

This means that inequalities in access to postgraduate qualifications have implications for social mobility and social justice. If those from certain social class backgrounds are less likely to acquire them they are also less likely to acquire the managerial and especially professional occupations and higher salaries with which postgraduate qualifications are associated. Additionally, the relative absence of those from working-class backgrounds among doctoral graduates threatens the diversity and richness of new knowledge production in much the same way as that threatened by the underrepresentation of women and minority ethnic groups. This threat is especially relevant to universities, since doctoral graduates are the university teachers and researchers of the future. Indeed the future 'climate' of the university for working-class students is at stake because this is conditioned by the attitudes of its faculty, as the testimony of academics from working-class backgrounds suggests (Wakeling, 2010b). At stake in access to postgraduate study then is the openness of high-status occupations, as well as the social composition of the university itself.

In order to better understand this process, I present evidence on transitions to postgraduate study in the UK, using three different but complementary datasets. These provide three views of the transition process at various stages in order to give a more longitudinal picture. Delayed entry to postgraduate study is common. The datasets provide an opportunity to investigate the extent to which social class background is associated with transition to postgraduate study, holding other factors constant and to examine whether parental background is associated with the timing of transition. Before describing these datasets in greater detail and analysing the results obtained from them, I first review sociological thinking on the relationship between higher education, social mobility and social reproduction, together with the limited previous research on postgraduate education in particular.

## Higher education expansion and paradoxes of inequality

In the UK, access to higher education has enjoyed almost 20 years of sustained policy, research, and bipartisan political attention, beginning in earnest with the report of the Dearing committee (National Committee of Inquiry into Higher Education, 1997). Substantial funding has been directed towards the 'widening participation agenda' to encourage and support those from underrepresented social class backgrounds to enter higher education. A veritable industry has arisen around this activity, involving dedicated organisational units in higher education institutions, funding and regulatory agencies including the funding councils and the Office for Fair Access (in England), and philanthropic organisations such as the Sutton Trust and Brightside which arrange summer schools and other events. While explicit discussion of *social class* and how it is implicated in the inclusion and exclusion of individuals within higher education is largely confined to the sociological and higher education research literatures, state bodies have incorporated socio-economic measures into the monitoring and reporting of undergraduate participation. Thus data is collected about the occupational and educational backgrounds of university applicants and entrants, and there has been development of geo-demographic measures as proxies for socio-economic position.

A fairly clear picture has emerged about social class and access to first degrees. Measured using the official National Statistics Socio-economic Classification, which is based heavily on the Erikson-Goldthorpe-Portacero neo-Weberian schema (Rose and O'Reilly, 1997), those from working-class backgrounds have slightly increased their rate of entry to higher education in the UK from 29 per cent in 2002/03 to 33 per cent in 2013/14.[4] This has occurred in the face of consecutive changes to undergraduate student funding in much of the UK, which were widely predicted to exclude and discourage working-class students from attending university (e.g. Wilkins *et al.*, 2013). Indeed, successive large-scale studies have provided robust evidence that a substantial part of the social class difference in overall rates of university entry in Britain can be accounted for by prior attainment (Chowdry *et al.*, 2013; Rees *et al.*, 2015). Doubts have been expressed regarding the extent to which these improvements in access result from the deliberate interventions and policies pursued, or instead would have happened anyway given improvements in working-class attainment in upper secondary education (National Audit Office, 2008). However, it remains the case that there are more working-class students entering full-time undergraduate study in the UK in 2015 than there were in 2005 or 1995.[5]

Uplift in university participation rates for previously underrepresented social classes should not be naively accepted as an indication of progress towards the reduction of social class inequality (see Tholen and Brown chapter in this volume). While those from disadvantaged backgrounds have made progress in absolute terms, they continue to experience a stubborn *relative* inequality. In other words, while those from lower social class backgrounds are more likely to enter higher education than in the past, so are their more advantaged peers. The chance of a lower-class young person entering higher education *relative to* those from a 'service class' (i.e. professional/managerial) background have shifted little (Boliver, 2011). Indeed large-scale cross-national comparative sociological research has suggested this relative social class inequality is persistent across time and place (Shavit and Blossfeld, 1993; Pfeffer, 2008). Although recent research has found some weakening in the persistence of educational inequality across generations (Breen *et al.*, 2009), class differences remain substantial.

The latest research on changes across cohorts in the UK finds no reduction in class inequalities if educational levels are treated as relative rather than absolute (Bukodi and Goldthorpe, 2015). This ties in to earlier influential sociological work which identifies a process of *credential inflation*, whereby the worth of higher levels of educational attainment is devalued by their ubiquity (Collins, 1979). This is seen close-up in the recognition by today's UK undergraduates that 'a degree is not enough' (Tomlinson, 2008) to secure 'graduate-level' employment, accompanied with various strategies to achieve distinction (Bathmaker *et al.*, 2013). This process implicates postgraduate education too: it has been argued that social class inequalities in education are *maximally maintained*, meaning they tend to 'pass up' to the next educational level once access to the preceding level approaches saturation (Raftery and Hout, 1993). Put simply, as the bachelor degree becomes widespread, so holding a postgraduate qualification begins to confer distinct advantage.

Research on the British case suggests the theory of maximally maintained inequality pertains to first-degree participation (Boliver, 2011). The same study also confirms a further trend of *effectively maintained inequality* (Lucas, 2001). Here, horizontal stratification across a level results in unequal value for different qualifications. In the UK this relates in particular to the value of degrees from different kinds of higher education institution. Sociologists have demonstrated clear social class differences in the type of higher education institutions entered, the experience within those institutions and the outcomes which result (Bathmaker *et al.*, 2013; 2016; Sullivan *et al.*, 2014; Wakeling and Savage, 2015).

A further process identified by educational sociologists appears contradictory to the preceding trends in social class inequality in higher education. This is the tendency for *background effects to decline* (Hansen, 1997; Mare, 1980). That is, at each successive educational transition the measured association between social class background and progression reduces in strength. Inequalities in attainment by socio-economic background are strongest in earliest transitions and weakest with transition into higher education. Since typically each successive educational transition is conditional on the previous one, it is perhaps not surprising that this trend is observed. In technical terms, we can say that the unobserved heterogeneity in educational transitions reduces with each transition; that is, students who remain in education are increasingly alike in their characteristics, regardless of background characteristics (Mare, 1980), including social class.

These various tendencies make postgraduate education something of a potential paradox for sociologists of education and social stratification. The expansion of higher education points to pressure for educational inequalities to pass up to the next level, so that increasing access to first degrees for lower class groups will open up inequalities in access to postgraduate study. On the other hand, the waning effect of background characteristics in later educational transitions generates the opposite expectation – social class inequalities should be reduced or even minimal for postgraduate entry. The findings presented in this chapter about social class inequalities in access to postgraduate study provide an empirical basis for adjudicating these rival claims.

## Previous research

There is surprisingly little research on inequalities in access to postgraduate study (Wakeling and Kyriacou, 2010). Research has shown that doctoral students are less likely to be from a working-class background than first degree holders in France (Ministère de l'Éducation Nationale et le Ministère de l'Enseignement Supérieur et de la Recherche, 2008), Germany (Bornmann and Enders, 2004), Finland (Silvennoinen and Laiho, 1994) and Australia (James *et al.*, 2008). However, these studies did not investigate whether such differences could be explained by differential attainment or other 'legitimate' factors. In contrast, in his seminal study of educational transitions, Mare (1980) found that background effects were not important in access to postgraduate study in the USA. This finding was confirmed by Stolzenberg (1994), but later research found the emergence of socioeconomic inequalities in entry to doctorates and 'first professional' postgraduate study (Mullen *et al.*, 2003; Zhang, 2005). Torche (2011) found background effects declined or even disappeared among holders of first degrees, only to re-emerge among holders of higher degrees. This gives a U-shaped pattern of background effects, which are accompanied by horizontal stratification across institution and field of study. English research has shown little social class effect in *immediate* transition to postgraduate study (HEFCE, 2013).

An interesting feature of transition to postgraduate study in the UK, which contrasts with earlier transitions, is the extended time period over which it can occur. Prior transitions are typically immediate, following completion of the previous educational level or after only a short delay. Differences in both the likelihood of making the transition to postgraduate study *and* in the timing of that transition by social class should therefore indicate the extent to which postgraduate qualifications figure as part of class strategies for reproducing advantage.

## Data and methods

### Datasets

In order to investigate access to postgraduate education, I utilise several different datasets about UK-domiciled first-degree graduates and postgraduates. This comprises an admittedly eclectic mix of population data, very large-scale surveys and smaller surveys collected at different points over the past decade or so and capturing data about transition to postgraduate study after shorter or longer periods post-first-degree. However, the key point is that messages across these various different datasets about patterns of transition to postgraduate study and social class are consistent.

The first – and most important – group of datasets cover 'first destination' data for the academic years 2001/02–2004/05 and 2010/11–2011/12 inclusive (pooled $N \approx 1.423$ million; annual $N$ in range 209,959–284,979). The data is sourced from the Higher Education Statistics Agency (HESA) Student Record and Destination of Leavers from Higher Education surveys. The first of these is an effectively obligatory annual census of all students in publicly funded higher education institutions in the UK. The second is an annual survey of students successfully completing their programme approximately 6 months to 1 year following graduation which attempts 100 per cent coverage.[6] Destinations include employment, further study, unemployment, travelling and so on. With these data it is possible to compare the background characteristics of those making different transitions, including from a first degree into postgraduate study.

As noted above however, most of those who enrol in postgraduate study have not entered directly from a first degree. This *is* a common transition, but does not represent the path taken by the majority. Only 42,650 (or 40 per cent) of the 107,210 new postgraduates in 2011/12 had completed a first degree in 2010/11 (Wakeling and Hampden-Thompson, 2013). There is a distinct possibility that later transitions to postgraduate study (i.e. those not contiguous with first-degree graduation) exhibit different patterns of background effect. The second dataset (the HESA Destination of Leavers from Higher Education (DLHE) Longitudinal Study) gives a slightly different view of postgraduate transitions, which will help to address this possible shortcoming of the first dataset. It comprises a follow-up survey of a small sample of 2002/03 graduates some 3 years after their graduation ($n = 12,766$) to ascertain their later (as opposed to first) destination. Data was weighted for nonresponse.

The final dataset considered was based on surveys undertaken as part of a project funded under the Higher Education Funding Council for England's Postgraduate Support Scheme (PSS) in which there were six participating universities, all members of the most selective (and typically most prestigious) 'Russell Group' of universities located in the north of England. This examined the background, post-graduation activities and motivations of graduates from the six universities who completed first degrees in 2009 or 2012.[7]

Taken together, these datasets provide a view of the process of transition to postgraduate study at two distinct points post-first degree: immediately after graduation; and approximately 3 or 4 years after graduation. Inevitably these datasets give a somewhat partial view of the process in general, being sample surveys of varying size and relating to particular points in historical time. By using the datasets in concert, however, one can gain a more holistic view of entry to postgraduate degrees than is possible with a single study.

## Key variables

I focus in this chapter on two particular outcomes: enrolment on a taught higher degree (i.e. a master's degree in the British system); or on a higher degree by research (typically a doctorate).[8] Enrolment is first of all computed across social class background, with a range of other salient variables subsequently added to the analysis, including gender, first-degree institution, first-degree attainment and subject discipline.

*Social class.* The measure used across the datasets is the UK's official category, the National Statistics Socio-Economic Classification (NS-SEC).[9] Essentially NS-SEC is an occupationally based scheme closely based on the neo-Weberian system developed by Goldthorpe and colleagues in the Nuffield Mobility Studies and after (Rose and O'Reilly, 1997). While some sociologists have been critical of the capacity of occupationally based class schemes to adequately characterise class in contemporary Britain, occupational schemes remain a practical choice for large-scale survey work (Crompton, 2008; Savage *et al.*, 2013). In any case, the NS-SEC scheme is ubiquitous in large-scale British research on social class and higher education participation.

*First-degree institution.* There is a well-established link between first-degree institution attended and progression to postgraduate study in the UK (House, 2010; Wakeling, 2009). The datasets used here all identify graduates' first degree institution (although in the case of the 2009/2012 alumni surveys this is limited to six particular universities). In the UK, as elsewhere, there is long-standing and growing stratification of institutions based on age, research profile, reputation and so on (Boliver, 2015; Halsey, 1992; Shavit *et al.*, 2007), with 'mission groups' emerging formed of similarly profiled institutions. These groups correspond to empirical regularities in the distribution of students by attainment, social class (Boliver, 2011), ethnicity and so on. To aid parsimony, a simplified categorisation of institution has been adopted. This divides the institutions into the Russell Group; other universities which attained university status prior to 1992 (often called 'old' universities in the UK); universities which obtained their status in 1992 or afterwards (all of which were formerly polytechnics or higher education colleges); higher education colleges which teach a range of subjects; and specialist higher education colleges (something of a mixed group, comprising *inter alia*, medical schools, art and design institutions, performing arts colleges and so on).

*Subject discipline.* This is an important confounding factor in this analysis because there is substantial variation in rates of progression to postgraduate study across different areas of higher education (Wakeling, 2009). Whereas those graduating in Medicine and Dentistry invariably immediately enter medical practice, Law graduates in the UK very often enter directly onto a postgraduate legal practice course to complete their professional training. In some disciplines, notably Chemistry, there is a high rate of progression to a research degree (this being an established route into both academic research and industrial chemistry). Furthermore, previous research has shown both the structured pattern of the distribution of students from different social class background across subject disciplines and the variation in outcomes for graduates along similar lines (Jackson *et al.*, 2008; van de Werfhorst and Luijkx, 2010; Wakeling, 2009). If graduates from different socio-economic backgrounds are unevenly distributed across subject disciplines, different gross enrolment rates in postgraduate study may simply be an artefact of this selection into subject areas.

*Degree classification.* As noted earlier, educational transitions are strongly conditioned by attainment. British degrees are typically graded using a four or five point scale, with first, upper second, lower second and third class honours and sometimes a 'pass' grade (without honours). Entry to a research degree usually requires at least upper second class honours and many masters programmes have a similar requirement, especially for recent graduates. As social class is known to be associated with attainment, including at degree level (HEFCE, 2015), it follows that unequal rates of progression to postgraduate study after a first degree could simply reflect differences in attainment (primary effects, in Boudon's [1974] terms).

We might charitably consider first-degree classification and discipline as 'legitimate' academic factors[10] influencing progression to postgraduate study. It would be naïve to believe they are perfect indicators of merit, but finding that they influence access to higher degrees would not perhaps be a direct cause for concern.

## Results

Looking first at overall rates of progression to higher degrees by social class and gender for UK-domiciled graduates, Figure 10.1 shows clear, consistent, although not especially stark, differences by social class background.[11] With just a few exceptions, the general pattern is for those from NS-SEC Class 1 to have the highest rate of progression, followed by Class 2, then Class 3, then the other classes. Women have lower rates of progression to higher degrees than men, particularly for entry to research degrees. These patterns appear constant over time, being robust to changes in overall participation rates. While there does not seem to be any evidence of the social class gap closing, neither does it seem to be growing. The notable exception is men's rate of progression to research degrees in 2009/10 and 2010/11 where Class 1 and Class 4–7 graduates diverge, but this represents two data points only. More generally, in comparison to class differences seen at earlier levels of the education system, this gap between Class 1 and Class 4–7 male graduates is relatively small. For instance, "in 2013 almost 90 per cent of boys from higher managerial and professional homes passed five GCSEs[12] but less than 50 per cent from homes where the parents were in routine employment or not in employment at all did so" (Mills, 2015, p. 3). However, it is worth noting that, while the absolute rate of progression to research degrees was low for both men and women across the classes, there are clear differences by gender, with men much more likely than women to make this transition.

The *relative* differences by social class are also substantial. To illustrate this, Table 10.1 extracts selected rates of progression to postgraduate study for 2010/11. This shows that around one in every 50 female graduates from Class 1 progressed to a higher degree by research, compared to only one in 100 for female Class 4–7 graduates. Male graduates from Class 4–7 were as likely as Class 1 women to progress to a research degree, but Class 1 men progressed at the rate of 1 in 25. So while entry to a research degree was a rare graduate destination overall, Class 1 male graduates were four times more likely to make this transition than Class 4–7 women in 2010/11.

In Figure 10.2, we can see the results from the other datasets, which give us a slightly more longitudinal view of entry to higher degrees. Taking the HESA Longitudinal Study first, we see for the 2002/03 graduates that the social class differential has increased over time for both men and women. Caution is needed in that the graduates in this dataset are a subsample of those in the DLHE 2002/03 data and hence there could be sampling error in these estimates. On the face of it however, the social class gap in entry to higher degrees has widened over time, whichever statistic we use to compare change. Thus the gap between Class 1 and Class 4–7 graduates in entry to taught higher degrees has increased for men (women) from 1.6 (2.1) percentage points to 5.7 (7.7). This means that the odds of a Class 1 man or woman entering a higher degree compared to a Class 4–7 man or woman are about 24 per cent (36 per cent) higher close to graduation, but increase to 64 per cent (115 per cent) higher approximately 3 years after graduation. In simple terms, class inequalities seem to increase in line with time from graduation. While those from Class 1 almost double their rate of entry to

*Table 10.1* Selected rates of immediate transition to higher degree by research by social class and gender, 2010/11

| Graduate group | Progression rate (%) | Approximates to . . . | Odds ratio |
| --- | --- | --- | --- |
| Male, Class 1 | 4.0 | 1 in 25 | 1.00 |
| Female, Class 1 | 1.9 | 1 in 50 | 2.15 |
| Male, Class 4–7 | 2.1 | 1 in 50 | 1.94 |
| Female, Class 4–7 | 1.1 | 1 in 100 | 3.75 |

Note: progression rates taken from Figure 10.1c and 10.1d

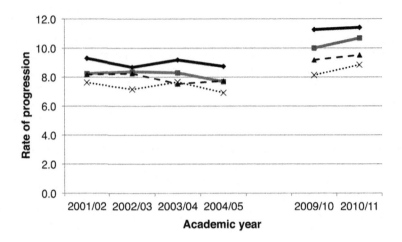

*(a) Taught higher degree – men*

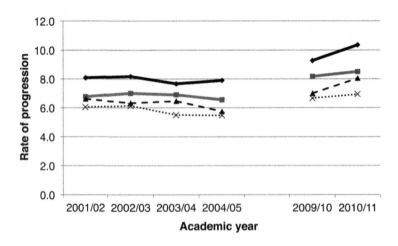

*(b) Taught higher degree – women*

*Figure 10.1* UK-domiciled graduates' rates of immediate progression to higher degrees by social class and gender, 2001/02–2010/11

Source: HESA First Destinations Survey 2001/02–2002/03; Destination of Leavers from Higher Education Survey 2003/04–2004/05 and 2009/10–2010/11.

Note: data weighted to adjust for survey attrition; y axis varies between qualification types to aid interpretation of social class differentials.

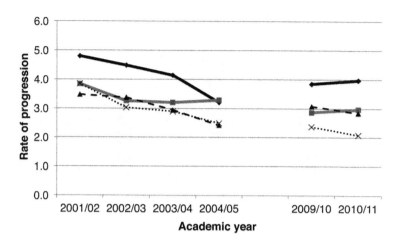

*(c) Higher degree by research – men*

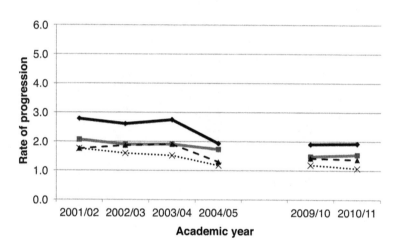

*(d) Higher degree by research – women*

──►── Higher managerial and professional occupations

──■── Lower managerial and professional occupations

─ ▲ ─ Intermediate occupations

···×··· Other occupations

*Key*

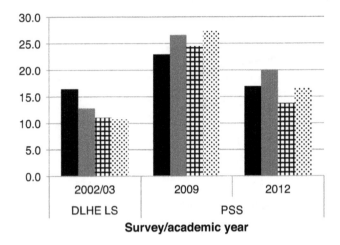

*(a) Taught higher degree – men*

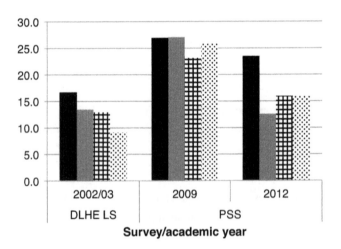

*(b) Taught higher degree – women*

*Figure 10.2* Per cent of UK-domiciled graduates reporting previously or currently studying for a higher degree by social class and gender, selected datasets

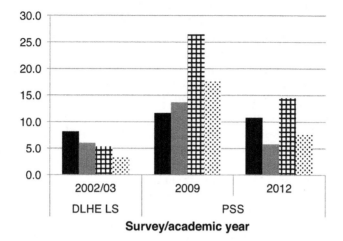

*(c) Higher degree by research – men*

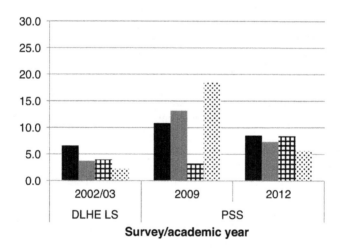

*(d) Higher degree by research – women*

taught higher degrees, the rate of increase for Class 4–7 graduates is only around half that. These findings are consistent with HEFCE's analysis (2013) using neighbourhood participation quintiles instead of social class. A similar pattern is seen in the data for higher degrees by research.

The dataset from the group of 'PSS' universities, also shown in Figure 10.2, gives a somewhat different picture. While those who graduated in 2009 were more likely, by the point of the survey in 2014, to have begun or completed a higher degree, there is no consistent or obvious pattern by social class evident. This is a slightly smaller dataset than the HESA Longitudinal Study. Nevertheless, the relative homogeneity of the six participating universities suggests that *within this set of institutions*, there does not appear to be any clear relationship between social class and progression to postgraduate study.

This disappearance of the association between social class and entry to post-graduate study seen in the group of research-intensive universities in the PSS study suggests that some – potentially most – of the aggregate social class differences observed could be down to compositional factors. That is, differences may appear because of the differential distribution of graduates from different social classes across institutions, subject disciplines and differential degree-level attainment across social classes. It is well known that rates of entry to postgraduate study are higher for those attaining a 'good' degree (in the British system, upper-second or first-class honours). Similarly graduates from older universities, especially those in the self-selecting Russell Group, tend to have higher rates of entry to higher degrees, as do those from particular disciplines (HEFCE, 2015; Wakeling, 2009; Wakeling and Hampden-Thompson, 2013). We also know that graduates from the most advantaged social classes are more likely to achieve a good degree (Zimdars *et al.*, 2015), are overrepresented among Russell Group institutions (Boliver, 2013) and in certain subject disciplines (National Audit Office, 2008). All things being equal then, even if there were no social class differences in progression to higher degrees within an institution group or for graduates with the same attainment level, we would still find overall social class differences in progression.

Focussing on the DLHE data on taught higher degrees we do indeed see compositional patterns appear to account for some of the overall social class differences in progression. Figures 10.3 and 10.4 show the results, aggregating 2009/10 and 2010/11, and men and women. There is a clear monotonic decline across degree classifications: the higher the degree classification, the higher the probability of progressing to a taught higher degree. However, within each degree classification there is also a monotonic decline across social class. Holding attainment constant then, there remain social class differences. Figure 10.3 is remarkable in its neatness though: Class 4–7 graduates are more likely to progress to a taught higher degree than Class 1 graduates with the next highest level of attainment, and so on. Thus a Class 4–7 graduate with an upper second class honours degree is only slightly more likely to progress immediately to taught postgraduate study than a Class 1 graduate with lower second class honours.

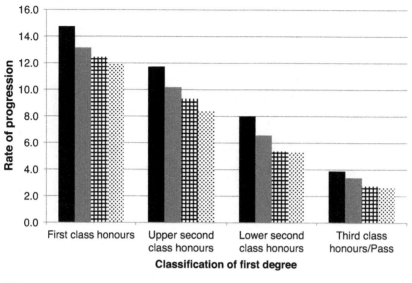

*Figure 10.3* Rate of progression by UK-domiciled first-degree graduates to taught higher degree, by social class and first-degree classification, 2009/10–2010/11

Source: DLHE 2009/10–2010/11.

Figure 10.4 presents similar results, substituting first degree classification with the type of institution attended for the first degree. The more prestigious, research-intensive and selective institutions – the Russell Group and the (now defunct) 1994 Group – have far higher rates of progression to taught higher degree study than the groups representing 'post-1992' universities such as Million+ and Guild HE. While Class 4–7 graduates of Russell Group universities have a substantially higher rate of progression than a Class 1 graduate from University Alliance, Million+ and GuildHE institutions, within each institution group there is the familiar social class difference in progression rates.

To investigate the contribution of these various 'academic' factors to the social class differential in progression to taught postgraduate study, logistic regression models were fitted to the DLHE dataset to investigate immediate progression to taught higher degree study for 2009/10 and 2010/11 graduates. A baseline model containing only gender and social class was fitted first, with the resulting odds ratios plotted as the dark grey bars in Figure 10.5. This shows, as already seen in Figure 10.1, that there are gender and social class differences in this transition. Here, male graduates and Class 1 graduates represent the reference categories (taking values of 1.0 for the odds ratio). Adding a set of controls for age, subject

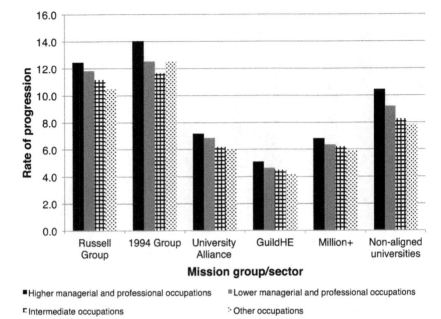

■ Higher managerial and professional occupations    ▪ Lower managerial and professional occupations

Intermediate occupations    ⁚ Other occupations

*Figure 10.4* Rate of progression by UK-domiciled first-degree graduates to taught higher
degree, by social class and first-degree institution type, 2009/10–2010/11

Source: DLHE 2009/10–2010/11.

discipline, degree classification and first-degree institution type produces the
change in odds ratios shown by the lighter grey portion of the bars. Controlling
for these factors thus accounts for some, but not all of the social class differences
– most in the case of Class 4–7 graduates – but very little of the gender difference.

## Discussion

What are the implications of these findings? Regarding the theory of declining
background effects, the results suggest that they do indeed decline in the
transition to postgraduate study in the UK. That is, socio-economic background
has a less apparent influence on whether an individual makes the transition to
postgraduate study, holding other factors constant, than is the case in earlier
transitions. Taking a longitudinal view of the transition, however, suggests that
rather than declining in a consistent way, the weakest effects of socio-economic
background are felt in the earliest transition, with something of a *revival* of effects
at later points. This is a somewhat novel finding. It extends, back into entry to
postgraduate study itself, Torche's (2011) observation of re-emerging income
inequalities by class background among advanced degree holders. It also contrasts

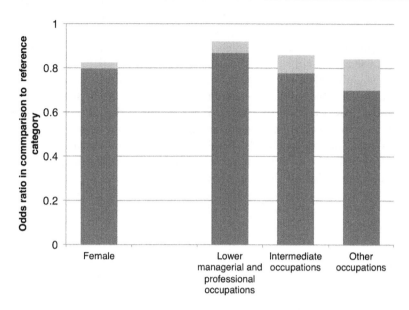

*Figure 10.5* Selected odds ratios from logistic regression model to predict progression to taught higher degree by UK-domiciled first-degree graduates 2009/10–2010/11

Source: DLHE 2009/10–2010/11.

Notes: dark grey bar represents odds ratios from baseline model containing gender and social class only. Light grey bar represents change to odds ratio for given category in subsequent model, which includes controls for subject discipline and classification of first degree, first degree institution type and age (parameters not shown). Full results are available from the author on request. Reference categories are male; and Higher managerial and professional occupations respectively. All coefficients are statistically significant.

with some previous findings for other countries about the continuation of class differences in postgraduate transitions (e.g. Mullen *et al.*, 2003, Triventi, 2013).

How might we understand the patterns observed? The results could be interpreted as showing relatively meritocratic *early* transitions to postgraduate study, with those most able and motivated to continue to able to do so, regardless of social class background. A potential explanation for the subsequent re-emergence of class inequalities is that in the face of 'credential inflation' and a glut of first-degree graduates, those from more advantaged backgrounds are better able to use postgraduate study as a means to circumvent underemployment. That is, among those entering the labour market with only a first degree, some graduates will be unable to find employment commensurate with their graduate status. A possible remedy open to them is to undertake further study, providing an edge in the competition for jobs. In such a situation, there is less advantage in immediate entry to a higher degree if suitable graduate employment opportunities are immediately available; however, when such a position is not obtained, further study becomes more attractive. Certain graduates will be able to call on family resources to support further study, which in the UK is largely unregulated and without large-scale public support. Others will not.

On a slightly different note, the evident importance of first-degree institution in progression to postgraduate study may mask the effects of socio-economic background An optimistic interpretation is that social class has only marginal effects on immediate transition to postgraduate study within university groups. If there is sorting into different kinds of institution on initial entry to higher education, the lack of further social class differences in later transitions may mean that one's later educational fate is set at an early stage. More pessimistically then, this suggests processes of institutional stratification are intensifying the separation into *de facto* tracks, despite formal equality across UK universities, with consequences for social mobility.

## Conclusion

This chapter has investigated whether the effect of background characteristics – specifically social class – continue to decline in importance at the ultimate educational transition into postgraduate study. The association of class background with immediate progression to postgraduate study is relatively slight once academic attainment and tracking factors are taken into consideration. However, the association appears to strengthen among those delaying their transition, with class differentials re-emerging when graduates are surveyed a few years after graduation. These findings suggest that comparative investigation of access to postgraduate study and of inequalities introduced through the timing of educational transitions would be fruitful developments for the sociology of educational inequality.

## Acknowledgements

I owe thanks to the anonymous respondents of the online surveys. Some of the data used in this chapter was collected as part of projects conducted collaboratively with Gillian Hampden-Thompson and Sally Hancock. Data from the First Destinations Survey 2001/02, DLHE 2002/03–2004/05, Student Record 2001/02–2004/05 and DLHE Longitudinal Study 2002/03 are reproduced by permission of the Higher Education Statistics Agency Limited. HESA cannot accept responsibility for any inferences or conclusions derived from the data by third parties. Thanks to Nicole Tieben, Peter Rudd and Adél Pásztor for their comments on an earlier version of this chapter. This work was supported by the Higher Education Academy Centre for Sociology, Anthropology and Politics, (grant number PG05–13); the Political Studies Association; the University of York; the Economic and Social Research Council (grant number PTA-030–2003–01311); and the Higher Education Funding Council for England (grant number G0166).

## Notes

1 There were just over 200,000 higher education students in 1960, compared to over 300,000 UK-domiciled postgraduates in 2013/14 (sources: Wakeling, 2009; and HESA Student Record 2013/14 respectively).

2 In the Labour Force Survey for July–September 2014, fewer than five per cent of those born before 1960 held a higher degree.

3 A notable exception is *The Big Bang Theory*, although technically the characters in that show have already completed postgraduate study.

4 Source: HESA performance indicators, Table T1a, available at www.hesa.ac.uk/pis/urg (accessed 19 October 2015). Figures refer to young entrants (under 21).

5 It is difficult to identify precise numbers of working-class students for any given year due to changes in definitions of social class and the reference population used in different official statistics over time. Using young entrants to full-time undergraduate study in the UK, we can see that 28.2 per cent of entrants were from NS-SEC groups 4–7 in 2004/05 ($N$ = 200,410); and 33.0 per cent in 2014/15 ($N$ = 254,210). NCIHE (1997, Table 1.3) reports 28.1 per cent of intake from Registrar General Social Classes IIIM, IV and V in 1995 but gives no denominator. However the Age Participation Index for 1995 is reported by NCIHE (1997, Table 1.1) as 15.1 per cent, compared to 20.3 per cent (Bolton, 2010, p. 10). Notwithstanding concerns about missing social class data (Gorard, 2008; Harrison and Hatt, 2009), it is evident that the *number* of working-class students has increased over time, even if their proportion has been more resistant to change, with around one in four undergraduates having fathers in manual occupations across the period 1920–1960 (CHE, 1963, cited in Bolton, 2010, p. 4).

6 The DLHE survey typically attains around 85 per cent response, meaning destination data is missing for some graduates. Data reported in this paper have been adjusted to account for nonresponse and missingness – full details are available in Wakeling (2009), Chapter 5.

7 Full details of the surveys are given in Hancock, Wakeling, and Hampden-Thompson (2015).

8 It is possible to proceed from a first degree immediately to a doctorate in the UK, although this transition is increasingly less common, particularly outside the natural sciences.

9 DLHE 2001/02 and 2002/03 and the DLHE Longitudinal Study instead use Registrar General's Social Class. This has been recoded into NS-SEC categories following Heath *et al.* (2003).

10 There is also a case for treating first degree institution as a (limited) proxy for attainment. The more prestigious institutions have stiffer entry requirements and a stronger performance in the UK's Research Excellence Framework, suggesting that undergraduates in those institutions may be more academically inclined, and therefore perhaps more amenable to postgraduate study.

11 Social classes 4, 5, 6, and 7 have been collapsed together for this analysis. This is because (i) this is the convention adopted in official widening participation 'performance indicators' published by HESA; and (ii) because the absolute number of graduates in these groups is smaller. Class 2 is the largest single group in the graduate data, reflecting the size of this group in the general population and differential rates of entry to first degrees. Class 8 graduates have been excluded from the analysis. This is a small group within the datasets (e.g. for 2010/11, $n$ = 370).

12 The General Certificate of Secondary Education is a set of public examinations taken at age 16 by pupils in England, Wales, and Northern Ireland.

# References

Bathmaker, A.M., Ingram, N., and Waller, R. (2013). Higher education, social class and the mobilisation of capitals: recognising and playing the game. *British Journal of Sociology of Education*, *34*(5–6), 723–743.

Bathmaker, A-M., Ingram, N., Abrahams, J., Hoare, T., Waller, R., and Bradley, H. (2016). *Higher education, social class and social mobility: The degree generation*. Basingstoke: Palgrave MacMillan.

Boliver, V. (2011). Expansion, differentiation, and the persistence of social class inequalities in British higher education. *Higher Education*, *61*(3), 229–242.

Boliver, V. (2013). How fair is access to more prestigious UK universities? *British Journal of Sociology*, *64*(2), 344–364.

Boliver, V. (2015). Are there distinctive clusters of higher and lower status universities in the UK? *Oxford Review of Education*, *41*(5), 608–627.

Bolton, P. (2010). *Higher Education and Social Class*. House of Commons Library Standard Note SN/SG/620. Retrieved February 8, 2016 from http://dera.ioe.ac.uk/22802/1/SN00620.pdf

Bornmann, L., and Enders, J. (2004). Social origin and gender of doctoral degree holders – impact of particularistic attributes in access to and in later career attainment after achieving the doctoral degree in Germany. *Scientometrics*, *61*(1), 19–41.

Boudon, R. (1974). *Education, opportunity and social inequality*. New York: Wiley.

Breen, R., Luijkx, R., Müller, W., and Pollak, R. (2009). Non-persistent inequality in educational attainment: evidence from eight European countries. *American Journal of Sociology*, *114*(5), 1475–1521.

Bukodi, E., and Goldthorpe, J.H. (2015). Educational attainment – relative or absolute – as a mediator of intergenerational class mobility in Britain. *Research in Social Stratification and Mobility*, 43, 5–15.

Chowdry, H., Crawford, C., Dearden, L., Goodman, A., and Vignoles, A. (2013). Widening participation in higher education: an analysis using linked administrative data. *Journal of the Royal Statistical Society (Series A)*, *176*(2), 431–457.

Collins, R. (1979). *The credential society: An historical sociology of education and stratification*. New York: Academic Press.

Committee on Higher Education. (1963). *Report of the Committee on Higher Education [The Robbins Report]*. London: Her Majesty's Stationery Office (Cm. 2154).

Crompton, R. (2008). *Class and stratification* (Third edition). Cambridge: Polity.

Department for Business, Innovation and Skills (BIS). (2015). *Statistical first release. Participation rates in higher education: Academic years 2006/2007–2013/2014 (Provisional)*. London: BIS.

European Commission, Eurydice and Eurostat. (2007). *Key Data on Higher Education in Europe. 2007 Edition*. Brussels: Eurydice.

Gorard, S. (2008). Who is missing from higher education? *Cambridge Journal of Education*, *38*(3), 421–437.

Gorard, S., Adnett, N., May, H., Slack, K., Smith, E., and Thomas, L. (2007). *Overcoming the barriers to higher education*. Stoke-on-Trent: Trentham Books.

Halsey, A.H. (1992). *Decline of donnish dominion: The british academic professions in the twentieth century*. Oxford: Clarendon Press.

Hancock, S., Wakeling, P., and Hampden-Thompson, G. (2015). *Technical Supplement to the Understanding the Student strand report*. University of York, Department of Education.

Hansen, M.N. (1997). Social and economic inequality in the educational career: do the effects of social background characteristics decline? *European Sociological Review*, *13*(3), 305–321.

Harrison, N., and Hatt, S. (2009). Knowing the 'unknowns': Investigating the students whose social class is not known at entry to higher education. *Journal of Further and Higher Education*, *33*(4), 347–357.

Heath, A.F., Martin, J., and Beertens, R. (2003). Old and new social class measures: A comparison. In D. Rose, and D.J. Pevalin (Eds.), *A researcher's guide to the national statistics socio-economic classification*. London: Sage, 226–243.

Higher Education Funding Council for England (HEFCE). (2013). *Trends in transition from first-degree to postgraduate study: Qualifiers between 2002–03 and 2010–11*. Bristol: HEFCE.

Higher Education Funding Council for England (HEFCE). (2015). *Differences in degree outcomes: Key findings*. Bristol: HEFCE.

Higher Education Statistics Agency (HESA). (2015a). *Higher education student enrolments and qualifications obtained at higher education providers in the United Kingdom 2013/14 (SFR 210)*. Cheltenham: HESA.

Higher Education Statistics Agency (HESA). (2015b). *Statistical First Release: Destinations of Leavers from Higher Education in the United Kingdom for the academic year 2013/14 (SFR217)*. Cheltenham: HESA.

House, G. (2010). *Postgraduate Education in the United Kingdom*. Oxford: Higher Education Policy Institute and The British Library.

Jackson, M., Luijkx, R., Pollak, R., Vallét, L-A., and van de Werfhorst, H.G. (2008). Educational fields of study and the intergenerational mobility process in comparative perspective. *International Journal of Comparative Sociology*, *49*(4–5), 369–388.

James, R., Bexley, E., and Maxwell, L. (2008). *Participation and equity: A review of the participation in higher education of people from low socioeconomic Backgrounds and Indigenous people*. Canberra: Universities Australia.

Lindley, J., and Machin, S. (2013). *The postgraduate premium: Revisiting trends in social mobility and educational inequalities in Britain and America*. London: The Sutton Trust.

Lucas, S. R. (2001). Effectively maintained inequality: Education transitions, track mobility, and social background effects. *American Journal of Sociology*, *106*(6), 1642–1690.

Mare, R.D. (1980). Social background and school continuation decisions. *Journal of the American Statistical Association*, *75*(370), 295–305.

McCulloch, A., and Thomas, L. (2013). Widening participation to doctoral education and research degrees: a research agenda for an emerging policy issue. *Higher Education Research and Development*, *32*(2), 214–227.

Mills, C. (2015). CSI 11: Is Class Inequality at KS4 decreasing? Centre for Social Investigation, Nuffield College, Oxford. Retrieved November 28, 2016 from http://csi.nuff.ox.ac.uk/wp-content/uploads/2015/03/CSI_11_Class_Inequalities.pdf

Ministère de l'Éducation Nationale et le Ministère de l'Enseignement Supérieur et de la Recherche. (2008). *Repères et Références Statistiques sur les Enseignements, la Formation et la Recherche (RERS 2008)*. Paris: Ministère de l'Éducation Nationale et le Ministère de l'Enseignement Supérieur et de la Recherche.

Moore, J., Sanders, J., and Higham, L. (2013). *Literature Review of Research into Widening Participation to Higher Education: Report to HEFCE and OFFA by ARC Network*. Bristol: Higher Education Funding Council for England.

Morgan, M. (2014) Patterns, drivers and challenges pertaining to postgraduate taught study: An international comparative analysis. *Higher Education Research and Development*, *33*(6), 1150–1165.

Mullen, A. L., Goyette, K.A., and Soares, J.A. (2003). Who goes to graduate school? Social and academic correlates of educational continuation after college. *Sociology of Education*, *76*(2), 143–169.

The National Committee of Inquiry into Higher Education. (1997). *Higher education in the learning society: The report of the national committee [The Dearing Report]*. London: Her Majesty's Stationery Office.

National Audit Office. (2008). *Widening participation in higher education: Report by the comptroller and auditor general*. London: The Stationery Office.

Pfeffer, F.T. (2008). Persistent inequality in educational attainment and its institutional context. *European Sociological Review*, *25*(5), 543–565.

Raftery, A.E., and Hout, M. (1993). Maximally maintained inequality: Expansion, reform and opportunity in Irish higher education, 1921–1975. *Sociology of Education*, *66*(1), 41–62.

Rees, G., Taylor, C., Davies, R., Drinkwater, S., Evans, C., and Wright, C. (2015). *Access to Higher Education in Wales: A Report to the Higher Education Funding Council for Wales*. Cardiff: Wales Institute of Social and Economic Research, Data & Methods.

Rose, D., and O'Reilly, K. (Eds.), (1997). *Constructing classes: Towards a new social classification for the UK*. Swindon: ESRC/ONS.

Savage, M., Devine, F., Cunningham, N., Taylor, M., Li, Y., Hjellbrekke, J., Le Roux, B., Friedman, S., and Miles, A. (2013). A new model of social class: findings from the BBC's Great British Class Survey experiment. *Sociology*, *48*(1), 219–250.

Shavit, Y., Arum, R., and Gamoran, A. (2007). *Stratification in higher education: A comparative study*. Stanford, CA: Stanford University Press.

Shavit, Y., and Blossfeld, H.P. (1993). *Persistent inequality: Changing educational attainment in thirteen countries*. Boulder, CO: Westview Press.

Silvennoinen, H., and Laiho, I. (1994). The hierarchy of academic education, gender and social background. *Scandivanian Journal of Educational Research*, *38*(1), 15–32.

Stolzenberg, R.M. (1994). Educational continuation by college graduates. *American Journal of Sociology*, *99*(4), 1042–1077.

Sullivan, A. (2014). Social origins, school type and higher education destinations. *Oxford Review of Education*, *40*(6), 739–763.

Tomlinson, M. (2008). "The degree is not enough": Students' perceptions of the role of higher education credentials for graduate work and employability. *British Journal of Sociology of Education*, *29*(1), 49–61.

Torche, F. (2011). Is a college degree still the great equalizer? Intergenerational mobility across levels of schooling in the United States. *American Journal of Sociology*, *117*(3), 763–807.

Triventi, M. (2013). Stratification in higher education and its relationship with social inequality: a comparative study of 11 European countries. *European Sociological Review*, *29*(3), 489–502.

van de Werfhorst, H.G., and Luijkx, R. (2010). Educational field of study and social mobility: Disaggregating social origin and education. *Sociology*, *44*(4), 695–715.

Wakeling, P. (2009). Social class and access to postgraduate education in the UK: A sociological analysis. PhD thesis. University of Manchester.

Wakeling, P. (2010a). Inequalities in access to postgraduate education: a comparative review. In E. Goastellec (Ed.), *Understanding Inequalities in and by Higher Education*. Rotterdam: Sense, 61–74.

Wakeling, P. (2010b). Is there such a thing as a working-class academic? In Y. Taylor (Ed.), *Classed Intersections: Spaces, Selves, Knowledges*. Farnham: Ashgate, 35–54.

Wakeling, P., and Hampden-Thompson, G. (2013). *Transition to higher degrees across the UK: An analysis of regional, institutional and individual differences*. York: Higher Education Academy.

Wakeling, P., and Kyriacou, C. (2010). *Widening participation from undergraduate to postgraduate research degrees: A research synthesis*. Swindon: ESRC and NCCPE.

Wakeling, P., and Savage, M. (2015). Entry to elite positions and the stratification of higher education in Britain. *Sociological Review*, *63*(2), 290–320.

Wilkins, S., Shams, F., and Huisman, J. (2013). The decision-making and changing behavioural dynamics of potential higher education students: The impacts of increasing tuition fees in England. *Educational Studies*, *39*(2), 125–141.

Zhang, L. (2005). Advance to graduate education: the effect of college quality and undergraduate majors. *The Review of Higher Education*, *28*(3), 313–338.

Zimdars, A., Sabri, D., Moore, J., Sanders, J., Jones, S., and Higham, L. (2015). *Causes of differences in student outcomes*. Bristol: HEFCE.

# Chapter 11

# Participation in paid and unpaid internships among creative and communications graduates

## Does class advantage play a part?

*Wil Hunt and Peter Scott*

## Introduction

With the expansion of higher education (HE) and the polarisation of jobs, the graduate labour market is increasingly competitive and positional (Ware, 2015a, b; Brown, 2013; Brown, Power, Tholen, and Allouch, 2014). Along with rising tuition fees and student debt, graduates can no longer rely on achieving the same graduate wage premium as previous generations (Conlon and Patrignani, 2011). The mere possession of a degree no longer guarantees access to the best jobs (Bathmaker, Ingram, and Waller, 2013; Tomlinson, 2008). Additional markers of achievements and potential ability thus become increasingly important in improving the individual's employability and life chances. Undertaking an internship has emerged as one possible strategy to try to gain advantage (Perlin, 2012). However, the consequences of internships for levelling the playing field for entry into competitive careers are still contested and unclear. Graduate internships are seen as a way of improving employability, but there remain concerns about social mobility and access to opportunities (Lawton and Potter, 2010; Milburn, 2009). Internships can potentially be seen as extending – maybe intensifying – the mechanisms of socio-economic reproduction already evident in the educational system itself.

Some insightful qualitative studies, discussed below, have provided partial support for both sides of this 'dual view' of internships. However, up until now there has been little in the way of quantitative research looking at the extent of the practice, or patterns of participation. Much of the quantitative research on 'internships' has been carried out outside of the UK and has focused on what might be more commonly referred to as 'work placements' carried out while studying (e.g. Callanan and Benzig, 2004; Divine, *et al.*, 2007; Wilson 2012; Saniter and Siedler, 2014). Meanwhile, quantitative studies of graduate internships in the UK have predominantly been limited to government backed schemes that may not be representative of the wider practice (e.g. Mellors-Bourne and Day, 2011; Oakleigh Consulting Ltd. and CRAC, 2011). The Futuretrack study provided some quantitative evidence on the wider practice of graduate internships, finding participation higher among graduates from higher tariff and specialist institutions, and among graduates from subjects such as: architecture, building and planning; social studies; law; languages; linguistics and classics; historical and philosophical studies; and creative arts and design (Purcell *et al.*, 2012). However, examination of participation patterns related to social class remains unstudied.

This chapter addresses questions about participation in graduate internships through data from a survey of creative and communications graduates several years after graduation from a subsample of UK universities. The data forms part of a wider study of the role of graduate internships in the labour market (Hunt, forthcoming). Our chapter looks at participation in paid and unpaid internships and explores the role of social class in determining who has access to different types of early labour market opportunities. The research finds that the factors related to participation in internships largely reflect measures of social and cultural capital, and of both 'hard' and 'soft' currencies of employability. Hard currencies defined as including various kinds of credentials such as educational credentials and work experiences, and soft currencies comprised of more nebulous qualities such as personal skills, appearance, drive, self-confidence, and charisma (Brown and Hesketh, 2004). Degree classification, institution prestige, and previous placement experience increase chances of doing an internship. Also, while those from less advantaged backgrounds were no less likely to do unpaid internships *ceteris parabus*, advantaged graduates were more able to access the better, paid opportunities. Social class therefore continues to stamp its imprint on the role of internships in the transition from education to employment. This finding challenges oft-held assumptions in the literature that access to paid internships is unproblematic by showing that, even after removal of financial barriers and controlling for grades and institution prestige, those from disadvantaged backgrounds still struggle to secure the better opportunities. Patterns of class advantage and disadvantage in access to internships run deeper than simple questions of geography and affordability.

## Internships and patterns of (dis)advantage

In this section, we review the competing claims to be found in the literature about the relationship between internships, their declared benefits and social mobility. Positive accounts suggest that internships can be routes for young workers to gain valuable work experience, develop industry specific skills and knowledge, increase participants' confidence and employability, allow employers to try out new job entrants and lead to positive employment outcomes (Chartered Institute of Personnel and Development [CIPD], 2010; Mellors-Bourne and Day, 2011; Oakleigh Consulting Ltd and CRAC, 2011). In a precarious labour market where it increasingly falls to individuals to develop, maintain and display employability, internships may represent a manifestation of an 'audition' or 'try before you buy' culture (Smith, 2010; Thompson, 2013; Siebert and Wilson, 2013). Internships may be a vehicle to help young workers improve their social networks, and could thus contain the potential to overcome deficits in social capital, but this would rely on access to them being open and equal (Gateways to the Professions Collaborative Forum [GPCF], 2013).

However, some argue that internships can operate as a further barrier to social mobility. One of the main purported benefits of internships is that they can help interns 'get a foot in the door' in their careers. This would imply that those lucky enough to be able to secure and complete an internship are at an advantage in the job market over those who have not done so, although this is by no means proven. In turn, this depends on the assumption that the content of all internships is of similar value. The literature indicates this is not the case, with some interns engaged in routine and mundane work with little developmental benefit (Lawton and Potter, 2010: Milburn, 2009; Frenette, 2013; Tholen and Brown this volume). Some have suggested that the best internships are those in which employers invest the most time and effort, and are more likely to be formal in nature and paid (Milburn, 2009; Gerada, 2013; CIPD, 2015). This implies that some opportunities may be more beneficial than others. Evidence suggests that the extent to which internships are paid or unpaid varies depending on subject area or industry with internships in government and administration, manufacturing and engineering, and retail and logistics being more likely to be paid, while unpaid internships are more prevalent in media-related, creative and cultural industries, and the voluntary sector (Mellors-Bourne and Day, 2011). However, it is generally assumed that in cases where internships are paid and recruitment is more formal, access will tend to be fairer.

Much of the literature concentrates on equality of opportunity to engage in internships. Some commentators argue disadvantaged groups are being excluded for financial, geographical, and informational reasons. First, where internships are unpaid or low paid it is likely that aspirants from disadvantaged backgrounds are unlikely to be able to forgo wages for any considerable length of time, whereas those from more affluent backgrounds are more likely to be able to rely on their parents for support (Milburn, 2009; Lawton and Potter, 2010). Although there is a paucity of quantitative evidence on this, the aforementioned policy reports, and some qualitative studies (e.g. Siebert and Wilson, 2013; Shade and Jacobson, 2015; Leonard *et al.*, 2016), have highlighted access as a potential problem. This may be the case in glamorous or attractive sectors in particular, where competition is fierce, such as media, fashion, politics and the creative industries (Milburn, 2009; Lawton and Potter, 2010; Shorthouse, 2010; Mellors-Bourne and Day, 2011; Oakleigh Consulting Ltd and CRAC, 2011). Second, the same authors note that accessibility problems are compounded because internship opportunities are often geographically focussed, with many key sectors centred around London and South East England, making internships more costly for candidates from farther afield who cannot commute from the parental home. Third, informational barriers mean those from lower socio-economic groups are less likely to have the social networks that more privileged graduates have to enable them to find out about and access opportunities, and help understand the qualities employers look for in interns (Milburn, 2009).

Citing the *Skillset survey on performing arts 2005*, a report from the Department of Culture, Media and Sport (DCMS) noted that access to unpaid internships in the creative industries may not be evenly distributed across socio-economic groups, claiming that 'for too many at the moment, the chance to start a career in the creative industries means moving to London, working for free or knowing someone who can get you a foot in the door' (DCMS, 2008: 7), findings echoed in Holgate and Mackay's (2007) study of the London audio-visual freelance labour market. Thus, in many cases internship opportunities, and particularly unpaid ones, may not be openly advertised, leading to an 'informal economy' where access to opportunities is based on personal contacts rather than the ability or potential of applicants, further limiting access and fairness (Milburn, 2009).

Moreover, studies have shown that being able to envisage a future career in the creative industries as plausible and then accessing the opportunities that will help make it happen depends upon the complex interplay of class- and place-based habitus (Allen and Hollingworth, 2013; Allen, *et al.*, 2013). In Allen and colleagues' studies, middle-class young people and students were able to draw on their social, economic, and cultural capital in order to learn about and access opportunities in the creative industries, whereas their working-class counterparts faced barriers in terms of the information, finances and networks.

The above policy and qualitative studies have provided partial support for both positive and negative accounts of graduate internships. However, as noted, little generalisable quantitative research looks at the extent of the practice, or at patterns of participation, which would help to fill out the gaps in the patchy picture of small-scale qualitative studies. This chapter aims to address this gap. The chapter draws on data from a survey of creative and communications graduates – two subject areas identified in the literature where internships are becoming commonplace and where concerns have been raised about openness of access and social mobility – in order to extend knowledge about participation in paid and unpaid internships, and examine the role of social class in determining who is able to access different types of opportunities. The survey forms part of a wider PhD study that incorporated quantitative data from primary and secondary sources in order to investigate participation in and access routes to graduate internships, as well as perceived benefits and labour market outcomes (Hunt, forthcoming).

## Method: the CGCS survey

The Creative Graduates Careers Survey (CGCS) was an original survey of creative art and design (CAD) and mass communications and documentation (MCD) graduates from UK higher education institutions (HEIs). Internships were found to be particularly prevalent in these two areas in a separate analysis of HESA data carried out earlier in the research project, and reflect sectors where concerns have been raised in the literature in relation to internships and social mobility. The survey methodology is detailed in Hunt (forthcoming). However, a summary of the key points is as follows.

The survey was a sample survey of graduates from twelve HEIs representing a good geographical spread, broadly reflecting UK provision in CAD and MCD. Graduates were sampled using a systematic probability sampling method. The eligibility criteria were:

Full-time or part-time first degree graduates from courses in the CAD and MCD subject areas (Joint Academic Coding System codes W and P); UK or EU domiciled; From the 2007/08, 2009/10 or 2011/12 graduating cohorts;

These criteria were chosen to: minimise double selection where graduates stayed on for further study, reduce non-response from non-EU overseas students returning home after studying, and allowed time for graduates' careers to have developed while minimising crossover with the Destinations of Leavers from Higher Education Longitudinal survey (LDLHE).

8,467 sampled graduates were emailed directly by their institution between September and December 2014 and invited to complete the survey online. 616 eligible responses were received, representing a response rate of 7.4 per cent after adjusting for any known undelivered emails. However, the true adjusted response rate is likely to be higher, as some of the larger institutions were unable to provide data on unreceived emails.

The questionnaire was loosely based on one used in the *Creative Graduates, Creative Futures* project (Ball, Pollard, and Stanley, 2010; Hunt, Ball, and Pollard, 2010), on which the lead author worked, as it was found useful for capturing the diverse work and career patterns of creative and mass communications graduates. The instrument was developed during summer 2014 and covered: course details and eligibility; current and previous work situation; details of up to three current jobs; perceived benefits of internships and other forms of employment; career satisfaction; and personal characteristics (including age, gender, ethnicity, region of domicile and parental experience of HE). Parental experience of HE was included as a measure of whether graduates were from a 'traditional' or 'non-traditional' background and as a proxy for social class (Roberts, 2010). Studies have shown that first generation HE students tend to have less favourable experiences of university, are more likely to need to work while studying, more likely to run into difficulty and are less likely to engage in extra-curricular activities (Johnson *et al.*, 2009; Purcell *et al.*, 2009; Purcell *et al.*, 2012), and thus can arguably been seen as an indicator of relative disadvantage.

When comparing to available HESA data (Table 0.1) the sample was broadly reflective of the wider population of CAD and MCD graduates in terms of: gender, age, ethnicity, domicile and subject area. However, there was a slight overrepresentation of graduates with a first class degree, and of graduates from the 2011/12 cohort. Also, despite a reasonably even geographical spread of institutions, there are slight overrepresentations of graduates who studied in Wales and Scotland, and under-representations of graduates who studied in London and the North of England. While it is worth noting these differences when considering aggregate figures, the multivariate analysis presented later in this chapter controls for these when examining the relative influence of different factors on participation in internships.

*Table 11.1* Sample profile and population comparison

|  | Sample, % | Population comparison, %* |
|---|---|---|
| **Gender** | | |
| Male | 33.9 | 40.0 |
| Female | 65.9 | 60.0 |
| Base, N | 615 | 531,555 |
| **Age at graduation** | | |
| Under 25 | 79.5 | 85.0 |
| 25–29 | 9.4 | 8.3 |
| 30+ | 11 | 6.7 |
| Base, N | 616 | 136,330 |
| **Ethnicity** | | |
| White | 93 | 86.0 |
| Black | 1.1 | 3.4 |
| Asian | 2.8 | 4.0 |
| Mixed/other | 2.4 | 4.2 |
| Unknown | 0.7 | 2.4 |
| Base, N | 616 | 129,250 |
| **Domicile** | | |
| UK | 89.7 | 94.8 |
| Other EU | 10.3 | 5.2 |
| Base, N | 602 | 136,330 |
| **Cohort** | | |
| 2007/08 | 24.4 | 31.0 |
| 2009/10 | 26.5 | 32.2 |
| 2011/12 | 49.2 | 36.5 |
| Base, N | 616 | 144,290 |
| **Classification of degree** | | |
| 1st | 27.3 | 14.2 |
| Upper second | 51.3 | 50.2 |
| Lower second | 18.8 | 27.9 |
| 3rd/pass | 2.1 | 6.0 |
| Unclassified | 0.5 | 1.7 |
| Base, N | 616 | 144,290 |
| **Subject area** | | |
| CAD | 83.4 | 78.0 (82.0) |
| MCD | 16.6 | 22.0 (18.0) |
| Base, N | 602 | 144,290 |
| **Region of HEI** | | |
| Scotland | 8.9 | 5.0 (3.0) |
| Wales | 16.9 | 5.5 (14.3) |
| NE/NW/Y+H | 14.9 | 22.3 (15.4) |
| Mid/East of Eng | 20.9 | 21.7 (21.0) |
| London | 13 | 21.1 (23.0) |
| SW/SE | 25.3 | 23.1 (23.3) |
| NI | – | |
| Base, N | 616 | 144,290 (20,535) |

Base: All respondents (N= 616)
Notes: Figures in parenthesis ( ) are for participating HEIs only
* Population comparison figures are UK and EU first degree qualifiers from CAD and MCD subjects in 2007/08, 2009/10 and 2011/12 combined, except for gender which are UK and EU first degree students from CAD and MCD subjects in 2009/10 and 2011/12 and undergraduate students in 2007/08. Population data for ethnicity is UK domiciled only.
Source: *Creative Graduates' Careers Survey* and HESA Student Record 2007/08, 2009/10 and 2011/12 Copyright Higher Education Statistics Agency Limited 2009, 2010 and 2013. HESA cannot accept responsibility for any inferences or conclusions derived from the data by third parties.

## All internships are not equal

The survey results shed new light on internship pathways, how graduates experience internships, and internships' role in influencing patterns of transferring class advantage. Crucially, not all internships are equal: clear differences emerged between paid and unpaid internships. We begin by investigating the incidence of different types of internship, and how graduates experienced them, in this section. The following section looks at differences in patterns of participation in internships.

The survey was designed to enable distinction between paid and unpaid internships because evidence from earlier DLHE analysis revealed notable differences between paid and unpaid internships in terms of motivations, skills level required and access routes (Hunt, forthcoming). In the DLHE analysis, compared to unpaid internships, paid internships were: more likely to fit with graduates' career plans, were more likely to require graduates' HE qualification (rather than it just being an advantage), and were relatively more likely to be accessed through formal routes (as opposed to personal contacts). The reverse was true for unpaid internships. Access routes were also found to vary by social class, with those from more privileged backgrounds relatively more likely to have found out about their internship through personal contacts than their less privileged counterparts. However, the relationship between social class, grades and internship type was complex: graduates appeared to rely on personal contacts either where they were able to (e.g. because they had the social and economic capital to do so) or in cases where they had to (e.g. because their grades meant that they would find it harder to secure internships through more formal routes).

By 2–6 years after graduation one quarter (25 per cent) of CGCS respondents reported having engaged in at least one internship since finishing their first degree. Of these, nearly half (46 per cent) had engaged in more than one and two-thirds (66 per cent) had done at least one unpaid internship. Nearly all respondents appear to have finished with internships by the time of the survey, with only 2 per cent currently doing an internship.

The differences between paid and unpaid internships identified in the analysis of DLHE data were carried through in the CGCS data. When asked how useful overall their internships had been in the development of their career so far, the majority of those with internship experience (92 per cent) indicated that they had been at least quite useful, with 61 per cent reporting that they had been very useful (Figure 11.1). However, those who had only engaged in unpaid internships were much less likely to say their internship(s) had been very useful than those who had only engaged in paid internships (51 per cent compared to 70 per cent)[1]. Caution should be taken in drawing conclusions based on comparison of two naturally occurring groups, such as these, due to differences in characteristics between those who have only done paid or unpaid internships. However, these findings suggest a difference in quality between the two types of experience, as confirmed by respondents' answers to a subsequent section asking about perceived

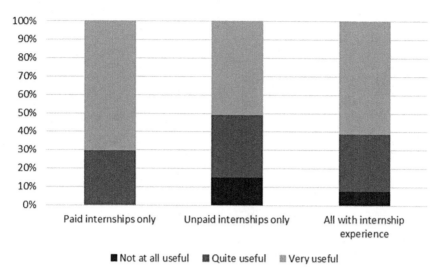

*Figure 11.1* Perceived usefulness of paid and unpaid internships

benefits of different types of employment. All graduates were asked to rate on a scale of one to five how well they believed different types of employment or working developed different career-related attributes. These comprised industry specific knowledge and skills, professional networks, general career development, and ability to be creative or develop their own ideas – something particularly important to creative graduates (Ball *et al.*, 2010). The different types of working/ employment they were asked to rate were: permanent employment (in their chosen sector), self-employment, their own creative work/developing a professional portfolio, paid internships, and unpaid internships.

In all cases unpaid internships were rated lower than paid internships and the lowest of all the types of employment listed. Paid internships were rated relatively highly in relation to most career-related attributes, although in all cases a permanent job in the industry was rated highest, except for allowing the ability to be creative and develop one's own ideas where own portfolio work and self-employment were rated highest (Figure 11.2). These findings support the view that paid internships may be more beneficial than unpaid internships in terms of development and helping develop a career, although they also suggest that a permanent job is preferred.

Taken together, the findings for the perceived usefulness and developmental benefits of graduate internships suggest clear differences between paid and unpaid internships in terms of career development. In addition, while internships, both paid and unpaid, tend to be rated as useful and are felt to have developmental benefits, permanent employment is still perceived as preferable in terms of most aspects of career development rated here, although self-employment and portfolio

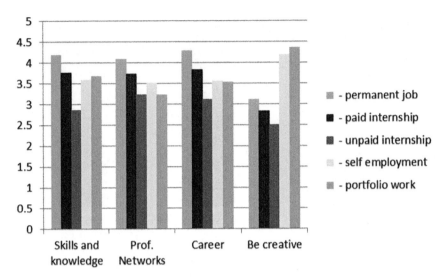

*Figure 11.2* Mean ratings for each employment type for each area of development

work are generally felt to be the best for allowing creativity and the ability to develop one's own ideas. These findings appear to support the idea that paid and more formal internships may be more likely to be beneficial for individuals in terms of development and employability (CIPD, 2015; Milburn, 2009; Gerada, 2013). They also raise questions about the utility of unpaid internships for individuals and about whom the practice really benefits. They have implications for questions of social mobility, as access to the better opportunities was not found to be equal, as discussed next.

## Patterns of participation

Having established that there are some substantial differences between paid and unpaid internships in terms of their potential usefulness for individuals, it is important to examine patterns of participation in order to assess any contours of advantage and disadvantage. In addition, while some have suggested that internships have the potential to help overcome class disadvantage in terms of a lack of networks needed to access the best jobs (Grugulis and Stoyanova, 2012; GPCF, 2013), others have argued that lacking the social capital needed to access internships combined with the lack of financial resources needed to work for low or no pay for any significant period of time may in fact have the opposite effect, presenting a barrier to social mobility and reinforcing socio-economic reproduction (e.g. Milburn, 2009; Lawton and Potter, 2010).

Findings from CGCS appear to support the latter view. It is often assumed that paying interns will help make internships more accessible to those from less advantaged backgrounds due to the removal of financial barriers and because paid opportunities may be more likely to involve more formal recruitment practices (Milburn, 2009; Gerada, 2013; Leonard *et al.*, 2016). This did not prove so for the creative and mass communications graduates surveyed. At a bivariate level, graduates whose parents were themselves graduates were more likely to have engaged in a graduate internship, paid or unpaid. However, when controlling for other factors (including grades and reputation of institution) using multivariate analysis the relationship between parental experience of HE and participation in internships was only found to be statistically significant for paid, but not unpaid, internships. In other words, after controlling for grades, institutional reputation and other factors it is the paid, and not the unpaid, internships that those from more disadvantaged backgrounds struggle to secure. Given the apparent differences in perceived benefits between paid and unpaid internships, this raises questions about potential disadvantages in access to the more beneficial opportunities. Those from more advantaged backgrounds, who arguably have better networks and social capital, appear more able to secure paid internships than colleagues from less privileged backgrounds: the latter are faced with less favourable, unpaid positions or doing something else.

The approach taken in this analysis was first to examine bivariate patterns of association between participation in paid and unpaid internships and a range of personal and study characteristics implicated in the literature as being related to internships, but then to control for other variables using a multivariate analysis technique. In this case multinomial logistic regression analysis was used to explore which personal and study characteristics increased the chances of graduates having engaged in either a paid or unpaid internship since graduation relative to not having done an internship. Although certain personal and study characteristics feature in the literature as being related to participation in internships, these relationships have either not been demonstrated empirically or have failed to adequately control for extraneous factors. Therefore, as the analysis was essentially exploratory, a backwards elimination model selection procedure was used in order to explore which variables were significantly related to increased propensity to undertake a graduate internship (Field, 2009).

Variables entered in the model were selected either where they have been linked with participation in internships from previous research discussed above, or where an association was found in the secondary DLHE analysis (Hunt, forthcoming). These were: age at time of graduation; ethnicity; gender; parental experience of HE; region of domicile; classification of degree; broad subject area of degree; graduating cohort; previous participation in work placements, or internships, while studying; and a measure of reputational value associated with the HEI attended based on recent league table scores[2]. An interaction term for classification of degree by parental experience of HE was also included in the analysis as the aforementioned DLHE analysis suggested that there may be differential patterns of access for graduates from different social backgrounds depending upon their grades. Full details of the method followed are provided in Hunt (forthcoming).

The results of the multivariate analysis can be seen in Table 11.2 and Table 11.3[3]. The results of multivariate analysis broadly reflected bivariate patterns of participation with age, grades, league table score, previous work placement experience, cohort and parental experience of HE all found to be related to participation in internships. All else being equal, propensity to have engaged in an internship (paid or unpaid) was higher if graduates were younger; from an institution with a higher league table score; achieved a higher degree grade.

Graduates with work placement experience were more likely than those without to have done an unpaid, but not a paid, internship (all else being equal), as were graduates from the 2009/10 graduating cohort relative to those from other cohorts. The former finding perhaps suggests that those who are able to afford to work unpaid while studying can continue to do so after graduation; the latter suggests the practice of unpaid internships may have peaked for 2009/10 graduates. Although the coefficient for the relationship between work placements while studying and paid internships was not quite statistically significant at the $\alpha = .05$ level, the relationship was in a positive direction.

Most importantly, parental experience of HE was also found to be significantly related to participation in internships, albeit not necessarily in the direction literature predicts. Having a parent who was a graduate increased the odds of having a *paid* internship by nearly double relative to not having a graduate parent (*ceteris parabus*). However, the relationship between parental experience of HE and propensity to engage in an *unpaid* internship was not statistically significant. This finding contradicts the oft-held view that unpaid internships exclude those from less advantaged backgrounds as, among respondents to this survey at least, those from such backgrounds were no less likely to engage in an unpaid internship than their more privileged counterparts after controlling for other factors.

Indeed, this was evident in bivariate patterns of participation (Table 11.4), which showed that graduates with no parental experience of HE were less likely to engage in internships in general (19 compared to 32 per cent) and paid internships in particular (nine compared to 17 per cent), although similar proportions had done unpaid internships only (11 per cent compared to 15 per cent). The fact that, even after controlling for differences in grades and league table score of institution, graduates from more advantaged backgrounds seem more able to access – arguably more beneficial – paid internships is concerning. It suggests that patterns of class advantage and disadvantage in access to internships run deeper than just questions of affordability and academic credentials. One possible explanation for this finding could be related to class differences in quality and levels of networks and social capital. However, the fact that in the analysis of DLHE data presented elsewhere (Hunt, forthcoming) it was unpaid internships, rather than paid ones, that were relatively more likely to be accessed through personal and family contacts complicates this analysis.

On the other hand, this apparent contradiction can be explained in a number of ways. First, in the DLHE analysis although paid interns were relatively less likely to be accessed via informal routes 17 per cent still found out about their internship through family and friends. Second, middle-class graduates were more likely than working-class graduates to use personal contacts to access internships regardless of whether they were paid or unpaid. Finally, even where recruitment is more formal, graduates from middle-class backgrounds may do better during application and in interview because they can present themselves more attractively to employers. Thus, the fact that more privileged graduates appear more able to access the more sought after paid internships may be an indicator of differences in social capital and/or the ability to 'play the game' and package themselves in a way that is attractive to employers, as also suggested by Brown and Hesketh (2004), Bathmaker *et al.* (2013) and other contributors to this volume (see e.g. chapters by Tholen and Brown and by Bradley and Waller).

By and large, however, the main factors found to be significantly related to participation in internships might be seen as reflecting practical considerations on the one hand (e.g. older graduates may be less inclined or less able to engage in internships due to financial considerations or family responsibilities, which are themselves overlain by social class dimensions) and reflecting measures of social and cultural capital on the other (i.e. grades, institutional reputation and social class). The results suggest that, while traditional credentials, or 'hard currencies' of employability, such as grades, university attended and previous work experience help graduates in the labour market, other factors related to social class still influence patterns of inclusion and exclusion.

*Table 11.2* Iteration history for backwards elimination multinomial logistic regression

| Iteration | Variable | Change in -2LI | Df | Sig. |
|---|---|---|---|---|
| | Intercept only (initial -2LI) | 777.427 | | |
| 0 | All variables | 108.093 | 30 | <.0005 |
| 1 | Classification of degree by parental experience of HE | 1.573 | 4 | 0.814 |
| 2 | Sex | 3.96 | 4 | 0.411 |
| 3 | Ethnicity | 2.37 | 2 | 0.306 |
| 4 | Region of domicile | 2.998 | 2 | 0.223 |
| 5 | Broad subject area | 3.568 | 2 | 0.168 |
| | Change in -2LI if removed | | | |
| | Age at graduation | 20.207 | 2 | <.0005 |
| | Whether did a work placement at uni | 9.894 | 2 | 0.007 |
| | Cohort | 8.499 | 4 | 0.075 |
| | Classification of degree | 14.602 | 4 | 0.006 |
| | Parental experience of HE | 4.904 | 2 | 0.086 |
| | League table score of HEI | 20.621 | 2 | <.0005 |

Base: Working age respondents in work (N= 538)

*Table 11.3* Propensity to participate in paid internships or unpaid internships only compared to non-participation (final model)

| | β | Standard error | Odds ratio | Lower bound 95% C.I. | Upper bound 95% C.I. |
|---|---|---|---|---|---|
| **Unpaid internships only** | | | | | |
| Intercept | −6.473** | 2.03 | | | |
| Age at graduation | −0.115** | 0.049 | 0.891 | 0.81 | 0.981 |
| **Work placement experience** | | | | | |
| Placement | 0.831** | 0.282 | 2.296 | 1.321 | 3.99 |
| No placement | 0b | . | . | . | . |
| **Graduating cohort** | | | | | |
| 2007/08 | 0.569+ | 0.344 | 1.766 | 0.899 | 3.469 |
| 2009/10 | 0.721* | 0.329 | 2.056 | 1.078 | 3.919 |
| 2011/12 | 0b | . | . | . | . |
| **Classification of degree** | | | | | |
| 1st | 1.27** | 0.468 | 3.561 | 1.423 | 8.912 |
| 2:1 | 0.934* | 0.443 | 2.544 | 1.068 | 6.06 |
| 2:2/3rd | 0b | . | . | . | . |
| **Parental experience of HE** | | | | | |
| HE parent | 0.190 | 0.284 | 1.209 | 0.693 | 2.11 |
| No HE parents | 0b | . | . | . | . |
| League table score of HEI | 0.077** | 0.023 | 1.08 | 1.033 | 1.13 |
| **Paid internships (inc. some with paid and unpaid internships)** | | | | | |
| Intercept | −4.798* | 2.263 | | | |
| Age at graduation | −0.18* | 0.073 | 0.835 | 0.724 | 0.963 |
| **Work placement experience** | | | | | |
| Placement | 0.464+ | 0.28 | 1.59 | 0.919 | 2.751 |
| No placement | 0b | . | . | . | . |
| **Graduating cohort** | | | | | |
| 2007/08 | −0.429 | 0.367 | 0.651 | 0.317 | 1.335 |
| 2009/10 | −0.201 | 0.342 | 0.818 | 0.418 | 1.598 |
| 2011/12 | 0b | . | . | . | . |
| **Classification of degree** | | | | | |
| 1st | 1.123* | 0.478 | 3.075 | 1.204 | 7.853 |
| 2:1 | 1.091* | 0.441 | 2.977 | 1.254 | 7.068 |
| 2:2/3rd | 0b | . | . | . | . |
| **Parental experience of HE** | | | | | |
| HE parent | 0.624* | 0.286 | 1.866 | 1.065 | 3.268 |
| No HE parents | 0b | . | . | . | . |
| League table score of HEI | 0.080** | 0.022 | 1.083 | 1.037 | 1.132 |

Base: Working age respondents in work (N= 538)
Note: R^2= .160 (Cox and Snell), .206 (Nagelkerke), .117 (McFadden). Model $\chi^2(16)$= 93.624, p< .0005.
Coefficient significant at $\alpha$ = +.1, *.05, **.01.

*Table 11.4* Participation in paid and unpaid internships by parental experience of HE

| | Previous internship experience, % | | | | | |
| --- | --- | --- | --- | --- | --- | --- |
| | No internships | Paid only | Paid and unpaid | Unpaid only | Total, % | Total, N |
| Parental experience of HE | | | | | | |
| Parents did not study at HE | 80.5 | 5.9 | 2.9 | 10.6 | 100 | 339 |
| Parent studied at HE | 68.5 | 11.6 | 5.1 | 14.9 | 100 | 276 |
| All respondents | 75.2 | 8.4 | 3.9 | 12.5 | 100 | 616 |

Base: All respondents (N = 616)

## Discussion and implications

In an increasingly competitive and positional labour market internships are thought to help interns improve their employability by providing relevant work experience and helping develop skills, knowledge and networks. However, there are concerns that not all graduates are able to profit from these purported benefits either due to financial considerations or deficits of networks and social capital. This chapter uses data from a survey of creative and mass communications graduates to provide generalisable quantitative evidence on graduate internships. We looked at the prevalence of paid and unpaid internships among graduates in two subject areas where the practice is thought to have become commonplace and uncovered differences in the perceived benefits. We also investigated patterns of participation in internships and explored whether some graduates are being excluded from some types of internships.

The first major finding is that internships were common among CAD and MCD graduates: around one in four reported having had at least one internship since leaving university. There was some evidence of 'serial internships', with close to half of those with internship experience reporting having undertaken more than one. However, most had finished engaging in internships by 2 years after graduation.

A second noteworthy finding is that unpaid internships appear to be more prevalent than had been thought previously, at least among CAD and MCD graduates. This is significant in view of increased recent scrutiny by HM Revenue and Customs and the Low Pay Commission of 'bogus' unpaid internships where the relationship of intern to employer is more akin to that of 'worker' than genuine volunteer. Previous estimates have suggested that around one-third of internships across all sectors are unpaid (CIPD, 2010; Mellors-Bourne and Day, 2011; Sutton Trust, 2014). However, two-thirds of creative and communication graduates surveyed reporting internships indicated that at least one had been unpaid. This figure reinforces findings of the analysis of DLHE data carried out as part of the wider study where around two-thirds of CAD and MCD interns were unpaid 6 months after graduating (Hunt, forthcoming). However, it is perhaps unsurprising that unpaid internships are so common among such graduates. Qualitative studies indicate a certain level of acceptance among creative aspirants that getting into the sector is likely to involve working for free as a 'rite of passage', or 'paying your dues' (McLeod, O'Donohoe, and Townley, 2011; Siebert and Wilson, 2013; Shade and Jacobson. 2015). Creative and media graduates may be particularly vulnerable to exploitation and self-exploitation in this respect given their commitment and drive to be creative (Ball et al., 2010; Hunt et al., 2010), and in light of the glamour, desirability and competitiveness that characterise the sector and its geographical centres (Hesmondhalgh, 2010; Allen and Hollingworth, 2013).

The prevalence of unpaid internships in these sectors is particularly concerning, considering the clear differences found between paid and unpaid internships, with unpaid internships viewed as less beneficial in terms of skills, networks and career development. Comments from informants in Allen et al.'s (2013) study suggested that in some cases unpaid student work placements, when carried out for prestigious employers, are held in high esteem among employers because they signify commitment to the industry. Evidence presented here and in the wider study on which it is based appears to contradict that assumption to some extent: unpaid internships were consistently rated as less beneficial in terms of developing employability and appeared to have little benefit in terms of labour market outcomes (Hunt, forthcoming). However, the current study did not distinguish between unpaid internships undertaken for prestigious employers and those carried out for other employers, which are likely to be far more numerous. In addition, there are good reasons to expect that unpaid 'work placements' carried out before graduation may be more beneficial than unpaid internships carried out after. Findings from the Futuretrack study showed that, although unpaid work carried out while studying improved labour market outcomes, unpaid work after graduation led to less favourable outcomes (Purcell et al., 2012). Similarly, in the wider study from which this analysis is drawn, while work placements and paid internships had a positive effect on pay and chances of having a graduate level job, unpaid internships did not (Hunt, forthcoming). Furthermore, evidence suggests some employers use university work placements as a low-risk recruitment tool, rather than just a means of providing students with useful experience (Pollard et al., 2015). This may not necessarily be true in the case of unpaid internships.

With the differences between paid and unpaid internships in mind and, given the prevalence of unpaid internships, it becomes increasingly important that access to the best opportunities is open and fair. However, this does not always happen. Our third main finding shows participation in internships, especially paid ones, remains moulded by social class. This deserves further consideration as it is often assumed, either explicitly or implicitly, that *un*paid internships rather than paid ones present the barrier to social mobility. While it is often noted that networks and social capital also play a part in access to internships, it is generally assumed that the removal of financial barriers and more transparent recruitment processes associated with paid internships makes access less problematic for those from less privileged backgrounds (e.g. Milburn, 2009; Lawton and Potter, 2010; Gerada, 2013; Leonard *et al.*, 2016). However, the findings presented here challenge that notion. The analysis shows that while educational credentials are a factor in accessing internships, social class still plays a significant part. And while those from less advantaged backgrounds were less likely to participate in internships in general, after controlling for other factors such as grades, institution reputation and prior placement experience it is the more beneficial, paid internships that they struggled to secure. Whereas, graduates with high levels of social and economic capital were more able to access the better, paid opportunities that are likely to be of more help in the graduate labour market.

From the survey data alone, it is not possible to say precisely why it is paid, rather than unpaid internships, that less advantaged graduates find it harder to access. However, findings from the wider study and literature provide some insights. First, it is likely that those from more advantaged backgrounds are deploying their dominant social and cultural capital in order to access the best opportunities. We have already noted how findings from the current survey and the DLHE analysis appear to show that paid internships are likely to be more prestigious and sought after, and a number of studies have shown how more privileged graduates are able to use their superior social and cultural capital in order to advantage themselves in the graduate labour market (Tomlinson, 2008; Bathmaker *et al.*, 2014; Brown *et al.* 2014;). In addition, qualitative studies provide examples of how having (or not having) the right personal and family networks was significant in securing internships and other opportunities, particularly in the creative industries (Lee, 2011; Allen and Hollingworth, 2013; Siebert and Wilson, 2013; Shade and Jacobson, 2015;). Second, a number of scholars have noted how middle-class graduates more readily recognise what employers are looking for and are more able to 'play the game' and package their 'self' in a way that will put them ahead of the competition (Bathmaker *et al.*, 2013; Brown and Hesketh, 2004). Third, it may be that employers in the sector, who are probably more likely to be middle-class themselves, may simply tend to recruit graduates that either reflect themselves or otherwise display middle-class dispositions and ways of being (Bourdieu, 1984). Finally, there may be some degree of agency involved, with more disadvantaged graduates being less likely to possess the class- and place-based habitus that enables them to see the more competitive paid opportunities as an option (Allen and Hollingworth, 2013).

In actuality, it is likely to be some combination of the above processes at work. Allen *et al.* (2013) describe how in order to construct and present an identity as an employable, 'ideal' creative worker depends upon having access to a range of unequally distributed resources, such as economic, social and cultural capital, and knowing how to display these in a way that aligns with broader institutional and social practices. In other words, creative aspirants must be able to accumulate and display the right experiences, tendencies and proclivities that fit in with dominant ways of being. When one considers also that those from more advantaged backgrounds are likely to fare better in the education system anyway, tending to go to more prestigious universities and to achieve better grades, then the practice of internships may act to exacerbate patterns of advantage and disadvantage, reinforcing patterns of socio-economic reproduction.

Some theorists have questioned the 'conventional' view of an increasingly meritocratic labour market, instead arguing that the labour market is increasingly positional and hierarchical (Tholen, 2012; Brown *et al.*, 2014; Ware, 2015a,b). The findings presented here support this latter 'alternative' view more than the former. Although academic and other credentials do appear to help in the graduate labour market it is clear that some hold more currency than others providing evidence of a hierarchy of opportunities. In addition, the fact that privileged graduates are more able to access the best opportunities even when controlling for grades and institutional reputation undermines the 'myth of meritocracy' – central to the conventional view – as it is clear that factors other than academic ability and credentials play a significant part. It would seem more advantaged graduates are still able to draw on their resources in order to maintain their privileged position in the labour market. Whether it is through social capital and access to better networks or a greater ability to 'play the game' and present themselves in a light that is more attractive to those offering internships (Brown and Hesketh, 2004; Bathmaker *et al.*, 2013), it would appear that class advantage persists. Thus, this research contributes to the growing body of literature that highlights the classed processes that persist in an increasingly competitive and positional labour market.

Concerns in existing literature about the roles that internships play in terms of access to certain sectors and social mobility are usually based on two assumptions: first, that internships (paid or unpaid) help graduates in the labour market and, second, that unpaid internships exclude disadvantaged graduates from some sectors. Our findings challenge this view on two levels. First, unpaid internships appear not to confer advantage, at least in the sectors we investigated; they are the 'consolation prize'. Second, it is paid rather than unpaid internships that disadvantaged graduates struggle to secure. This is particularly important, as there is emerging evidence to suggest that paid internships may be better than unpaid internships in terms of employability and developmental benefits. And therefore, it is the inequalities in access to these better, paid, opportunities – and arguably in the labour market more widely – that is the real problem for social mobility.

## Acknowledgements

This chapter is based on part of Wil Hunt's doctoral thesis, *Internships and the Graduate Labour Market*, submitted to the University of Portsmouth, September 2016. A considerably expanded discussion of this research can be found there. The assistance of the Higher Education Statistics Agency, the Council for Higher Education Art and Design and the participating HEIs is acknowledged. The authors remain responsible for the interpretation of the data.

## Notes

1 All differences between paid and unpaid internships highlighted in this section were statistically significant at the α =.05 level (for further details see Hunt, forthcoming).
2 League table score was computed based on the institution respondents attended by compiling and averaging the most recent data available for the relevant subject areas for each participating HEI from the Complete University Guide and the Guardian's University Guide.
3 Bivariate patterns of participation in internships can be found in Hunt (forthcoming).

## References

Allen, K., and Hollingworth, S. (2013). 'Sticky subjects' or 'cosmopolitan creatives'? Social class, place and urban young people's aspirations for work in the knowledge economy. *Urban Studies, 50*(3), 499–517.

Allen, K., Quinn, J., Hollingworth, S., and Rose, A. (2013). Becoming employable students and 'ideal' creative workers: Exclusion and inequality in higher education work placements. *British Journal of Sociology of Education, 34*(3), 431–452.

Ball, L., Pollard, E., Stanley, N., with Dumelow, I., Hunt, W., and Oakley, J. (2010) Creative Graduates Creative Futures. Council for Higher Education in Art and Design, Report 471. London: University of the Arts London.

Bathmaker, A., Ingram, N., and Waller, R. (2013). Higher education, social class and the mobilisation of capitals: Recognising and playing the game. *British Journal of Sociology of Education, 34*(5–6), 723–743.

Bourdieu, P. (1984). *Distinction: A social critique of the judgement of taste.* Translated by R. Nice. Cambridge: Harvard University Press.

Brown, P. (2013). Education, opportunity and the prospects for social mobility. *British Journal of Sociology of Education, 34*(5–6), 678–700.

Brown, P., and Hesketh, A. (2004). *The mismanagement of talent: Employability and jobs in the knowledge economy.* Oxford: Oxford University Press.

Brown, P., Power, S., Tholen, G., and Allouch, A. (2014). Credentials, talent and cultural capital: A comparative study of educational elites in England and France. *British Journal of Sociology of Education, 37*(2), 191–211.

Callanan, G., and Benzig, C. (2004). Assessing the role of internships in the career-oriented employment outcomes of graduates. *Education and Training, 46*(2), 82–89.

Chartered Institute of Personnel and Development (CIPD). (2010). *Internships: To pay or not to pay?* London: Chartered Institute of Personnel and Development.

Chartered Institute of Personnel and Development (CIPD). (2015). *Internships that work: A guide for employers.* London: Chartered Institute of Personnel and Development.

Conlon, G., and Patrignani, P. (2011). *The Returns to Higher Education Qualifications.* (BIS Research Paper No. 45). London: Department for Business, Innovation and Skills (BIS).

Department of Culture, Media and Sport (DCMS). (2008). *Creative Britain: New talents for the new economy.* London: DCMS.

De Vries, R. (2014). *Earning by Degrees Differences in the Career Outcomes of UK graduates.* Sutton Trust.

Divine, R.L., Linrud, J.K., Miller, R.H., and Wilson, J.H. (2007) Required internship programs in marketing: Benefits, challenges and determinants of fit. *Marketing Education Review, 17,* 45–52.

Field, A.P. (2009). *Discovering statistics using SPSS* (3rd ed.) London: Sage.

Frenette, A. (2013). Making the intern economy: Role and career challenges of the music industry intern. *Work and Occupations*, *40*(4), 364–397.

Gateways to the Professions Collaborative Forum (GPCF). (2013). *Common best practice code for high-quality internships*. London: Trades Union Congress.

Gerada, C. (2013). *Interns in the voluntary sector: Time to end exploitation*. London: Intern Aware and Unite the Union.

Grugulis, I., and Stoyanova, D. (2012). Social capital and networks in film and TV: Jobs for the boys? *Organization Studies*, *33*(10), 1311–1331.

Hesmondhalgh, D. (2010). User-generated content, free labour and the cultural industries. *Ephemera*, *10*(3–4), 267–284.

Holgate, J., and Mackay, S. (2007). *Institutional barriers to recruitment and employment in the audio visual industries: The effect on black and minority ethnic workers*. London: Working Lives Research Institute.

Hunt, W. (forthcoming*) Internships and the Labour Market*, PhD thesis submitted to University of Portsmouth.

Hunt, W., Ball, L., and Pollard, E., Khambhaita, P., Oakley, J., Brown, G., and Stanley, N. (2010). *Crafting futures: A study of the early careers of crafts graduates from UK higher education institutions*. Institute for Employment Studies, University of the Arts London and the Crafts Council.

Johnson, C., Pollard, E., Hunt, W., Munro, M., Hillage J., Parfrement, J., and Low, N.A. (2009). *Student Income and Expenditure Survey 2007/2008: English-domiciled students*. (DIUS Research Report RR0905). London: Department for Innovation, Universities and Skills (DIUS).

Lawton, K., and Potter, D. (2010). *Why interns need a fair wage*. London: Institute for Public Policy Research.

Lee, D. (2011). Networks, cultural capital and creative labour in the British independent television industry. *Media, Culture & Society*, *33*(4), 549–565.

Leonard, P., Halford, S., and Bruce, K. (2016). 'The new degree?' Constructing internships in the third sector. *Sociology*, *50*(2), 383–399.

McLeod, C., O'Donohoe, S., and Townley, B. (2011). Pot noodles, placements and peer regard: Creative career trajectories and communities of practice in the British advertising industry. *British Journal of Management*, *22*(1), 114–131.

Mellors-Bourne, R., and Day, E. (2011). *Evaluation of the graduate talent pool scheme. (BIS Research Paper number 28)*. London: Department for Business, Innovation and Skills (BIS).

Milburn, A. (chair). (2009). *Unleashing aspiration: Final report of the panel on fair access to the professions*. London: The Stationery Office.

Oakleigh Consulting Ltd, and CRAC. (2011). *Increasing opportunities for high quality higher education work experience*. London: Higher Education Funding Council England.

Perlin, R. (2012). *Intern Nation: How to earn nothing and learn little in the brave new economy*. London: Verso.

Pollard, E., Hirsh, W., Williams, M., Buzzeo, J., Marvell, R., Tassinari, A., and Ball, C. (2015). *Understanding employers' graduate recruitment and selection practices: Main report*. (BIS Research Paper NO. 231). London: Department for Business, Innovation and Skills (BIS).

Purcell, K., Elias, P., Atfield, G., Behle, H., Ellison, R., Hughes, C., and Tzanakou, C. (2009). *Plans, aspirations and realities: Taking stock of higher education and career choices one year on – Findings from the Second Futuretrack Survey of 2006 applicants for UK Higher Education. (HECSU Research Report).* Manchester: Higher Education Careers Services Unit (HECSU).

Purcell, K., Elias, P., Atfield, G., Behle, H., Ellison, R., Luchinskaya, D. and Tzanakou, C. (2012). *Futuretrack Stage 4: Transitions into employment, further study and other outcomes (Full Report).* (HECSU Research Report). Manchester: Higher Education Careers Services Unit (HECSU).

Roberts, K. (2010). Expansion of Higher Education and the Implications for Demographic Class Formation in Britain. *Twenty-First Century Society, 5*(3), 215–228.

Saniter, N., and Siedler, T. (2014). *Door opener or waste of time? The effects of student internships on labour market outcomes.* (IZA Discussion Paper No. 8141). Bonn, DE: Institute for the Study of Labor (IZA).

Shade, L.R., and Jacobson, J. (2015). Hungry for the Job: Gender, unpaid internships, and the creative industries. *The Sociological Review, 63*(S1), 188–205.

Shorthouse, R. (Ed.) (2010). *Disconnected: Social mobility and the creative industries.* London: Social Market Foundation.

Siebert, S., and Wilson, F. (2013). All Work and No Pay: consequences of unpaid work in the creative industries. *Work, Employment and Society, 27*(4), 711–721.

Smith, V. (2010). Review article: Enhancing employability: Human, cultural, and social capital in an era of turbulent unpredictability. *Human Relations, 63*(2), 279–303.

Sutton Trust. (2014). *Internship or indenture? Research brief.* London: The Sutton Trust.

Tholen, G. (2012). The social construction of competition for graduate jobs: A comparison between Great Britain and the Netherlands. *Sociology, 47*(2), 267–283.

Thompson, P. (2013). Financialization and the workplace: Extending and applying the disconnected capitalism thesis. *Work, Employment and Society,* 27(3), 472–488.

Tomlinson, M. (2008). The degree is not enough: Students' perceptions of the role of higher education credentials for graduate work and employability. *British Journal of Sociology of Education, 29*(1), 49–61.

Ware, A. (2015a). The Great British education 'fraud' of the twentieth and twenty-first centuries. *The Political Quarterly, 86*(4), 475–484.

Ware, A. (2015b). Yes a fraud: A response to Johnston. *The Political Quarterly, 86*(4), 489–492.

Wilton, N. (2012). The impact of work placements on skills development and labour market outcomes for business and management graduates. *Studies in Higher Education, 37*(5), 603–620.

Chapter 12

# Gendered and classed graduate transitions to work

## How the unequal playing field is constructed, maintained, and experienced

*Harriet Bradley and Richard Waller*

## Introduction

> *That's the scary thing, like there's so much choice and, you know, you're out of University and for your whole life, it's almost kind of like stages. You have choice in terms of like what you want to do but now you're an adult, literally, you can do anything within reason if you succeed in doing it. But it's, it's scary 'cos like once you make a choice that's kind of like the path you lead and you can't do it all, and time is like limited and the choices that I make now will have like huge ramifications for me later on so I'm very, it feels like a bit of a burden.*

(Martin, middle-class, UoB)

As a *rite de passage* from adolescence into the adult world, university education in the UK has never been more popular. For children from middle-class families, 'going to uni' has become very much an unquestioned norm. For many working-class families, too, who in the past might have wanted their children to leave school aged 15 or 16 and get quickly into jobs, university education has become an aspiration (Bathmaker *et al.*, 2016). In an increasingly precarious economic climate marked by short-term contracts and low-paid work (Standing, 2011) the degree seems one way of grasping at some kind of security and hope for the future.

Certainly, gaining a degree still conveys some kind of economic advantages. Graduates are less likely to experience long-term unemployment. There is a very pronounced graduate pay premium. Official figures for 2014 (BIS, 2015) showed that the median average earnings for all in the 16–64 age group with postgraduate degrees is £40,000, for graduates £31,000, compared with £22,000 for non-graduates. For those aged 21–30 the differentials are lower, with median earnings at around £28,000, £26,000 and £18,000. Of course, the premium will also vary according to the type of degree gained: doctors and lawyers are better paid than philosophers and drama teachers. A young person who is determined to find well-paid and secure employment would make a wise choice in opting for engineering. Sociologists do tend to find a career in the end, but the path may be circuitous and rocky!

However, though research (e.g. Crawford and Vignoles, 2014; BIS, 2015) shows that the graduate salary premium persists and that those with degrees are less likely to be unemployed, there is no doubt that the labour market for graduates is changing in the first decades of the twenty-first century. The major Future Track study has highlighted the changing nature of occupational options facing graduates: as the supply of graduates increases, a smaller proportion will be able to access 'traditional' graduate jobs, (such as law, accounting, and medicine) and more will have to move into 'new' graduate jobs (e.g. event organising, new media jobs, social enterprise) or non-graduate jobs (e.g. leisure industry, retail) (Purcell *et al.*, 2013). Phil Brown's research into the graduate labour market has highlighted 'the opportunity trap' and the 'global auction' (Brown, 2003; Brown *et al.*, 2011). He argues that the promise of success and money lures many into higher education (HE) but the system is increasingly unable to fulfil the demand for graduate-level jobs. While the search for 'good jobs' has always been competitive, there is no doubt that the continued expansion of recruits to HE, especially since the lifting of the cap on student numbers at many universities, along with competition from students from overseas for top jobs in London, has led to a kind of hyper-competitiveness, as highlighted in the following comment from a middle-class Bristol University graduate seeking a permanent teaching job:

> It is very competitive and at the moment it is all of the PGCEs, all of the year three undergrads plus every other teacher in Bristol who decides that they want to move jobs and inevitably you are competing very fiercely for what is often one, two jobs – one school reckoned that they were going to get 85 applications for one job. It's no wonder really is it? Because it is very competitive.
>
> (Justin, middle-class, UoB)

This *hyper-competivity* combines with the multiplicity of choices faced by young people to create an environment of uncertainty and anxiety, as highlighted in the opening quotation from Martin. This is compounded by the neoliberal ethos of individual responsibility which makes young people believe that success or failure lies in their own hands entirely and is not shaped by structural forces (Roberts, 1995; Furlong and Cartmel, 2007; Woodman and Wyn, 2015; Bradley, 2016). It is not surprising if graduates find their situation 'scary' as they contend with the 'burden of choice'. Young people from all backgrounds face these conditions. However, middle-class young people may have resources behind them to cushion them from precarity, which their working-class peers lack. They are more familiar with the 'rules of the game' of professional life, their parents have the financial capital to help them through unpaid internships and placements and fund them for masters degrees or helping with rent in London. Especially importantly, through their parents young people can tap into networks which can help them gain access to elite organisations. This type of social capital is also crucial in accessing useful internships which so often serve as the first steps into permanent jobs (Redmond, 2010; Stevenson and Clegg, 2010; Bathmaker *et al.*, 2016). Working-class students lacking such resources have to rely on their own initiatives and resilience to see them through. As this chapter will show, at least some of them succeed in this.

## Methods

The data used here is primarily taken from interviews towards the end of the final year of a *Leverhulme Trust* funded longitudinal study exploring the progress of a cohort of students through their 3-year undergraduate degree course in England (2010–2013). The *Paired Peers* study aimed to compare systematically the experiences of pairs of students from different social classes, attending university in the same English city. The 'new' (i.e. 'post-1992') teaching-focused University of the West of England, Bristol (UWE) is a member of the University Alliance mission group, while the traditional 'elite' University of Bristol (UoB) is a member of the high status, research-intensive Russell Group of universities. As we shall see, this is an important discriminator.

Pairs of students studying one of eleven subject areas taught across both universities were matched by class, by institution, and by discipline. Among our objectives were to identify the various kinds of capital that students from different classes brought into their university experience (economic, social, cultural etc), and to explore the types of capital they acquired over the 3 years. In this way we aimed to examine differing processes of capital mobilisation and acquisition by students that might enhance future social positioning and career prospects.

By attending the programme induction sessions in 2010 and asking all students to complete a questionnaire (n=2,130), we recruited a sample of 90 students from the eleven disciplines (Biology; Drama; Economics and Finance; Engineering; English; Geography; History; Law; Politics; Psychology and Sociology). There were at least eight from each subject (e.g. two middle-class and two working-class Biology students at UoB and the same at UWE), enabling us to compare the experiences of students from differing class backgrounds. Our primary concern was to operationalise class, despite this necessitating a simplification of its complexities (Savage *et al.*, 2015). We classified students using seven different factors, including the occupation and educational attainment of both parents, the type of school the participants had attended, the number of their school friends who were going to university, and their self-reported class. Using their responses, we divided all responses into three groups: clearly working-class, clearly middle-class and those 'in between' which we rather aptly if jokingly named 'the muddle in the middle'. While we observed differences in the class fractions of students between the two institutions (middle-class students at UoB often had parents in the 'higher professions' such as law, finance or medicine, as opposed to nurses and teachers who were typical parents of our UWE recruits)), we readily found sufficient participants at both universities who pretty clearly belonged to the middle-classes; the relative paucity of unambiguously working-class students, particularly at UoB, led us to draw from the intermediate grouping in some disciplines. We tried to make sure that these displayed some feature of disadvantage (e.g. coming from a lone parent family).

This chapter focuses on social class. To avoid the additional variable of age, we only included 'young' (18- to 21-year-old) students, and there were insufficient students in our sample with disabilities, or members of black and minority communities to enable a meaningful discussion of disability or 'race', but we do refer to some emerging differences along the lines of gender. However, we do offer a more detailed consideration of other experiences of social or demographic demarcation elsewhere (e.g. Bradley and Ingram, 2012; Abrahams and Ingram, 2013; Ingram and Waller, 2015; Ingram and Abraham, 2016; Bathmaker *et al.*, 2016).

All interview data has been analysed and thematically coded using NVivo data analysis software, and we present some of this interview data in this chapter. Currently the Paired Peers project has entered a second phase (2014–2017), following a group of our participants into the labour market after graduation; some interview data from Phase 2 is also drawn on here.

## The contemporary graduate careers market

When we asked our participants to look back at their final year of study, many highlighted the considerable level of stress they had felt. In addition to completing course work and revising for their final exams, most felt the growing pressure from the need to secure an appropriate outcome following their studies, i.e. a graduate level job or further study. Many also needed to decide where to live the following year, a choice which for many came down between moving back to the family home (often in an attempt to save money), to stay in Bristol or to move elsewhere in pursuit of work. For some this meant re-locating to London, a move which would generally come at considerable expense in terms of rental costs, a phenomenon which Bristol also is increasingly suffering from. As stated above, our participants were confronted upon graduation in 2013 with an incredibly competitive careers' market, with greater numbers of graduates than ever before due to the expansion of higher education in the preceding decades, but without a commensurate growth in 'graduate level' jobs. This situation had evolved especially since the global financial crash of 2008 and the politics and economics of austerity that it heralded in in the UK and beyond. Thus Sally who had taken, along with many hopefuls, the prestigious law degree at UoB reflected:

> Basically hardly anyone I know who did the Law degree actually went on to become a lawyer. Like there's a couple of sort of like events management sort of things, sort of business. And then there's a few people who have gone into law but not as a lawyer, so they're sort of like paralegals or legal secretaries, that sort of thing, because it was just so difficult to get into a law

firm and do a training contract there because there just aren't enough and there's too many graduates, so actually not many of them are lawyers at all.

(Sally, middle-class, UoB)

Our participants were often painfully aware of the message that, to compete in the contemporary graduate careers market 'a degree is not enough' (Tomlinson, 2008; Bathmaker *et al.*, 2016), and that to thrive within the highly competitive field of graduate careers, they must undertake CV enhancing activities alongside their studies (Redmond, 2010; Stevenson and Clegg, 2011; Bathmaker *et al.*, 2013). It is also worthy of note that the process of applying for 'top' graduate jobs has become extremely onerous, something akin to 'a global war for talent' (Brown and Tannock, 2009; Brown, Lauder, and Ashton, 2011). The burden of recruitment has shifted from graduate employers to the students themselves, witness the decline of the so-called 'milk round'. Many major employers no longer take part in this, except at a handful of elite universities, among which UoB is usually numbered. Graduate recruitment fairs at UWE tend to focus more on local firms, who are targeted by the university in its employability strategies, reflecting its view of itself as a locally oriented and 'down to earth' organisation, a self-proclaimed 'university for the real world'.

This chapter explores the strategies of our participants as they moved into the labour market. We identify patterns among the group, in respect of their progress in seeking a 'good job'. We examine the influence of their class backgrounds and their gender upon these processes, and how they mobilised the capitals (Bourdieu, 1986) acquired through their family backgrounds or at university

## The impact of class and gender on graduate destinations

I think it's getting more and more difficult to get a job after university unless you go down like a specific career path. Like for me when I specifically decided I'm going to be a teacher and there's a sort of chain of like events, just like steps that you have to take and then you sort of get there. But I think if you're a graduate and you graduate and then that's it and you just have to go and find a job by yourself, I think it's getting more and more difficult to get on to like a graduate work sort of programme or into a graduate job straightaway. So many people I know have just . . . are working in like shops and cafes and bakeries and that sort of thing just sort of applying for jobs and then just like waiting to find a better one. Yeah. I think it's sort of slow progress after university, you sort of expect to go straight into a job and then suddenly it's like you can't actually find one.

(Sally, middle-class, UoB)

In terms of moving out of what many called the 'student bubble' (Reay *et al.*, 2009) and into work, we would expect some undergraduates to be doing this with greater success than others. Generally speaking we could make a number of assumptions, for instance that those taking more vocational courses (e.g. Law) will be closer to establishing a career than others, as Sally acknowledges in the quotation above. Likewise, those achieving well in their courses will probably find it easier moving into desirable jobs than those who struggled. This is why, as any lecturer will testify, undergraduate students may become fixated on getting a first class degree or a 2:1.

Some students have personal circumstances limiting them to certain locations (e.g. where their family lives), while others can effectively go wherever the fancy takes them – upon graduation some of our participants moved abroad to work for instance. Meanwhile some undergraduates have the financial resources necessary to enable them to immediately commence further study, while others need to earn money before embarking on an MA. And, perhaps most tellingly, some have a clear idea of what they would like their future lives to be like, while others barely have a clue! Our remaining cohort of 71 participants (we had lost 19 across the 3 years of the study who had either left university altogether or simply left the project) were no different.

While we acknowledge that each student was moving along their own individual trajectory, upon analysing their narrative accounts we were able to group them into four broad clusters, (leaving aside the few who were going onto a 4th year of their course). Some had already got a destination fixed by the end of their final year (e.g. a course, a job, or an internship). These we defined as being 'on track'. We identified another group who had not yet secured a destination upon completing their studies, but who had a fairly clear idea of where they wanted to go and were actively taking steps to get there,(e.g. they were applying for jobs or placements); we labelled these as 'pushing forward'. A third if smaller cluster was made up of people who felt they needed some kind of break before moving on to a career, some of whom had already been offered jobs or places on courses but had postponed the start in order to recharge their batteries. We referred to this group as having 'deferred careers'. The final group seemed to have had very little idea of what they wanted to do, or how to go about it, and we named them 'drifters'. Some of them were vaguely oriented to specific sectors – overseas development, charities, local government – but without much idea about particular occupations or career paths. Graduates in these latter two groups spoke of needing 'time to think' about where they should go next.

The table below shows how the students from the two universities are clustered by class background. We distinguish here between the two 'on track' groups, those going into work and those undertaking further study.

The above table suggests that while there are clear class differences between the backgrounds of those making up the clusters, they are strongly mediated by attendance at the two rather different universities. Although it is only data from the start of the students' working lives, the most striking feature is that those who attended UoB, whatever their class, are making a speedier and smoother transition into work than those who attended UWE. This is a crucial finding in terms of the

*Table 12.1* Student destinations by university and class of origin

|  | UoB middle-class | UoB working-class | UWE middle-class | UWE working-class | Total |
|---|---|---|---|---|---|
| Further study | 7 | 5 | 2 | 1 | 15 |
| On track | 4 | 3 | 1 | 0 | 8 |
| Pushing forward | 2 | 2 | 3 | 3 | 10 |
| Drifting | 5 | 4 | 8 | 3 | 20 |
| Deferred career | 1 | 3 | 1 | 3 | 8 |
| Final year study | 2 | 2 | 3 | 3 | 10 |
| Total | 21 | 19 | 18 | 13 | 71 |

debates over widening participation and social mobility (e.g. Milburn, 2009; 2012; 2014; Waller *et al.*, 2014; 2015). It suggests that attending a Russell Group university does indeed heighten the chances for working-class students of upward mobility and securing professional employment, while for middle-class students it is likely to help them maintain their original class status. While UWE has a strong record of getting its graduates into employment – at 95.6 per cent one of the highest in the sector (HESA, 2016), it may be that they will take longer to find a niche, or, more worryingly, end up in non-graduate jobs. While it is too early at this stage to be sure, we can say that the Russell Group graduates have a head start.

In terms of how we would explain this phenomenon, we suggest that the working-class young people who make it to UoB – often against significant odds and through demonstrating significant resilience – are generally highly aspirational, well-motivated, and determined to achieve. They are more likely to learn how to 'play the game' in terms of enhancing their CVs or using their newly acquired capitals than their counterparts at UWE. (see Bathmaker *et al.*, 2013, 2016, and Ingram and Waller 2015, for a detailed discussion of this process). The other side of the picture is the action of employers who appear to seek out Russell Group applicants. Our students told us of the '(University of) Bristol cachet':

Because I was in such a bubble before I never realised how rare like say a Bristol graduate is actually with these 'A' levels and GCSEs are, and you don't realise the value of yourself. So you're just like 'oh I'll take any job' but then you realise that actually we're actually quite hard to come by. But in a search engine, that will search there . . . all the key words . . . anything technical like language wise that they'd search, like graduate . . . biology, Bristol. I did Bristol on like loads of pages, I knew they were looking for that, Bristol University, A* as well, that was like just a big ream of that.

(Luke, middle-class, UoB)

But I shouldn't let it define me and what I do to the point that I give up and do a big corporate job because that option is there with you know you have a degree from Bristol you can do those jobs.

(Elliot, middle-class, UoB).

The table also demonstrates how over 20 per cent of the working-class students (although mainly those from UoB) were utilising their cultural gains in proceeding to PGCE qualifications or higher degrees, with ambitions to pursue careers as teachers or in some cases academics. These students had achieved well academically, gaining upper second or first-class degrees, and across the cohort as a whole the working-class students had performed as well in their degrees as their middle-class peers. Since most had attended non-selective state schools this shows that doing so does not present a barrier to subsequent high academic achievement. Indeed, as we suggest elsewhere (Bradley and Waller, 2014), in common with other 'non-traditional students', the difficulties they had faced in getting into university had apparently made them predisposed to work harder than their middle-class and public-school counterparts. This replicates the findings of earlier research by Brown and Scase (1994) and more recently the report from the Higher Education Funding Council for England (HEFCE) (2014).

A more surprising finding was that middle-class students were more likely to end up as drifters. This may partly be because going to university has become a middle-class norm whether or not young people have formed career plans, while for working-class students the motivation for university attendance may be more focused in terms of 'getting a good job', or 'giving something back' (Brine and Waller, 2004) or 'bettering themselves' (Bathmaker et al., 2016). Another factor may be the ability of their parents to support them for a period through the transition. This means that the pressure to find a job and become independent is less acute. Generally, the working-class students who were not yet 'on track' seemed to have a clearer idea of what they wanted to do, although it might take them longer to achieve it, for instance by taking non-graduate work in the short term to be able to save for a master's degree course, while many middle-class parents could – and would – pay outright. Thus Kyle, a working-class student from UWE, was working as a carer for learning disabled people to pay his way through his LPC (legal practice course). However, it is also possible that the phenomenon of the middle-classes drifting reflects a genuine decline in their fortunes in austerity Britain, particularly as the public-sector jobs which past cohorts were able to access in significant numbers have been in significant decline.

Thus some doubt may be cast on whether having a university degree may continue to serve as a way of maintaining middle-class distinction as clearly as it has done in the past. As we touched on earlier, the middle-class is fractionalised. The children of doctors, lecturers and lawyers who attend UoB may do better than the children of nurses, teachers and social workers at UWE. But the data do suggest, that for working-class young people who manage to overcome the systemic barriers and disadvantages and get into university, it appears to remain

Table 12.2 Student destinations by university and gender

|  | UoB males | UoB females | UWE males | UWE females | Total |
|---|---|---|---|---|---|
| Further study | 3 | 9 | 0 | 3 | 15 |
| On track jobs | 5 | 2 | 0 | 1 | 8 |
| Moving on | 2 | 2 | 3 | 3 | 10 |
| Drifting | 3 | 6 | 4 | 7 | 20 |
| Deferred career | 2 | 2 | 1 | 3 | 8 |
| Final year | 2 | 2 | 5 | 1 | 10 |
| Total | 17 | 23 | 13 | 18 | 71 |

a vehicle for upward social mobility and a potential route into more secure employment, especially if they attend elite universities (Savage *et al.*, 2015).

Analysis of the students' destinations also suggests that initial career outcomes for graduates are shaped by gender as well as class, as is shown in Table 12.2. Interestingly, while at the start of our research there seemed to be little difference in the aspirations and expectations between our male and female participants, there was an apparent 'cooling-out' process where the women's horizons contracted. The table reflects this is in the higher numbers of women who were either drifting or deferring their careers.

Especially notable was a tendency for women move towards teaching. Table 12.2 shows that women were more likely to go on to further study than men, but whereas all the men were taking masters of various kinds, six of these twelve women were taking PGCEs (the one-year postgraduate course in education).

Some young women came to university already intending to teach, often themselves the children of teachers. Indeed, many of the middle-class students had parents who were education professionals. Teaching has historically been seen as an appropriate job for women, and can be considered more compatible with the responsibilities of domesticity and motherhood, given that the hours and holidays coincide with children's. This is even truer in the context of today's 'long hours' work culture and lengthy commutes into work. It also chimes with the desire expressed by many of the female undergraduates to 'give something back' (Brine and Waller, 2004) to their communities. For example, Anna was a working-class student at UoB, who was keen to do something with her politics degree to challenge social injustices and inequalities. But she was deterred from a more academic career by the behaviour of male students and tutors which she found overbearing, and decided that a better choice for her would be to teach maths to children in disadvantaged areas.

Another who abandoned her original aspirations was Sally, a middle-class student studying law at UoB. She was differentiated from the rest of the sample in having a small child but her mother took on much of the necessary childcare for her. At first Sally seemed typically ambitious, set on becoming a barrister. In her second year she had decided being a solicitor would be her preference: 'I'm doing a law degree so I'll be a lawyer'. But doubts began to set in in her third year:

> I think I still want to be a solicitor but it's just really hard to be a solicitor. You have to work really long hours and things like that, so it's sort of not a particularly practical route to go down. Because I was thinking for a while over summer about teaching.

Sally decided that the legal profession was too competitive and demanding for her, especially as a lone parent. She reported seeing how lawyer friends of her parents worked long hours and then brought work home and this led her to a new decision:

> Because I think I would much prefer to teach and then sort of maybe be able to teach Law than have the stresses of having to practice it as a profession. Because everyone seems so stressed about it, all the lawyers that like I know who live on my road, they're all up at three in the morning ringing China every day and it just doesn't . . . the more I think about the less it appeals to me.

Sally struggled with this career switch, because she knew her parents had been set on her becoming a well-paid lawyer, and she did not want to disappoint them. This might inform her middle-class aspirational take on her potential career path:

> I don't see being a teacher as like what I'm going to do for ever. I feel like I could do a lot more than just being a teacher. After like maybe two years as a teacher, so in like three years' time, I would have started thinking about trying to go for Head of Department or an external examiner for something, or like something a bit different. I feel like being a teacher is just like a stepping stone to something like bigger and more elaborate.

Interestingly when we interviewed her two years' later she was still in a temporary post and told us that her ambition was to be headmistress of a girls' private school, but acknowledged it might take 20 years!

This clinging to aspirations to career progression, to be as Sally put it, 'a hotshot teacher' if she couldn't be 'a hotshot lawyer', contrasts with the statement of Jackie, a working-class UoB student also headed for a PGCE:

> Like if I went on a special educational needs course. I'd be interested in that. But I'm not particularly interested in being head teacher or deputy or anything, like senior member of staff.

Another working-class graduate, Ruby, described herself as 'driven' and ambitious', but also emphasised the importance of security as shaping her job choice:

I've chosen a secure career and I've chosen a career that I'm able to work up and become . . . you know to take it as far as I want to, I can do as little as I want or I could do as much as I want to. So I think in that respect I'm really optimistic that I'll be able to continue with this. So I think yeah I am, yeah.

For Ruby and Jackie, both of them were the first in their family to go to university, the achievement of a teaching career was a considerable step upward in occupational terms. While both of them looked set for possible early promotion if they wanted it, there was no pressure from their families to go further.

## On track: moving on up

Many of those we categorised as being 'on track' had known before coming to university what they wanted to do, and had chosen courses which would lead them towards that destination. Engineering was an obvious example. For instance, Marcus was a highly motivated student who had wanted to be an engineer since childhood and had clear plans to achieve this goal:

> I definitely want a first, it's just something else to have. I'm already doing a Masters' degree which you have to do for engineering, but going to careers fairs it is all a 2:1 required, and 80 per cent of Bristol students, I believe is the quoted figure, achieve a 2:1. So ideally I want a first. I will be a manager of some sort, hopefully a chartered engineer if I go into engineering – this is based on my chosen career path.
>
> (Marcus, working-class, UoB)

Marcus subsequently got his first and moved straight into a graduate scheme at a top firm.

A similarly strategic route was planned out by Tony, who studied economics at UoB:

> It's gone the way that I wanted it to go actually, get an internship, get a graduate role, go straight into work . . . I think I can kind of rise quite well within the industry. It's what I like so if it's what I like I'd assume that I can at least kind of motivate myself to do it well. Yeah I'm reasonably confident. I think a bit of confidence will probably help.
>
> (Tony, working-class, UoB)

Nathan was another who throughout his degree had been remarkably focused on obtaining his goal: a very well paid job in the City (see Ingram and Waller (2015) for a fuller discussion of this). He was contemptuous of fellow students whom he saw as wasting their time. By contrast he was doing everything he could to get the high-status career he aspired to:

Get exposed to the companies and the industries that you might want to work for as early as possible. Research the opportunities available, (which I did), and summer internships (which I did and got the job off the back off). Join societies and clubs and try and take up leadership positions in those clubs that are relevant to the potential career that you want – if the society doesn't exist, create it . . . Just try and do everything to build up your CV, just add little bits of experience, add little bits of training, competitions if you can, and make yourself look busy.

(Nathan, middle-class, UoB)

Nathan got a first-class degree in Law and gained a place at a leading merchant bank which would start him off on a high salary destined for a high-flying career. In this first stage of his career he was still carefully planning his next moves, which now focused on using his position as a base for setting up his own company:

The job market for people with two to three years of banking experience is ridiculously hot, you know I would typically get maybe an email or two in a week for potential jobs. It's not a very big industry, there may be a couple of hundred people who do the kind of thing that we do in London, and so once you have a little bit of a reputation or some people have worked with you on a couple of deals, they start thinking 'oh this guy might be alright, he's a good guy, and he's also good at his job'. So you start to get invites from head hunters, generic ones and also ones that people have referred you for. And you just kind of filter through and see if there's anything you might like.

(Nathan, middle-class, UoB)

While Table 12.2 shows that male graduates are more likely than female to be on track, there were one or two women who fell in to this category. One such was Lizzie, a very bright young working-class woman doing engineering at UoB. Interestingly, unlike Marcus, Lizzie had had one or two wobbles along the way wondering whether this was really the direction for her. But her story of how she got her first job after graduating with a first-class degree illustrates the advantages of attendance at a Russell Group research intensive university:

Well I was invited by the professor at the University to go to Farnborough Air Show with him in July, cos he'd been invited as a guest and he could bring a student with him to go to. So the company have a chalet at Farnborough Air Show so we went there to watch the Air Show and whilst I was there they approached me and told me that they would like me to join the graduate scheme next year, so this is in 2016, because they'd heard, my professor told them all about me and they knew that I wanted to go travelling so they offered me some work experience before I went travelling, with no commitments, so if I didn't want to join them next September I don't have to. But, you know, they put my name around in the company and then one of the managers picked up my CV and name and stuff and he contacted me, and so, yeah it was quite fortunate.

(Lizzie, working-class, UoB)

A bright working-class young woman had been pushed forward by her tutor using his social capital to get her on the scheme; it is indicative that unlike the self-motivated young men mentioned above, she had needed that intervention from her tutor.

## Pushing forward: progress towards a goal

As we mentioned earlier, many of the students found the final year of their degree stressful, especially the run up to the final assessments. Preoccupations with exams stopped them from getting ahead with securing placements or internships, even when they had a good idea what they wanted to do, as in the following account from Sophie who told us 'I think I should get the grades first and then look for jobs':

I'm looking for like graduate schemes at home, so like with the councils. But because I've got my job I can leave it a bit because I can live on my wages at the moment because I'll be moving back home. But I think I need to focus more on getting the grades first rather than looking for jobs because I could apply like in the summer.

(Sophie, working-class, UWE)

Sophie's case is also an interesting example of the 'cooling off' process we observed among young women. She came from a local working-class family taking Politics at UWE. Her account tells of the way many working-class students deliberately impose limits on their aspirations.

I didn't really want to choose universities that were too high, I wanted to become like my level, I didn't want to aim 'above my station', so I only applied for three places, like here, Aston and Coventry.

(Sophie, working-class, UWE)

Her apprehension of a class ceiling, however, was not reflected in the aspirations she expressed in her first interview for the project when she spoke of possible jobs in the civil service, foreign office or diplomatic service. Such ambitions seemed to conflict with her self-analysis which again were redolent of delineated class horizons: 'I don't like to fail, I like to be comfortable'. Indeed by the second year she was contemplating voluntary sector or council work. The latter must have appeared both familiar and attainable as she had a relative working there. She still aspires to work for the council but currently has a permanent job with an accountancy firm.

Like others in this cluster, Sophie's immediate plan was to move back home to her parents and start looking for jobs. Such was the fate of Leo, another working-class student who had nothing fixed at the end of his three years and was anticipating moving home to Wales while he sought a place on a graduate scheme:

> I've only applied for two, and got turned down for one, still waiting on the other one, but yeah I haven't really put as much effort into finding a graduate scheme as I should have. But that's what I'm hoping to do. I'm applying to go anywhere over the country, usually in the finance departments for large businesses.
>
> (Leo, working-class, UWE)

Leo, also a UWE student, was interesting because he had left school, gone straight into an accountancy firm, got fed up and went off to university hoping for a 'good time' and improved career prospects. Leo achieved a first –class degree, but was unable to find his way into a top job like Tony and Nathan, partly no doubt because he lacked the 'Bristol cachet', but also because he not 'played the game' as carefully as they had and had no social contacts to unlock closed doors for him. Finally he secured himself a moderately well-paid job in a large public sector organisation's finance office which satisfied him (see Ingram and Waller, 2015 for a further discussion of this).

Leo and Sophie, it seems to us, are typical of working-class students from the new university sector with moderate ambitions. Furthermore, these ambitions may have been moderated over the course of their degree to something realistic in terms of their qualifications and achievements. Such students are not' driven' in the same way as the Nathans and Sallys of this world. Moreover, in terms of their class backgrounds they have achieved much in getting decent reasonably secure jobs, as have Jackie and Ruby. They have escaped the traps of unemployment and precarious work which are the fate of many of their school fellows and probably made their families proud.

## Deferred career: time for a break

Given that many of the students, particularly the young women, found the last year of their degree so stressful and draining as they sought to achieve good results in the final assessments, some of those who were well 'on track' decided they needed a break from the pressure. Jasmine wanted to go into social work, but told us of her need for temporary relief from the intensiveness of university study, which appeared overwhelming. This would allow her to focus on practical life arrangements:

> I was going to go straight into a masters, but I want a year out, to save up, get a flat and stuff. Cos I just can't cope. So I'm moving in with my boyfriend.
>
> (Jasmine, working-class, UWE)

Jenifer was another who wanted time out. She had secured a first-class engineering degree and was thus on track for a well-paid secure job, but preferred to defer for a year. She had taken a waitressing job and was living with her grandmother:

> It was a bit intense, but that year was worth 75 per cent of my degree grade, so yeah I felt I had to work hard that year. So I sort of decided that I needed an engineering break after that and that's why I haven't sort of gone straight into a graduate job like most people do . . . and that's why I'm living here now with my granny in (name of town) for the time being, and then I want to go travelling before I start my job.
>
> (Jenifer, middle-class, UoB)

The desire to spend some time travelling was strong among many of the students and could be another reason for deferment. Several of the participants were living abroad, either travelling, working or studying. Megan for instance had gained a place on the Teach First programme but decided to take time off so she could indulge her great passion for horses and riding.

> I've deferred it so I'm having a year out. One thing I will do is the four months in Canada. There's a Work Away placement where I would work with training young horses on a ranch, which is my dream . . . And because it's Work Away I work at their ranch for four to six hours a day and they pay for my food and board, so I don't pay for any of that so it will be quite cheap. There's another horse-related thing I really want to do, which is a project where you live and ride with Mongolian nomadic people for a month.
>
> (Megan, working-class, UoB)

The choice to defer for these young women can be seen as way to recuperate from the strains of competition and achievement which so many of them told us about. One wonders if psychologically it is a chance to spend time as a 'free spirit' before the traps of adult responsibilities finally close upon them. This certainly appeared to be the case with Megan.

## Drifting: what shall I do with my life?

While over half of the students who were not still carrying on with studies fell into one of these three former groups, the largest number was of those we categorise as 'drifters'. It can be argued that there is a bit of an issue about expecting young people of school age to pick a career and carry that straight through sixth form and into university or college. Many other countries allow for a more leisurely approach to career choice and development. A 'gap year' may be helpful in giving some experience of the world of work, but in many cases it is spent backpacking and acquiring that addiction to 'travelling' which was displayed by many of our respondents. Given the young age of most graduates (typically 21 to 23) and their lack of experience of the wider world and its opportunities, it is quite predictable that many graduates have still no idea about what they want to do with their lives.

The drifters had arrived at university with no clear career ambitions and were still in that condition on graduation. Although nowadays universities, especially those like UWE, make much of 'employability' and preparing the students for the 'real world' (one of UWE's branding slogans), it is understandable that with the intensity of study, social life and changing relationships, undecided students find little time, especially in the final year, to think about future directions. It was noticeable and somewhat surprising that the drifters were mainly women (13 out of 20). This may reflect the fact that despite social change young men are trained towards a future as breadwinners, while for young women things are more ambiguous.

For the drifters, then, it is a question of going out and seeing what the labour market has to offer. Realistically, some of these drifters knew that they were likely to change over the coming years, as Lauren expresses:

> I'm not going to initially start looking for a career as soon as I've done my exams because I don't think that's practical, I don't think that's realistic, so I think it will take time. I can't see myself in the future. I try and like think about what will I be like in like five or ten years and I just . . . I can't vision anything, I just can't imagine it.
>
> (Lauren, middle-class, UoB)

Amber was another drifter, although unlike Lauren she had arrived at university with a clear ambition to do engineering and work with cars: however, she had become disillusioned and quit after three years of the degree (which normally includes a fourth year qualifying the engineering students for a masters)

> I'll probably just move back home and I have a job at a pub at home. Hope-fully . . . I will be able to find a job for either starting in September or like starting in the summer, really just for a year, and then hopefully within that year I'll figure out, like try at maybe do some work experience in different sectors and see what sort of thing I fancy going into I've not decided on anything yet. Just try and get some work experience in different areas.
>
> (Amber, middle-class, UWE)

Both these middle-class young women moved back to the family home. Perhaps such a strategy offers them a sense of stability and security in a precarious and shifting world. In a time of austerity families become even more important as places of refuge and economic support, especially given the high costs of rented accommodation in the southern part of the country, where many of the city's undergraduate students originate.

As the tables show, we identified drifters from both universities and all classes, although male students from both classes at UoB were least likely to drift. It may be the case, however, that working-class students end up as drifters not because of personal indecisiveness but because they lack insider knowledge of the professional world and its cultural and social parameters. Entering HE they do not have the cultural capital that middle-class students possess. They have no topographical overview or map of this terrain to guide them so they can only learn by experimenting.

It is important to stress we should not equate drifting with laziness. Sussing out the labour market, applying for jobs and trying out jobs can be hard work as the following comments imply:

> It's been really difficult, really, really difficult and just in a sense that it's quite disheartening when you're kind of filling out loads of job applications, it's time consuming as well because obviously you've got work, you've got a life but I always make sure, 'right you know, I've got to at least do one or two applications a week', which doesn't sound like a lot but when you're kind of doing your personal statement and obviously you're taking a bit of time to tailor it, it's quite disheartening when you don't hear back from people and you kind of think 'oh what am I doing wrong'. The jobs I have been going for have been mainly in like the third sector or the public sector and for charities as such – also for universities as well. And I haven't really got much kind of luck in kind of getting interviews or anything.
>
> (Adele, working-class, UWE)

> I had this wonderfully naïve notion that I'd just kind of come up and . . . with a personal interest in Politics and a degree to boot, you know really it would just be a case of picking from the job offers which obviously would come my way! God, it was pretty bleak at first, I mean it very quickly becomes apparent that it's just like a very horrible environment. I saw some ads saying, you know, graduate job opportunities and the requirements were like three Olympic gold medals or world records, you know it's like that because the stuff they're advertising is entry level. I applied for I think about 32 jobs, no . . . it was mid 20s . . . but each one of these was like 'monolithic', some of them just wanted a CV and a cover letter . . . if I'm going do this I'm going to do it really well and not have any trace of reciprocation across different stuff so I'm going to research each company, research each organisation and write something tailor made. So that ended up being like three weeks of just doing that full time.
>
> (Oscar, middle-class, UWE)

## Conclusions

In this chapter we have focused on the difficulties faced by our cohort of graduates as they make the transition from university into adulthood, the labour market and eventually into a career. Our data has concerned the first phase of the transition: as time passes, a different picture may emerge, with more of the drifters finding their way into a job they value. These initial phases, however, are already revealing classed and gendered differences in the pace and direction of individual trajectories.

As stated at the beginning of this chapter, a degree still brings economic advantages, in the form of greater job security and a graduate premium in lifetime earnings. It remains to be seen whether this premium will persist given the changes in the labour market noted at the start of our discussion. It may be that the young adults will achieve higher levels of pay over their lifetime, especially when and if the economy picks up; on the other hand, it might be the case that, as some commentators have argued, that this generation may find itself trapped in a 'high-skill, low-wage' economy (Shildrick *et al.*, 2012; Howker and Malik, 2013; Gardiner, 2016). However, university remains a gateway into high- and medium-level professional employment, and is also seen as a guarantee of calibre by recruiters and employers who can be mistrustful of young people's work ethic and capabilities.

We have argued in this chapter and elsewhere (e.g. Bradley and Waller, 2014; Waller and Bradley, 2015) that this gateway is open to at least some of the young people from less advantaged background who have grit and determination to overcome barriers into higher education. This is increasingly described as 'resilience' and we have used this term previously (Bradley and Waller, 2014). While we have observed this strength in the face of obstacles among our sample, we recognise that this is an individual attribute, and that requiring working-class students to demonstrate it in itself can serve to exclude more vulnerable youths. Our sample performed as well in their exam results as their middle-class peers and were no more likely to end their undergraduate degrees without a job. However, there is a major advantage for students of all classes if they attend an elite university like UoB, compared to even a leading post-1992 one such as UWE. We find this deeply disappointing, given that many of the UWE students had worked very hard and gained as good degrees as their UoB counterparts. The blame must fall upon employers and recruiters who focus so narrowly on a handful of 'top' universities and do not widen their search for talent into newer arenas. Nonetheless, if we consider the role of universities in offering social mobility to well-qualified and aspirational talented working-class youths (albeit only ever a limited number of them), there is evidence here to suggest that role continues. The problem is that far fewer people from working-class backgrounds make it to the most successful universities. Cherry-picking a few of the most academically able will not make a great difference to this systemic problem as pupils from private schools are steered into mass uptake of Russell Group places. Parents and schools combine to steer privileged youth towards elite careers (Reay *et al.*, 2005; Khan, 2012; Bathmaker *et al.*, 2016).

We have also pointed to a gender dimension as young women appear more likely to abandon or moderate initial ambitions to be lawyers, engineers, politicians and employees of elite city firms. Our female graduates seemed deterred from the competitive environments into which they were being inducted. Many of them are channelled into teaching, a job which appears to offer a better work-life balance (although that is disputable) and is certainly more compatible with motherhood. Moreover there are gender differences in motivations. When we asked our undergraduates what kind of job they wanted, women often mentioned 'working with people', 'working with children', or 'making a difference' while young men were more likely to talk of money and status. The frame of mind associated with the patriarchal concept of the 'male breadwinner' appears to be still entrenched.

Meanwhile, our cohort of young graduates did not seem too daunted as they set forth on their journey to adult independence. We might describe their mood as apprehensive but hopeful. Some appeared already on the way to traditional graduate employment, as accountants, lawyers, teachers and engineers. Others are resigned to starting out in 'non-graduate' jobs, while they take further steps to better their chances, for example by applying to graduate-entry schemes. Finally, some appear quite directionless, with no real idea of how their lives may turn out.

It is early days yet, however, and, whatever their place on the road to the future, our student participants had few regrets about the choice they had made to attend university. Even if they had not yet attained the economic rewards they had hoped a degree would bring, the vast majority acknowledged the pleasures, intellectual, social and cultural, which their student experience had brought them. A degree indeed may not be enough to secure upward mobility (Tomlinson, 2008) in the climate of hyper-competivity, but it is still a source of personal pride in achievement, especially to those from working-class backgrounds.

## References

Abrahams, J., and Ingram, N. (2013) 'The chameleon habitus: local students' negotiations of a multiple fields', Sociological Review Online, 18 (4) 2 www.socresonline.org.uk/18/4/21.html

Bathmaker, A-M., Ingram, N., and Waller, R. (2013) 'Higher education, social class and the mobilisation of capitals: Knowing and playing the game', British Journal of Sociology of Education, special issue on education and social mobility, 34, 5–6: 723–743.

Bathmaker, A-M., Ingram, N., Abrahams, J., Hoare, T., Waller, R., and Bradley, H. (2016) Higher education, social class and social mobility: The degree generation, Basingstoke: Palgrave MacMillan.

Bourdieu, P. (1986) 'The forms of capital' in Richardson, J. Handbook of Theory and Research in Education, Westport, CT: Greenwood pp. 241–258.

Bradley, H. (2016) Fractured Identities 2nd edition, Cambridge: Polity.

Bradley, H., and Ingram N. (2012) 'Banking on the Future: Choices, aspirations and economic hardship in working-class student experience' in W. Atkinson, S. Roberts and M. Savage (eds.) Class Inequalities in Austerity Britain, Basingstoke: Palgrave Macmillan, pp. 51–69.

Bradley, H., and Waller, R. (2014) 'Social class, resilience and the struggle to adjust to university life: comparing the experiences of working- and middle-class students'. Presentation to British Sociological Association Annual Conference University of Leeds 23–25 April.

Brine, J., and Waller, R. (2004) Working-class women on an Access course: Risk, opportunity and (re)constructing identities, *Gender and Education*, 16 (1), pp. 97–113.

Brown, P. (2003) *The Opportunity Trap: Education and Employment in a Global Economy*, Paper 32, Cardiff University Working Paper Series.

Brown, P., Lauder, H., and Ashton, D. (2011) *The global auction: the broken promises of education, jobs and incomes*, Oxford: Oxford University Press.

Brown, P., and Scase, R. (1994) *Higher education and corporate realities*. London: University College Press.

Brown, P., and Tannock, S. (2009) Education, meritocracy and the global war for talent, *Journal of Education Policy*, 24, 4: 377–92.

Crawford, C., and Vignoles, A. (2014) 'Heterogeneity in graduate earnings by socio-economic background'. *IFS Working Paper W14/30* London: Institute for Fiscal Studies.

BIS (2015) *Graduate labour market statistics: October to December 2014* London: Department for Business, Innovation and Skills.

Furlong, A., and Cartmel, F. (2007) *Young people and social change*, Buckingham: Open University Press.

Gardiner, L. (2016) Stagnation generation: *the case for renewing the intergenerational contract*. Intergenerational report, London: Resolution Foundation.

HEFCE (2014) *Differences in Degree Outcomes: Key Findings*, Bristol: Higher Education Funding Council for England.

HESA (2016) *UK Performance Indicators 2014/15: Employment of leavers*, Cheltenham: Higher Education Statistics Agency.

Howker, E., and Malik, S. (2010) *Jilted Generation: How Britain Bankrupted its Youth*, London: Icon Books.

Ingram, N., and Abrahams, J. (2016) Stepping outside of oneself: how a cleft-habitus can lead to greater reflexivity through occupying "the third space", in J. Thatcher, N. Ingram, C. Burke and J. Abraham (eds.) *Bourdieu: the next generation. The development of Bourdieu's intellectual heritage in contemporary UK sociology*, Abingdon: Routledge, pp. 140–156.

Ingram, N., and Waller, R. (2015) Higher education and the reproduction of social elites, *Discover Society* 20 www.discoversociety.org/2015/05/05/higher-education-and-the-reproduction-of-social-elites/

Khan, S.R. (2012) Privilege: the making of an adolescent elite at St Paul's School, Princeton: Princeton University Press.

Milburn, A. (2009) Panel on Fair Access to the Professions. 2009. *Unleashing aspiration: the final report of the Panel on Fair Access to the Professions* (also known as the Milburn Report). London: Cabinet Office.

Milburn, A. (2012) Fair Access to Professional Careers: A progress report by the Independent Reviewer on Social Mobility and Child Poverty. London: Cabinet Office.

Milburn, A. (2014) Elitist Britain? A report by the Independent Reviewer on Social Mobility and Child Poverty. London: Cabinet Office.

Purcell, K., Elias, P., Atfield, G., Behle, H., Ellison, R., and Luchinskaya, D. (2013) *Transitions into employment, further study and other outcomes. The Futuretrack stage 4 Report*, Manchester/Coventry: HECSU/Warwick Institute for Employment Research, University of Warwick. Retrieved June 2014 from www2.warwick.ac.uk/fac/soc/ier/people/kpurcell/publications/

Reay, D., Crozier, G., and Clayton. J. (2009) Strangers in paradise: working class students in elite universities. *Sociology* 43 (6): 1103–1121.

Reay, D., David, M.E., and Ball, S. (2005) *Degrees of choice: social class, race and gender in higher education*, Stoke-on-Trent: Trentham Books.

Redmond, P. (2010) "Outcasts on the inside: Graduates, employability and widening participation", Tertiary Education and Management, 12: 119–135.

Roberts, K. (1995) *Youth and employment in modern Britain*, Oxford: Oxford University Press.

Savage, M., Cunningham, N., Devine, F., Friedman, S., Laurison, D., McKenzie, L., Miles, A., Snee, H., and Wakeling, P. (2015) *Social class in the 21st century*, London: Penguin.

Shildrick, T., McDonald, R., Webster, C., and Garthwaite, K. (2012) *Poverty and Insecurity: Life in low-pay, no-pay Britain*. Bristol: Policy Press.

Standing, G. (2011) The precariat: the new dangerous class, London: Bloomsbury.

Stevenson, J., and Clegg, S. (2010) Possible selves: students orientating themselves towards the future through extracurricular activity, *British Educational Research Journal*, 37: 231–246.

Tomlinson, M. (2008) 'The degree is not enough': Students' perceptions of the role of higher education credentials for graduate work and employability, *British Journal of Sociology of Education*, 29, 1: 49–61.

Waller, R., and Bradley, H. (2015) 'What a difference an A makes': Towards a typology of university entry routes'. Paper presented to the *Society for Research in Higher Education's Annual Conference*. Newport 9–11 December

Waller, R., Holford, J., Jarvis, P., Milana, M., and Webb, S. (2014) Widening participation, social mobility and the role of universities in a globalized world, *International Journal of Lifelong Education* 33 (6), pp. 701–704.

Waller, R., Holford, J., Jarvis, P., Milana, M., and Webb, S. (2015) Neo-liberalism and the shifting discourse of 'educational fairness', *International Journal of Lifelong Education* 34 (6), pp. 619–622.

Woodman, D., and Wyn, J. (2015) *Youth and generation*, London: Sage.

# Conclusion

## Social class, participation, and the marketised university

*David James*

While they are all focused in one way or another on social inequalities in higher education admissions, experiences, and outcomes, the chapters in this volume cover a great deal of ground. Their loose arrangement in three parts ('getting in', 'getting on' and 'getting out') works well, as it did for Haselgrove's rather different edited book *The Student Experience*, published over two decades ago (Haselgrove, 1994). Where Haselgrove's book signalled an urgent need for institutional thinking and practice to catch up with the realities of an expanding and more diverse student body, this book has a related but more defined focus. Its various contributions add up to compelling evidence that class remains a fundamental and constitutive feature of what it means to become a student, to be a student and then to be a graduate. In this short final chapter, I avoid the strong temptation to summarise and celebrate each contribution or segment of the book, worthy though they are of that. Instead, I offer some reflections directly triggered by reading all of the chapters together.

### Challenging popular myths

Taken together, the contributions in this collection do a great deal to challenge, or at least question, popular myths about higher education. One such myth is around the inexorable forward march of progress in all things, so that the shift from an 'elite' to a 'mass' system of higher education is seen rather like other major historic advances (perhaps the abolition of slavery, universal adult suffrage, universal schooling up to secondary level) and taken to signal a mature and civilised democracy, or a society and economy in which talent can be nurtured to the highest level. I mention this because the rise of 'mass' higher education is all-too-easily perceived as *simply* or *only* a wholly positive development, a modern version of those earlier extensions of elementary and then secondary schooling.

As the chapters in this book make clear, there has been a range of motives for the expansion of higher education. The shift in these is apparent if we make a comparison between the 'Robbins Report' (Committee on Higher Education, 1965), the 'Dearing Review' (National Committee of Inquiry into Higher Education, 1997) and the 'Browne Review' (Browne, 2010). The most recent (though now quite long-standing) impetus gears higher education expansion to the needs of a knowledge economy in which 'UK PLC' might maintain or improve its global economic position. A 'human capital' view of the relationship between education and economic growth continues to be at the heart of policy, despite evidence and analysis of its limitations (e.g. Brown *et al.*, 2011; Piketty, 2014). It most certainly underpins the view that students themselves are the main beneficiaries of higher education and should therefore individually pay for the investment being made in their own 'human capital'. At the same time, the extending of higher education is also something that educationalists themselves generally support, and by no means solely because they have a vested interest in nurturing demand for their services. They may have more humanistic reasons, such as the belief (for which there is research evidence – see Pew Research Center, 2016) that more educated societies tend to be more liberal. They may also have ambitions to nurture innovation or change, or operate in partnerships that can foster local or regional economic growth or community development. In a more immediate and practical sense, many of those who teach will have seen many instances of children, young people or adults gaining new capabilities, new knowledge, understanding and skills, new self-confidence or perhaps a new criticality, and this is highly rewarding for all concerned. Given all this, who could possibly argue with increasing investment in education and in particular, expanding the opportunities to gain a degree?

I am not primarily concerned with questioning either the economic or the humanistic arguments for education or its expansion. Rather, and as many of the contributions to the book illustrate, there is a need to recognise and confront the darker side: that is, we need to investigate in what ways any given educational activity is *generating* inequality, even simultaneously with other effects, as it interacts with various social and economic factors. A great deal of existing work in the sociology of education would suggest that this is one of the things that educational activity does do as a matter of course. I have argued elsewhere that this is one of several areas of tension or strain between (on the one hand) the beliefs and practices of educators, and (on the other hand) the tools of a Bourdieusian approach. In a nutshell, where educational activity is only seen through the lens of individual growth and development, then it is likely to be seen as positive or (at worst) neutral; where it is also seen as a process of social differentiation, some educators are likely to find the portrayal considerably at odds with their core values. This is one probable reason that some educational research has made superficial use of Bourdieu's concepts (James, 2015). The 'myth' here, then, is that educational activity can only do good.

Despite a rising public awareness of inequality over the last decade or so, and despite sociologists and others offering detailed examinations of social class and its ramifications (see e.g. Sayer, 2005; Savage, 2003; Savage *et al.*, 2015), there seems at the same time to be a wider cultural tendency to continue to deny the significance of class and perhaps to assume that it belongs to a more divisive and divided past. It could be argued that UK Prime Ministerial declarations about class signify concerted efforts to re-shape its place in popular consciousness. Margaret

Thatcher's famous declaration of 'there's no such thing as society' is a complete denial of class, despite its salience for her own trajectory and for the changes to the industrial landscape under her leadership. While John Major's wish for 'a genuinely classless society' acknowledged that it was still to be achieved, Tony Blair's declared end to the class war and focus on social exclusion was effectively a denial of the relevance of class by the turn of the millennium. More recently, 'diversity' can sometimes indirectly acknowledge class concerns, and David Cameron expressed the view that there needed to be more diversity in the top positions in parliament, the judiciary, the army, and the media. Theresa May has set out her vision for Britain becoming the 'great meritocracy', and while this includes some recognition of 'barriers' to be overcome, which could perhaps include social disadvantage or class, the dominant message is that of the American Dream: anyone can become anything provided they want it enough and provided they are prepared to work sufficiently hard. Dubbed by one commentator as 'Mayritocracy', this 'neoliberalism with borders' (Littler, 2016: 1) arrives at a time of greatly amplified inequalities, when perhaps a consciousness of class is most likely to re-emerge through collective shared experiences. In the everyday, and especially in everyday institutionalised education, many people do indeed seem to operate as if class was a thing of the past, even though class suffuses more or less everything we do, in one way or another, often as the source of familiarity and strangeness, comfort or anxiety. Where it explicitly enters consideration, class is usually confined to sanitised concepts or palatable proxies, such as 'postcode', or 'member of an under-represented group'.

This latter point comes through clearly in several of the contributions to this volume, perhaps especially in the consideration of the processes of 'getting in'. For example, Coulson *et al.* illustrate how policy discourse around HE entry seems to avoid class, and how in the processes of institutions considering applications, class can be '. . . added or taken away'. It is not treated as '. . . a constituent part of the applicants' selves, their experience, or their educational success'. These authors also point to the way that social disadvantage is often 'marked', but that socio-economic *advantage* is not, in a sense making the latter normal and the former abnormal. These are troubling insights, and also reminders of a set of more widespread and fundamental problems or 'misrecognitions' that run through the world of education. One of these is that our assessment regimes and mechanisms for HE entry, partly for reasons of bureaucratic manageability, encourage us to see identical educational credentials as signifying identical achievements, when the 'distance travelled', 'obstacles overcome' or 'support received' can be vastly different from person to person. A related problem is the almost universal tendency to misrecognise privilege or relative advantage as evidence of individual (and sometimes institutional) achievement. A common example of this, reproduced on an almost daily basis, would be the widespread assumption that a secondary school where 90 per cent of students gain 5+ A* to C grades at GCSE is somehow intrinsically better than another school where 60 per cent of students attain this level (when the complete opposite is just as likely to be true). In higher education, a slightly different example would be to assume that the presence of highly rated research – or the absence of it – is always a major determinant of the quality of teaching or the richness of student experience.

Perhaps less directly, the evidence and analysis put forward in the foregoing chapters might make us question another popular and widespread understanding that seems to run through educational policy, institutions and activity. This is the idea that the more 'academic' institutions, processes and credentials have a mono-poly in the legitimate nurture and measurement of intelligent human endeavour, and that everyone sees this in the same way. Yet such understandings are far from universal. Some families and young people will know graduates who are unem-ployed or under-employed, and perhaps also individuals who are happy, fulfilled and even economically comfortable but have never been to university. Discussions like those in the middle part of this book remind us that we can only understand student experience of higher education *relationally*: it will not mean the same thing to everyone, and the risks, costs and implications of participation vary greatly, especially (though not only) by social class.

## What could be different?

There have been a number of reforms and mechanisms put in place to try to achieve widened access to higher education, and Harrison's chapter gives a very helpful account of these since the Dearing Report of 1997. The overall picture is one of net failure. This is in part because different types of university have been able to *conceive* and *define* 'Widening Participation [WP]' in different ways. This point was made powerfully a few years ago by McCaig and Adnett (2009), who studied a cross-section of original and revised institutional access agreements. They concluded that in the increasingly marketised system, the institutions were using these agreements to promote their own programmes rather than for wider system-level objectives, and distinctions between pre- and post-1992 institutions were consolidated as a consequence. Thus, while some institutions could set up or expand 'profitable' programmes in the name of WP, in others (as Harrison also notes), WP is sometimes narrowly conceived as being about 'the missing', a small group of high-ability socially disadvantaged students who should be in elite universities. These analyses suggest that more clarity about national objectives could help. I return below to the prospects of this becoming manifest.

Perhaps the most useful distinction here is between actions that are currently possible, and then other actions that might be pursued, if there was sufficient political will. I begin here with a personal reflection. My own PhD studies, completed part-time during the early 1990s, focused on mature student experience in higher education. On reflection, one of the reasons I wanted to research this topic was that I both met and read about a number of mature students who said that higher education had not served them well, and this was in sharp contrast to my own largely positive experience. I had myself been a mature undergraduate student between 1978 and 1981, a decade earlier. My sixth-form A level results had been very modest, but some four years after leaving school I attended an A level evening class in Sociology and applied to Bristol University, where I was offered a conditional place. I gained the required 'B' grade. On arrival, I found – to my complete astonishment – that all but one of my cohort of fifteen were mature students, ranging in age between their early 20s and early 40s. This made the group highly unusual (possibly unique) in Bristol University. I later found out that this was the result of unilateral action by a specific group of academic staff, and was achieved in the face of some powerful opposition. I mention all this not so as to engage in self-indulgent reminiscing, but to signal a form of WP that could yet be more widely utilised in the sector, perhaps especially in those subject disciplines where some post-school experiences (of work, volunteering or just life in general) can really help to enrich study and indeed help students appreciate it for the precious opportunity that it can be.

Sticking for a moment with what is currently possible, we should note that the remit of England's Office for Fair Access [OFFA] is somewhat more restricted than is often assumed. All institutions must have an access agreement with OFFA if they wish to charge higher fee levels. OFFA has the power to impose fines or refuse to renew an access agreement with an institution. But when are these sanctions used? The sanctions can be applied '. . . if a university or college seriously and wilfully breaches its access agreement'. The organisation '. . . would not do this solely because an institution had not made progress against its targets or milestones' (OFFA, 2016a: 1). There is less to OFFA's role than might be expected, and the current arrangements enable a situation in which 'Higher education providers with the most unequal student bodies are the least likely to hit access and progression targets' (Havergal, 2016; and see OFFA, 2016b).

For those institutions failing to meet the access targets that they themselves helped to shape, OFFA can and does act as a source of mild rebuke, via the ensuing bad publicity. However, this could have a further unintended consequence, if such institutions take action to improve their image, such as a well-publicised initiative offering a small number of places at lower entry grades to young people from local schools in areas of relative disadvantage. This may counter the negative publicity, demonstrating that an institution really is concerned about its role in social inequality – all the while leaving in place a dominant pattern of social reproduction.

Institutions can choose to recruit more part-time students, whose profile in terms of age and background can be very different to full-time school leavers. It is likely that the recent collapse of mature student part-time study (from roughly 250k to 100k between 2008 and 2014) will have done much to affect the overall composition of the student body in terms of social class. This 'demand side' shift appears to have a number of economic and social causes, and the earlier level of activity is unlikely to be restored solely by institutions making more attractive offers of part-time routes, important though this is. Institutions vary quite widely in what they explicitly offer part-time. It is possible that the Equalities Act of 2010 may yet produce legal challenges in this area: while class is not itself a 'protected characteristic' under the Act, universities have a duty not to discriminate in the provision of education against potential, current or former students under any of the protected characteristics, and the groups most affected are likely to have a more diverse social class profile than school-leavers aiming for full-time degrees.

On the face of it, the current set of arrangements in the UK, especially in England, engender pessimism, and this may encourage us to look beyond the reforms and mechanisms that are currently available. The current admissions landscape contains tendencies that are so marked and persistent, and clearly reflective of relative wealth and privilege, that – following Alan Milburn's terminology – they could be called 'social engineering'. It is interesting that this phrase is usually applied pejoratively to attempts to improve equity. However, recognising that the issue is about both structure and agency at the same time, a better term might be *cycle of advantage*. The term 'cycle' is often applied to poverty, or disadvantage, and contains the idea that in families, some actions or behaviours can become entrenched after three generations or so, and are therefore extremely difficult to 'break' or 'break out of'.

There is undoubtedly a cycle of advantage in higher education admissions. A high proportion of undergraduate places at the most prestigious universities continues to be taken by young people from the minority of secondary schools that are fee-paying and private, which are themselves supported by the taxpayer via their charitable status. In many of these schools, relatively small class-sizes and high levels of individual attention (and of course dedicated teachers and leaders) continue to produce exceptionally high results in public examinations. Furthermore, as if this efficient conversion of economic capital into cultural capital was not enough, (and as Boliver explains in her chapter), university admission decisions are not then determined by academic achievement alone, and those applying from more advantaged backgrounds are more likely to be offered places than their less-advantaged peers with identical academic achievements.

The first step to changing this situation is to stop seeing it naively, as if it were some kind of small malfunction in an otherwise thoroughly rational and meritocratic system. Rather than requiring adjustment to current systems, the problem here can surely only be tackled with a more radical move. One route may be the more systematic use of contextual information, though as Boliver notes, it is very early days in terms of having something robust enough as a mechanism. Meanwhile, there could be scope for research-informed training for university admissions staff which could mean that even the *unsystematic* use of contextual information may assist with making admissions processes a little more equitable. Despite one recent government Opposition initiative, there has not as yet been an effective political will to remove the charitable status of private schools on the grounds of reducing the capacity of some families to purchase advantage. Yet these may not be the only ways in which to work towards a more equitable admissions process. Universities' access agreements (or some future equivalent) might include a baseline expectation that the proportion of their entrants who have attended independent secondary schools is somewhere nearer the proportion of the relevant age-group in those schools (i.e. around 7 per cent), with a special case having to be made to increase beyond this.[1] Another may be if the most prestigious universities (measured perhaps through demand) could be required to put a high proportion of their undergraduate places in a pool, and applicants with the required credentials could be allocated those places in a centralised process, taking as much account as possible of their preferred destination. Given that the current arrangements are not even meritocratic in a narrow or naïve sense, this could represent a considerable advance.

## Some implications for research

The implications for further research vary across the three broad issues used to organise this collection, but I would like to start here by mentioning one that we can take from all parts of the book. It is that a range of concepts of social class can be productively employed in examining higher education, provided we remain clear about which ones are being used, and aware of their limitations. Contributions to the book demonstrate that class *categories* such as those used in official statistics continue to be useful, but also that classed *practices* are an important focus. While they are related, it would be naïve in the extreme to expect these differently derived concepts of class to somehow 'line up' with each other, and then to reject the whole idea of social class on the grounds that there is some disagreement about how it is to be defined.

Work in the general area of 'getting in' is well advanced and has some clear directions of travel to pursue. The four chapters in the first part of the book represent a welcome balance between work that gets close to practices, and that which draws on several of the large existing datasets. The latter is now becoming a substantial body of work, some parts of which link to what has been dubbed a 'WP industry'. It promises to become even more informative if a wider range of UCAS data is to become more accessible. However, under this general heading, I would also suggest that there is scope for more work directly addressing two related issues. One is the question of the extent to which the immense current faith in A levels is warranted. As is well known, these examinations have their origins in university entry some 65 years ago and were reformed via a subdivision into AS and A2 at the turn of the century. While their longevity may not itself be a reason to question them, they do span a period in which higher education provision and participation have been transformed, and this alone would be more than sufficient to justify a thoroughgoing examination of their continued fitness for purpose. More specifically, it may be very helpful to know more about the extent to which they are used as a proxy for ability and/or capacity to study for a degree, and connected to this, the sorts of concepts of ability that are, practically speaking, in circulation around them. Another issue worth closer consideration is how different school cultures construct, shape or influence the development of pupil dispositions in relation to possible higher education futures. Recent work by Abrahams (2017) closely examined three secondary schools in one city in England, each with a distinctive social class pupil profile. Differences in the aspirations of the young people in each location appeared to be consolidated and amplified by a range of school-level processes, despite strong claims to be doing the opposite.

Second, the work presented in this volume on experiences of 'getting on', using a (mainly) 'class' lens to examine what it is like to be a student, presents us with a series of highly insightful analyses, covering: working-class students managing 'the academic' in relation to their social selves and identities (Reay); student life and the night-time economy (Cheeseman); social class, ethnicity and 'fitting in' among young Bangladeshi women students (Scandone); and class in cultural consumption and display among students (Mountford). Rightly, the methods employed are mainly qualitative, and the resulting analyses are rich, informative and often troubling. They can to some extent be pieced together to give a bigger picture, though this is not always an easy thing to do.

While these accounts of students 'doing student' demonstrate that the potential research questions in the field of 'student experience while at university' are virtually infinite, they are also a reminder of how, generally speaking, sociological study of higher education differs from that applied to schools, and to a lesser extent, colleges. I would argue that there is scope here for a larger comparative study of student 'lived experience', perhaps sharing some elements of the 'paired peers' study which underpins Bradley and Waller's chapter, but encompassing more institutions. Such a study might adopt a *learning cultures* perspective (James and Biesta, 2007) which has some theoretical anchorage in Bourdieu, Dewey, and Lave and Wenger. It might attempt to understand examples of higher education being 'done', so would need to get close to staff-student encounters. It would encompass student lifestyle and identity, including class and other dispositional facets, but also more directly address issues of learning, learner identity, curriculum and pedagogy. It might look at: how learning is defined and what activities are done in its name, by whom and with whom, from course to course; the range of relationships between paid work and study; whether some provision draws profitably on aspects of student's lives outside their course, past or present; whether there are equity issues inherent in pedagogic arrangements. There are a few examples of work on higher education that goes in this general direction (see Ashwin *et al.*, 2014; Boni and Walker, 2013; James, 2014), but also ample further scope. Arguably, we should be doing more to study the experiential side of higher education in some of the ways we do already when we look at schools (and to a lesser extent, colleges).

'Getting out' is the third cluster of concerns in the volume. Again the work presented is important and insightful. As I read the chapters in this segment, three particular points seemed especially fundamental to understanding what happens to students when they graduate. The first is that higher education institutions (which are often seen as being very powerful players in the overall education landscape) appear to have succumbed to an artificially individualised view of graduate employability. As Tholen and Brown put it in their chapter, '. . . the drive to make both students and HE providers solely responsible for improving labour market outcomes is disingenuous'. It takes no account of congestion, graduate over-supply and deep-rooted inequalities, all of which structure the labour market. Moreover, 'employability' remains highly problematic as an organising device for parts of the higher education curriculum. In a recent study of graduates' work (as lawyers, journalists and teachers) Higgins shows how current skills- and employability based conceptions of a higher education for employment, which take a narrow, standardised view of graduates' work, do not accurately represent the nature and demands these kinds of jobs actually make of the people performing them, and are inadequate for the task. At the same time, the capacities developed through academic study, such as the critical analysis of competing evidence and claims, or research skills, *are* fundamental to successful working in such 'graduate jobs' (Higgins, 2017).

The second striking point, again running right through the section, is that class continues to frame a great deal of what happens, post-graduation. This is another example of something that might be expected by those who think sociologically, but not by a more general public. As with university entry, successful completion of a degree, it turns out, does not level the playing-field very much. This may also come as something of a surprise to students themselves, especially those who may be expecting benefits to balance the costs they have incurred, whether these are financial, social or psychological.

Third, and related to the above, if students somehow were to remain unaware, while studying, of the significance attached to the institutional location of their degree, then this will surely make itself readily apparent once they graduate. There have always been hierarchies of university, and even whole character traits attributed to people who have been to this or that kind of institution, such as the idea of 'the Oxford man' (see e.g. Cartwright, 2008). Recent research has confirmed that there is an institutional hierarchy that is deeply embedded in wider social structures and which reflects the social reproduction role of higher education, and is very stable over time (Croxford and Raffe, 2015; Savage *et al.*, 2015). What the contributions here draw attention to is the persistence and depth of this differential valuing, and to the fact that when labour market conditions worsen, the significance of credentials as positional goods increases. A move towards greater marketisation of the higher education sector seems likely to further entrench this stratification.

## The increasingly marketised university

These are difficult and confusing times in higher education. While the relatively recent introduction of loans and fees was a major 'demand side' reform, we may be about to see an equally radical 'supply side' shift. At the time of writing, the Higher Education and Research Bill has just had its second reading in the House of Lords. The Bill has the explicit purpose to open up the sector to increased competition and choice, so that new providers can start up, be granted degree-awarding powers, and achieve university status. A new body, the Office for Students, will act as a single market regulator, assisted by a new mechanism for judging the quality of teaching, the Teaching Excellence Framework, which will take into account destinations including employment. The Bill continues a now very well established direction of travel in UK (especially English) higher education policy, most clearly articulated in the 2011 White Paper *Students at the Heart of the System* (BIS, 2011). It is worth pointing out that neither document offers a vision in respect of the rationale for, and purposes of, a higher education sector. There is nevertheless a strong vision of a different kind, one of market-isation, consumerism and certain measures of employment success. Arguably, the absence of any reasoning as to why this should be pursued is itself telling, as if it is so self-evidently necessary that it requires no comment.

There are strong parallels in all this with recent shifts in the conception and governance of schools. In their international comparison of school choice policies, Plank and Sykes (2003) pointed out how:

> The enthusiasm of economists and others for the 'magic of the market' has produced recommendations for privatising virtually all the activities of the public sector . . . Arguments that urge governments to 'unleash' market forces in the education system have been powerfully influential in a number of countries including Chile, the Czech Republic, the United Kingdom, and the United States.
>
> (Plank and Sykes, 2003: xii)

Forsey *et al.*, also commenting upon the rise of school choice policies glo bally, point out how the claim to increase choice has appeal to many different groups and interests, regardless of whether they would share anything else of 'market thinking' (Forsey *et al.*, 2008). Similarly, in a study of 'against the grain' school choices in London and two other English cities, Reay *et al.* note that 'choice is . . . easily conflated with ideas like freedom and respect for individual rights' (2013: 65).

This brings us to a final, and somewhat uncomfortable issue that sits behind much of the research discussed in this book. Put simply, in English higher education, we are moving rapidly from something partially conceived as a *system*, towards something rather different, where there are customers who purchase a service, and a series of providers of variable quality or qualities, to be regulated through mechanisms like the Teaching Excellence Framework. There is little room in such arrangements for general, agreed purposes. To put this another way, general purposes *other than* the normally unarticulated one of social reproduction appear to have diminished in importance, at least at the level of policy. Of course institutions will continue to have distinctive features, and will declare their own purposes: indeed, with heightened competition they must surely do so in order to survive. Yet looked at collectively, it is increasingly difficult to answer the question 'what is higher education for', and the question itself may eventually begin to sound odd. Though always diverse, contested and multi-layered, there have been periods in which such purposes have been clearer and more directly designed.

The clearest new requirement is to satisfy students as consumers. We can expect 'brands' to become more important than they already are, and for all the costs associated with study for a degree to reflect, increasingly, the market position of this or that university. Inequalities may become more entrenched but also more individualised and masked, since they will increasingly appear to be the result of 'good' and 'bad' choices made by individuals. The illusion of the market is that it offers a kind of natural mechanism for justice, though it is fairly clear that those best resourced will benefit the most. Consumers will make what Bourdieu terms 'the choice of the necessary', which is to say that their position in the field structures their habitus and therefore shapes their horizons for action: would-be students can be expected to adjust their ambitions well in advance of making an application, as many do now, but perhaps more so. It remains to be seen what implications this new landscape would have for how social class enters student experience during their period of study and after they graduate, but it already seems likely that it will further deepen existing inequalities. What we must hope (and do whatever we can to ensure) is that there continue to be sociologically inclined researchers with time, resources, interest and commitment similar to those represented in this book. Such researchers will need to keep their sociological imagination and critical faculties very sharp, because the field in question is a particularly dense thicket of entangled interests and not many features of it are quite as simple as they seem, or as simple as some would have us believe.

## Acknowledgement

I am very grateful to the book editors (Richard Waller, Nicola Ingram, and Michael Ward) for their comments on an earlier version of this chapter.

## Note

1   I am grateful to Nicola Ingram for reminding me of this suggestion.

## References

Abrahams, J. (2017). *Schooling inequality: Aspirations, institutional practices and social class reproduction*. PhD Thesis, School of Social Sciences, Cardiff University.

Ashwin, P., Abbas, A., and McLean, M. (2014). How do students' accounts of sociology change over the course of their undergraduate degrees? *Higher Education, 67*(2), 219–234.

BIS. (2011). *Higher Education: Students at the heart of the system*. London: Department for Business, Innovation and Skills, Cm 8122.

Boni, A., and Walker, M. (Eds.) (2013). *Human development and capabilities: re-imagining the university of the twenty-first century*. London: Routledge.

Brown, P., Lauder, H., and Ashton, D. (2011). *The global auction*. Oxford: Oxford University Press.

Browne, J. (2010). *Securing a sustainable future for higher education: an independent review of higher education funding and student finance*. London: Independent Review of Higher Education Funding and Student Finance.

Cartwright, J. (2008). *This Secret Garden – Oxford Revisited*. London: Bloomsbury.

Committee on Higher Education. (1965). *Report* (The 'Robbins Report') London, HMSO.

Croxford, L., and Raffe, D. (2015.) 'The iron law of hierarchy? Institutional differentiation in UK higher education'. *Studies in Higher Education*, 40(9), 1625–1640.

Forsey, M., Davies, S., and Walford, G. (2008). *The globalisation of school choice*. Oxford: Symposium Books.

Haselgrove, S. (Ed) (1994). *The Student Experience*. Society for Research into Higher Education and Open University Press: Buckingham.

Havergal, C. (2016). Elite universities least likely to hit access goals. *The Times Higher*, Retrieved from www.timeshighereducation.com/news/elite-universities-least-likely-hit-access-goals

Higgins, H. (2017). *Meeting the demands of graduates' work: Re-imagining a higher education for work*. PhD Thesis, School of Social Sciences, Cardiff University.

James, D. (2014). 'Investigating the curriculum through assessment practice in higher education: the value of a "learning cultures" approach'. *Higher Education*, 67(2), 155–169.

James, D. (2015). How Bourdieu bites back: recognising misrecognition in education and educational research. *Cambridge Journal of Education*, 45(1), 97–112.

James, D., and Biesta, G.J.J. (2007). *Improving learning cultures in further education*. London: Routledge.

Littler, J. (2016). *Mayritocracy: Neoliberalism with new borders*. LW Blog, Lawrence and Wishart. Retrieved from www.lwbooks.co.uk/blog/mayritocracy-neoliberalism-with-new-borders

McCaig, C., and Adnett, N. (2009). English universities, additional fee income, and access agreements: Their impact on widening participation and fair access. *British Journal of Educational Studies*, 57(1), 18–36, DOI: 10.1111/j.1467–8527.2009.00428.x

National Committee of Inquiry into Higher Education [NCIHE]. (1997). *Higher education in the learning society (The 'Dearing Report')*. London: HMSO.

OFFA (2016a). *Frequently Asked Questions (Journalists)*, Bristol: Office for Fair Access. Retrieved November 24, 2016 from www.offa.org.uk/press/frequently-asked-questions/

OFFA. (2016b). Outcomes of Access Agreement Monitoring for 2014–15. *Bristol: Office for Fair Access*. Retrieved November 24, 2016 from www.offa.org.uk/wp-content/uploads/2016/05/2016.04-Outcomes-of-access-agreements-monitoring-1.pdf

Pew Research Center. (2016). *A Wider Ideological Gap Between More and Less Educated Adults*. Washington DC: Pew Research Center. Available at www.people-press.org/2016/04/26/a-wider-ideological-gap-between-more-and-less-educated-adults/

Piketty, T. (2014). *Capital in the Twenty-First Century (Trans. Arthur Goldhammer)*. Cambridge, MA: Harvard University Press.

Plank, D.N. and Sykes, G. (Eds). (2003). *Choosing choice: School choice in international perspective*. New York and London: Teachers College Press.

Reay, D., Crozier, G., and James, D. (2013). *White middle class identities and urban schooling*. Basingstoke: Palgrave Macmillan.

Savage, M. (2003). 'A new class paradigm?' *British Journal of Sociology of Education*, 24(4), 535–541.

Savage, M., Cunningham, N., Devine, F., Friedman, S., Laurison, D., McKenzie, L., Miles, A., Snee, H., and Wakeling, P. (2015). *Social class in the 21st Century*, London: Penguin.

Sayer, A. (2005). *The Moral Significance of Class*. Cambridge: Cambridge University Press.

# Index